BEYOND THE
EARTH SUMMIT

BEYOND THE EARTH SUMMIT

Conversations with Advocates of Sustainable Development

by Steve Lerner

COMMON KNOWLEDGE PRESS
COMMONWEAL
Bolinas, California

Commonweal is a health and environmental research institute located in Bolinas, California. Founded in 1976, Commonweal has been concerned with disadvantaged children, people with cancer and other life-threatening illnesses, and major environmental issues. Its work has been supported by grants and gifts from foundations and individuals from across the United States.

Acknowledgements:
The following people worked on the production and development of *Beyond the Earth Summit:*

Michael Lerner and Albert Wells: Co-directors of the Commonweal Sustainable Futures Project.
David Parker: Executive Vice-President of Commonweal
Mary Ellin Barrett and Thomas Weston Fels: Editors
Frank Urbanowski: Consulting Editor
Karl W. Stuecklen: Cover Art

Design and production: John Wilton Associates, New York, NY
Printed by Bookcrafters, Chelsea, MI

This book was made possible by grants to Commonweal from The Nathan Cummings Foundation, the Hale Fund, and the Jennifer Altman Foundation.

Beyond the Earth Summit: Conversations with Advocates of Sustainable Development is available from Commonweal, P.O. Box 316, Bolinas, California 94924, USA. The price is $12.50. For shipment at book rate in the U.S., add $2.00, for Canada, add $3.00. For shipment to all other countries by surface mail, add $4.00 postage and handling. All orders must be prepaid in U.S. funds.

ISBN 0-943004-07-1
First printing May, 1992
Printed on Enviro-Text recycled paper in the USA ♺

Contents

Section III:

Defending Biological Diversity

Preface

*T*he purpose of *Beyond the Earth Summit* is to raise the level of public dialogue about the architecture of a just and sustainable future. As the conversations recorded in this book indicate, there is widespread agreement in the international environment and development communities that the peoples of the world must come together with unprecedented speed to transform global patterns of resource use and consumption toward equity and sustainability if we are to achieve a sustainable future. Our intention in publishing *Beyond the Earth Summit* is to make a small contribution to that task.

Beyond the Earth Summit is a record of conversations that Steve Lerner, Research Director at Commonweal, held with leading environmentalists, development specialists, social activists and policy specialists from around the world during the months leading up to the United Nations Conference on the Environment and Development (UNCED) in Rio de Janeiro in June, 1992. A companion volume, entitled *Earth Summit,* was co-published by Commonweal and Friends of the Earth, U.S., in 1991.

In *Beyond the Earth Summit,* the reader will find in-depth interviews with key North American players in the Earth Summit that include Maurice Strong, Secretary General of UNCED; Lester Brown, President of the Worldwatch Institute; James Gustave Speth, President of the World Resources Institute; Ambassador Robert Ryan, Jr., Director of the U.S. Coordination Center for UNCED; and Senator Al Gore (D-Tenn.).

Some formidable leaders of non-government organizations (NGOs) in the less industrialized nations of the South are present, including three whose voices are being heard around the world: Wangari Maathai from Kenya, who has led a grassroots tree-planting and pro-Democracy movement, and been beaten and imprisoned by the government for her efforts; Vandana Shiva from India, who is close to the historic Chipko Movement in which women are saving trees in the Himalayas by putting their bodies between the loggers and the trees; and Martin Khor from Malaysia, whose Third World Network has articulated one of the most comprehensive analyses of North/South economic and environmental relations.

There are fascinating interviews on the role of indigenous peoples in protecting biodiversity with Thomas E. Lovejoy of the Smithsonian Institution; Darrell Posey, an American researcher who lives and works with the indigenous people of the Amazon; Jason Clay, the Harvard-based researcher and Director of a remarkable entrepreneurial organization called Cultural Survival Enterprises; and Oren Lyons, a Chief of the Onondaga Nation in the United States.

Some of the most thoughtful policy specialists on the design of international institutions for a sustainable future are also interviewed, including David Runnalls of the Institute for Research on Public Policy in Canada; Hillary French of the Worldwatch Institute; Peter Davies of InterAction and Scott Hajost of the Environmental Defense Fund.

This is a partial list of the interviews with southern and northern activists and policy specialists that *Beyond the Earth Summit* contains. Some of the less widely known interviewees offer some of the most insightful observations in their areas of expertise.

Why interviews? There are few people who are currently conducting and publishing serious, full-length, interviews with leading figures in the global sustainable development movement. But connoisseurs of interviews as a form of communication know that in conversation many people say what they are really thinking more forcefully than they do in their written work.

Steve Lerner has devoted his full time for over two years to reporting on the Earth Summit negotiations, so he is a well-informed interviewer. The result is that these interviews go far deeper into the heart of the mystery of how we can save the earth than less informed conversations do.

Lester Brown of the Worldwatch Institute, in his interview with Steve Lerner, compares the magnitude of the transformation necessary to achieve a sustainable future to the magnitude of change that took place in the Agricultural Revolution at the dawn of human history and in the Industrial Revolution that ushered in the modern era. The difference now, he says, is how little time we have to carry out the transition to a sustainable future.

It is clear to everyone concerned with these issues that governments will only make changes of this magnitude if there is strong and consistent pressure from citizens. "When the people lead," the wise saying goes, "the leaders will follow." But for the people to lead, they must first understand the fundamental issues and the necessary solutions.

We hope these interviews will evoke a heightened awareness of the dangers we face, a deeper humility about the difficulties of addressing these dangers, and a broader recognition of the limitations of our own knowledge and belief systems as we encounter the perspectives through which the global struggle is viewed by knowledgeable people from around the world.

—*Michael Lerner*
President, Commonweal

Introduction

Every year the earth's forest cover is diminished, its topsoil is further eroded, the ozone layer is thinned, the oceans and air are more polluted, fresh water is contaminated, and an unknown number of species become extinct. Yet despite overwhelming evidence that the world's natural resources and regenerative capacity are being rapidly depleted, the nations of the world cannot seem to agree on an effective joint response.

Instead, a fractious debate has broken out between developed and developing nations over who is responsible for accelerating environmental degradation and who will bear the costs of remedial action.

The incremental nature of the damage humans do to the earth's ecosystems adds to the difficulty of marshaling collective action to meet this unprecedented threat. With creeping environmental degradation it is impossible to point to any moment in time as being the turning point in the ecological fate of the earth. It is equally hard to know if we are approaching some critical threshold, which, if breached, will cause irreversible damage to the web of life.

While few argue with the fact that the state of the environment deteriorates more every year, many policy makers remain unconvinced that we need to rush to do anything about it. They believe that if something goes seriously wrong with the environment, humans will be ingenious enough to find a technological fix. They think that if we run out of one resource we can always switch to using another.

The public, however, is less sanguine about the environmental outlook. Surveys suggest that the public is more concerned about environmental degradation than are political leaders who tend to focus only on short-term problems. Yet it remains to be seen if the people of the world will recognize that an ecological crisis is upon us and that collective action is required to keep the earth habitable for future generations.

Twice in the last 20 years the nations of the world have attempted to find comprehensive solutions to accelerating environmental degradation. The first such effort took place at the Stockholm Conference on the Human Environment in 1972, which achieved some measure of success by establishing the United Nations Environment Program (UNEP). UNEP became a catalyst for a number of international environmental agreements, including the 1987 Montreal Protocol on Substances that Deplete the Ozone Layer. The Stockholm Conference also resulted in the creation of environmental protection agencies in many nations around the world.

Another product of Stockholm was the launching of the World Commission on the Environment, chaired by Norway's Prime Minister Gro Harlem Brundtland. This commission held meetings around the world on the state of the environment and produced a seminal report entitled *Our Common Future*. Known as the Brundtland Commission Report, this document suggested that the international community would not be able to solve environmental problems without meeting basic human needs at the same time. It further contended that a new type of development that was ecologically sustainable would have to be practiced if the interconnected problems of meeting basic human needs and protecting the earth's vital ecosystems were to be solved.

For the next 20 years the concept of sustainable development was discussed in learned circles and it achieved a certain intellectual currency. Yet, while sustainable development sounded unobjectionable, few practiced it. Recognizing that the Stockholm Conference had failed to reverse the trend of environmental destruction, the United Nations General Assembly decided in December, 1989 that it was time for the nations of the world to grapple once again with the environment/development nexus of problems. Thus was established the United Nations Conference on Environment and Development (UNCED), the most comprehensive negotiation ever held on environment and development issues. Under its auspices the connections between environmental degradation and the development crisis in the Third World have been thoroughly explored. In two years of negotiations a variety of texts have been formulated that spell out what the international community should do about these problems.

The outcome of UNCED will most likely include a treaty on climate change, a treaty on protecting biological diversity, a set of principles on deforestation, an agenda for action on environment and development issues for the next century, and an Earth Charter that briefly sets out the rights and responsibilities of humans as stewards of the earth. The signing of these agreements is to take place in June, 1992, at the Earth Summit in Rio de Janeiro — a gathering that promises to be the largest U.N. summit of world leaders ever held.

Those of us in the non-government organization (NGO) community who have closely watched the UNCED negotiations in Nairobi, Geneva, New York, and now Rio have been alternately inspired and frustrated. Initially a sense of hope was kindled by the fact that the nations of the world were finally focusing on the problems posed by environmental deterioration and the unequal distribution of the earth's wealth. Many of us are convinced that the Rio Conference will usher in a new era of environmental diplomacy that will dominate the international agenda in the years to come. It appears as if the nations of the earth are finally beginning to take seriously the threat posed by human activity to the earth's vital ecosystems.

On the other hand, progress at UNCED has been frustratingly slow. Many of us from environment and development organizations were discouraged to see 160 nations squabble and defend their own narrow interests while the common good often went ignored. We were also largely unprepared for the extent of the rift between developed and developing nations that emerged during the UNCED negotiations.

The lack of cooperation among nations has been particularly disappointing in light of the fact that the end of the Cold War has raised hopes that the U.N. will be able to function more effectively now that it is no longer paralyzed by an ideological standoff. It has become apparent, however, that as the East/West ideological conflict has subsided, North/South tensions are increasing over the control of natural resources and the question of who will pay for a global environmental cleanup. This conflict between developed and developing nations has seriously slowed progress at UNCED.

Of course it should not be surprising that nations find it hard to agree about how to reverse environmental damage. Making the transition from an unsustainable to a sustainable global economy will require fundamental change. Not only will those in industrialized nations have to reduce consumption and shift from fossil fuels to renewable sources of energy, they will also have to learn to share the resources of the earth more equitably. Changing patterns of economic activities all over the world will inevitably challenge vested interests and require changes in ingrained patterns of behavior.

In retrospect, it is also perhaps less than surprising that the North and South would have different priorities and perspectives on how to achieve a sustainable pattern of development. The highest priority of the wealthier nations has been signing international agreements that will protect the global environment. Less prosperous nations have insisted that meeting basic human needs should be the global priority and that measures to protect the environment should not hinder their ability to develop and attain a better standard of living.

This difference in North/South perspectives was placed in stark relief during the UNCED negotiations when the North, led by an initiative from the United States, proposed that UNCED should fashion an international treaty to halt deforestation. Southern nations balked at negotiating such a treaty, fearing that a forestry convention would prevent them from earning desperately needed hard currency by cutting trees for export. Developing nations also argued that they needed to clear some of their forests to make room for new industry, housing, crops, and pasture.

What is particularly galling to some Third World delegates is that it appears as if the North, now that it enjoys the creature comforts of industrialization, wants to change the rules of the game. Having cut down all but a small fraction of its own old-growth forests, the North wants to impose restrictions that would prevent the South from following the same path to development. Delegates from southern nations also contend that the North wants to keep forests standing in developing nations as a sink for greenhouse gases emitted by industrialized nations. Delegates from the Third World are concerned that developing nations could be turned into bioreserves in which nature would be protected but the inhabitants would be prohibited from attaining a reasonable standard of living.

During the course of the negotiations it has become apparent that while the United States wants to impose all kinds of restrictions on people who live in the Third World that would require them to protect biological diversity and refrain from cutting down trees, it does not see any reason for such restrictions in the U.S. This impression is reinforced by the recent passage of legislation in the U.S. Senate that would open up to clear-cutting four million acres of what is left of old-growth forest in Montana, just as we are calling on developed nations to preserve their old-growth forests. Many in the developing world feel that they are being asked to make sacrifices to protect the global commons while the U.S. Administration has been unwilling to develop a sustainable energy policy or set targets or timetables for the reduction of carbon dioxide emissions that are driving global warming.

Faced with this double standard, the developing nations have invoked the "polluter pays" principle and argued that responsibility for global environmental problems should be laid at the feet of industrialized nations. After all, it is the wealthy nations that manufactured and used in large quantities those chemicals that depleted the ozone layer. Similarly, it is disproportionately the wealthy nations that can afford to burn fossil fuels in large quantities, which in turn release the greenhouse gases that are heating up the planet. Thus it is the North that should pay for stabilizing the climate, not the less prosperous nations of the South.

Some delegates from southern nations take this analysis even further by suggesting that an ecological debt is owed by the North to the South for the damage that industrialized nations have done to the global commons. This ecological debt of the North to the South dwarfs the $50 billion annual debt paid by the Third World to the First World, they contend.

Seeing the North as largely responsible for the global threats to the environment, the Group of 77 (G-77) developing nations have demanded that additional funds be made available by the industrialized nations to help developing nations meet the terms of the proposed international treaties. In addition to asking what financial resources the North would make available to the South, developing nations also want to know if the North is willing to reduce the consumption levels that have caused many of these environmental problems.

INTRODUCTION

Ambassador Robert J. Ryan, Jr., Director of the U.S. Coordination Center for UNCED, does not want to see the focus of the negotiations shift from issues such as the burning of the Amazon rain forest and pollution of the oceans to excessive consumption patterns in the North. Other countries would consume as much as the United States if they could, he argues. Instead of attempting to talk Americans into living in smaller houses and apartments, he continues, we should be trying to see how to heat, light, and insulate those homes more efficiently, thus reducing the burden on the environment. In short: the U.S. life style is not up for negotiation.

The United States has placed itself in an awkward situation at UNCED. Throughout the negotiations the U.S. position has been described by many observers as being characterized by three negatives: (1) it would provide "no new and additional resources" for sustainable development, (2) it wants no new U.N. bureaucracy created for the coordination of U.N. activities on the environment, and (3) it refuses to set targets or timetables for the reduction of carbon dioxide emissions. These three U.S. positions have become known as "the three no's".

As a result, the U.S. has been widely criticized for dragging its feet at the UNCED negotiations. Some observers have described the U.S. position as a damage-limitation exercise. The fact that as of this writing, six weeks before the Earth Summit, President Bush has still not committed to going to Rio is symbolic of the Administration's lack of commitment to these negotiations.

Late in the negotiations, however, the U.S. appears to be abandoning or retreating on some of its negative positions. The U.S. recently has conceded that new and additional financial resources will be needed in order to help developing nations practice sustainable development and meet the terms of the climate change and biodiversity treaties. The U.S. "will not be found wanting" when it comes time for the industrialized nations to provide these financial resources, a U.S. delegate is reported to have promised. So, while there is not yet a precise figure on how much the U.S. is willing to pledge for the promotion of sustainable development, there is now a signal that the U.S. recognizes it will have to make a significant contribution.

Similarly, as to whether or not a new commission should be created to coordinate U.N. activities on environment and development, the U.S. has now backpedaled to say that while it opposes the creation of a big new bureaucracy, it does not oppose the creation of a commission within the U.N. to coordinate activities on these issues.

Finally, on targets and timetables for the reduction of carbon dioxide, the most important greenhouse gas, the U.S. appears to be looking for a compromise. The Europeans have warned that they will not sign a meaningless climate change convention that lacks targets and timetables for the reduction of carbon dioxide emissions. The U.S. wants to avoid a costly cap on CO_2 emissions and instead come up with a package of initiatives that would reduce overall greenhouse gas emissions. It remains to be seen whether or not an agreement can be forged out of these conflicting approaches prior to the Earth Summit.

One can look at the change in the U.S. negotiating position from two perspectives. Either one can be glad that the U.S. appears to be abandoning the wrongheaded positions it adopted at the beginning of the negotiation; or annoyed that the Administration took these positions to begin with. In either case it is clear that the U.S. has not taken a position of leadership at these negotiations and has, in a number of instances, obstructed progress.

To be fair, however, it is important to give the U.S. credit for a number of positive contributions to the UNCED process. The U.S. has tabled significant proposals to protect the oceans, provide for good housekeeping practices in the handling of toxic wastes, and lobbied for an agreement that would require that citizens around the world should be given access to information about the environment.

Had the U.S. and other industrialized nations entered the UNCED negotiations willing to commit to making cuts in their greenhouse gas emissions, willing to give substantial financial assistance to developing nations to meet the terms of the new environmental treaties, and willing to cut consumption of virgin materials, it might have convinced people in the Third World that those in the First World were genuinely interested in joining in a partnership to meet basic needs in the developing world and protect the earth's ecosystems.

Had the nations of the industrialized world signaled their willingness to make sacrifices in order to protect global ecosystems, it might have convinced those in developing countries to make efforts to reduce population growth, democratize their societies, combat corruption, use aid more responsibly, provide their people with access to information about the environment, cut military expenditures, and put in place incentives for sustainable development. As it turns out, however, while a start was made on exploring a North/South partnership, these kinds of bargains over reciprocal reforms in the North and the South remain to be made in the years ahead.

It is easy to become so immersed in the details of the UNCED negotiation and the prospects for the Earth Summit that one misses their context. The Earth Summit must be seen as the beginning of a period of international environmental negotiations, not the end of it.

This collection of interviews is entitled *Beyond the Earth Summit* because, while all of those interviewed discuss the UNCED negotiations, most of them are preparing for the years ahead in which the transition from an unsustainable to a sustainable world economy will have to be carried out.

The lasting impression from having done the interviews in this book is that the focus of the environment/development movement is beginning to shift away from an endless recitation of environmental problems to a description of what changes humans must make in our relationship with nature.

In the years ahead, we must all look for examples of communities that have evolved sustainable patterns of development and see how those models can be applied more widely. We must also look for ways to share the bounty of the earth more equitably both between developed and developing nations and within every society. Unless we do this it will be impossible to engage large populations in changing their behavior in order to protect the ecosystems that support life.

Some will argue that it does not make sense to link protecting the environment with helping the poor. But the environmental movement must keep pace with a changing world dynamic.

In a thoughtful essay in the *Utne Reader,* David Morris, Co-Director of the D.C.-based Institute for Local Self-Reliance, identifies four stages in the environmental movement. The first stage, the conservation movement, concentrated on the preservation of wilderness. The second stage focused on reductions of toxic substances. In the third stage there was a recognition that some of the nontoxic industrial by-products — such as CFCs and CO_2 — could overwhelm nature's absorptive capacity when released in large quantities. In this third stage the emphasis shifted from environmental protection to the need for ecologically sustainable practices. The fourth stage, which we are now entering, involves a recognition that the world cannot achieve widespread ecologically sustainable practices without solving some of the larger equity issues that have created overconsumption in the North and crushing poverty in the South.

In the past, most of the major threats to the global environment — ozone depletion, global warming, transboundary air pollution, overfishing of the oceans — have been caused by the industrialized nations of the North. Clearly, these industrialized nations must be prevailed upon to reduce the strain they place on the absorptive capacity of nature. In the years to come, however, another potentially more intractable problem is emerging. The cumulative impact of large populations in developing nations will also cause a strain on the global commons. While northerners release more greenhouse gases per capita than do people in the South, in a few years the total amount of greenhouse gases released by the developing world will exceed the amount released by industrialized nations.

While wealthy nations can afford pollution control technologies or a switch to a more expensive but less environmentally damaging product or process, people in poorer nations do not have this luxury. Enlisting people who live a subsistence life in the collective task of saving the earth's ecosystems will require that we first meet their basic human needs.

Clearly, some very ingenious bargains will have to be made in order to keep the world's ecosystems from being overwhelmed. Ultimately, each person on the planet may be allocated a certain portion of nature's absorptive capacity. This would place considerable pressure on those of us in industrialized nations to make significant reductions in per capita releases of greenhouse gases. It might also lead to an international system of selling pollution permits. These are the kinds of trade-offs we will be dealing with in the decades to come.

Unfortunately, many of those who occupy positions of power in business and politics see this transformation to a sustainable future as threatening. They see environmentalists as neo-Luddites who oppose all varieties of business and industry. Nothing could be further from the truth. While there are some extremists in the environmental movement, most favor transforming technology by inventing a new generation of environmentally friendly technologies. The new vision suggests that if we control population growth and transform our technologies, human needs around the world can be met while placing less of a strain on the ecosystems that support life.

Industrialists, miners, oil producers, farmers, ranchers, loggers, regulators, bankers, investors, and others can either fight a rear-guard action in which they try to maintain the status quo and resist the transition to green technologies or they can recognize that, as environmental regulations tighten, those products that are most ecologically benign will become tomorrow's best sellers.

Inventing more ecologically benign technologies will obviously entail some dislocations as old, polluting industries are phased out and new ones brought on line. Workers will have to be retrained. People will have to adapt their life-styles to new patterns. New tax and accounting systems will have to be put in place. But there is no reason, as the current U.S. Administration suggests, that we should have to choose between having a job or a reasonably healthy environment. It is possible to have work and take care of the environment at the same time.

To make this transition to an ecologically sustainable future will require that we begin to listen to some of the wise people around the world who have been studying long-term environment/development trends and thinking about how we can build an ecologically friendly culture. The interviews in this book describe what people in different parts of the world have been doing to promote sustainable development in their communities. Some are activists, some are organizers, some are thinkers, but they all have in common an interest in solving the environment/development crisis.

The book is divided into five sections. In the first, we hear from

people who offer an overview of the environment/development movement and who have insights into how the transition from unsustainable
to sustainable economies can be promoted. In the second section, activists from around the world describe what it is like to be on the front lines
in protecting local ecosystems and promoting a sustainable way of life.
The third section is devoted to an exploration of the movement to preserve both biological and biocultural diversity. The fourth section offers
two opposing perspectives on the North/South debate over sustainable
development. And the fifth section examines the institutional arrangements that will best coordinate activities to solve the environment/de-
velopment crisis.

I hope that you will find that listening in on these conversations is as
thought-provoking for you as it has been for me.

—*Steve Lerner*
Washington, D.C., April, 1992

Section I:

The Road from Rio: An Overview

Lester R. Brown:

The Environmental Revolution

*L*ester R. Brown is President of the Worldwatch Institute. He is co-author of *Saving the Planet: How to Shape an Environmentally Sustainable Global Economy*. The Worldwatch Institute also publishes an annual *State of the World* report as well as the Worldwatch Environmental Alert Series.

Steve Lerner: You have said that the principal message to emerge out of the United Nations Conference on Environment and Development (UNCED) may be that we can no longer separate the future habitability of the planet from the current distribution of wealth. Would you elaborate on that?

Lester R. Brown: There has been an economic gap between the industrial and developing countries for a long time. Up until now a major rationale for rich nations assisting Third World countries has been the East/West ideological conflict. Providing assistance to Third World countries has been used to get them to line up on one side or the other of the ideological divide. There has also been a certain humanistic rationale for providing assistance to Third World countries. But I think we are now moving into a period where the nature of the relationship may change because poor countries now have something that rich countries want and need: namely, their cooperation in helping to protect the earth's basic life-support systems.

One of the differences between the Rio conference and its predecessor in Stockholm in 1972 is that the Stockholm conference focused mainly on industrial pollution of air and water that was largely seen as a local problem, although even then there were some transboundary issues evolving. The principal issues at Rio will be global warming, the need to protect the earth's remaining biological diversity, and, to a lesser degree, the depletion of the stratospheric ozone layer.

One of the interesting characteristics of these problems is that no country can solve them alone. These are threats that can be successfully dealt with only by collaborative international action. If, for example, a single developing country of some size were to continue to manufacture and use CFCs it would eventually deplete the stratospheric ozone layer over the entire planet.

3

There are many people in poor countries who are trying to survive until the next harvest. And not all of them make it. For them, concerns about the stratospheric ozone layer — which they have never seen and don't understand — or the protection of biological diversity, or the stabilization of climate, are rather remote. These issues don't have anything to do with surviving the next several months.

These circumstances, in effect, define the challenge. The question is: How do you create a situation in which people who are preoccupied with short-term survival needs can begin to think about the long term both for themselves and for everyone else?

Finding a solution to this will require some new thinking at the international level. It will require a focus on satisfaction of basic human needs, creating conditions that will lead to population stabilization, which in turn will mean raising education levels, improving health care, and providing opportunities for women other than child bearing. It will also require some new thinking about development, international cooperation, and working together in new ways to insure the future habitability of the planet. This is what I think will distinguish the Rio conference from those that have gone before.

What do you think is the importance of the Earth Summit?

I see the Rio conference as the event that will officially mark the transition from the old era, which was one dominated by the East/West ideological conflict, to a new era that will be dominated by the need for ecological sustainability — the need to build an environmentally sustainable global economy. This latter effort inevitably brings together the two great issues of our time: namely, poverty and environment. And it brings them together in a way that they have not been brought together before except in a conceptual sense. Many people have recognized the environment/poverty link. But these two issues have not officially been linked in the way that I think they will be at the conference in Rio.

In a sense, the organizing principle in the old era, the one that stretched over the last four decades or so, was ideological conflict. It determined the political coalitions of countries, it dominated the setting of national priorities and use of public resources. It dominated international affairs completely. In the new era the organizing principle will be not ideological conflict, but rather ecological sustainability. This will bring countries together in a way that they have not been brought together before.

The Rio conference, I believe, will underline the extent to which we all now share a common destiny, something that we may have talked about from time to time in the past, but which we have not really faced in a concerted way.

While the ideological conflicts of the Cold War may be subsiding, at the UNCED negotiations the conflict between North and South is re-emerging.

LESTER BROWN

In the new era the North/South conflict will replace the East/West
ideological conflict. And the new conflict between North and South will
be about the terms of cooperation. So, it is not as if everyone will suddenly decide to live together happily ever after Rio, but rather that we
are going to begin to realize that we have to work together if we are
going to respond to the threats that the North perceives and the threats
that the South perceives. Those threats that the North perceives center
more around the future habitability of the planet; those that loom large
in the South are basic day-to-day survival issues. Both these issues are
necessarily fused in the new order that is emerging. The terms under
which they are fused are going to shape international affairs for years if
not decades to come.

In your book, Saving the Planet: How to Shape an Environmentally
Sustainable Global Economy, *you write about the concept of ecological
debt owed by industrial nations to the rest of the world for the ecological damage they have inflicted on the biosphere. Do you think that concept will enter into the negotiation over debt relief and the need to
provide new resources for developing nations so they can develop sustainably? Is it reasonable for developing nations to argue that their debt
to the developed nations is offset by the ecological debt owed to them by
northern industrialized nations?*

As you look at the world today and the global environmental threats,
including both global warming and the depletion of the stratospheric
ozone layer, it is the industrial countries that are primarily responsible
for that damage and disruption. If global warming is a prospect, and
indeed it is probably already underway, it will be an extraordinarily
disruptive process. For example, just two of the effects of global
warming are a change in agricultural cropping patterns and the longer-
term rise in sea level. All countries will, in various ways, bear the costs
and have to deal with the consequences of global warming even though
some countries may have contributed very little to the buildup of
greenhouse gases that is driving that process. So we have that set of
issues on the table.

We also have a situation in Third World countries where the principal
ecological deficits are local deficits in the form of deforestation, grass-
land degradation, and soil erosion. What we are seeing is that growth in
human population is slowly but steadily destroying basic resources on
which life depends. What we have to do is think of how to reverse that
process of deterioration, because if it continues there is very little
prospect that the political stability needed for international cooperation
will even exist in those countries.

When I am asked what are the major environmental problems in the
world today, I always respond that there are two that stand at the top of
the list. One is the need to stabilize population; the other is the need to
stabilize climate. Both are extraordinarily difficult. The first requires a

revolution in human reproductive behavior; the second requires a restructuring of the global energy economy, in effect, essentially phasing-out fossil fuels in order to check the buildup of greenhouse gases.

When we look at what needs to be done we see the need for an enormous change. We look back to the Stockholm conference on the Human Environment that took place in 1972 as having officially launched the international environmental age. Since then we have seen a lot of changes. Scores of countries have created environmental protection agencies. Thousands of laws have been passed to protect the environment, ranging from clean air laws to endangered species legislation. There have been thousands of environmental success stories at the local level.

However, in the last 20 years, we have not succeeded in reversing even one of the major trends of global environmental degradation. The forests continue to shrink and the deserts continue to expand. Indeed the forests are shrinking faster now than they were 20 years ago. We are losing topsoil from our croplands at a record rate. Each year the world's farmers are losing an amount of topsoil comparable to the amount of soil in Australia's wheatlands, which is not an inconsequential amount. Each year the number of plant and animal species with which we share the planet is diminishing. Each year the concentration of greenhouse gases in the atmosphere rises in an all too predictable fashion. Each year the stratospheric ozone layer gets a little thinner. That process, too, appears to be accelerating.

If these trends continue for much longer, civilization as we know it will not survive. There is no way that civilization can survive the continued loss of plant and animal species at the rate of the last two decades; or that we can survive economically the ecological devastation and continued deforestation of the earth.

It is now clear, I think, that although we have done a lot of things, our efforts have been minor compared to the scale of change. We have made an adjustment here, we have made an adjustment there, thinking that if we made enough adjustments the trends would be reversed. In reality they are not being reversed, they are not close to being reversed.

Here at Worldwatch Institute we do an annual *State of the World* report and we would like to be able to write an upbeat report one of these years. We would like to be able to report that last year the earth's tree cover expanded for the first time in the lifetime of anyone now living. We would like to report that last year world population growth slowed dramatically as birth rates fell throughout the Third World. We would like to report that last year carbon emissions dropped again as the effort to stabilize climate in the industrial countries gained momentum. But we can't say any of these things and we are not close to being able to say them.

It is going to take an enormous social and economic transformation, something that we have started calling the Environmental Revolution. It is a revolution comparable in scale to the Agricultural Revolution and the Industrial Revolution. The Agricultural Revolution set the stage for an enormous demographic change leading to population growth that continues today. The Environmental Revolution, if it succeeds, will also set the stage for enormous demographic change, in the form of a rapid shift to smaller families and stabilization of world population growth. The Industrial Revolution was based on a shift to fossil fuels; the Environmental Revolution will be based on a shift away from fossil fuels.

The big difference between the Agricultural and the Industrial Revolutions, on the one hand, and the Environmental Revolution, on the other, is not so much the scale of change as the time available for the change. The Agricultural Revolution started more than 10,000 years ago. The Industrial Revolution has been under way for two centuries. But the Environmental Revolution must be compressed into a matter of decades. We don't have generations or centuries to reverse the trends that are undermining our future. If our generation does not succeed, future generations will not have the opportunity, because environmental degradation will lead to economic decline and the two will feed on each other, leading to social disintegration.

That is a point that a lot of people don't grasp. You have written of the 1990s as the "turn-around decade" or the "environmental decade." Whether we want it to be the environmental decade or not, the acceleration of environmental degradation is going to make it that. Many people understand that the environmental problems are serious, but they see these problems as being something we will have to confront in the future. Why is it that you think that this decade is so critical in the race to save the planet? Why won't my child, when he comes of age, have a chance to solve these problems?

If we look around the world at the basic trends I mentioned earlier — trends of environmental degradation that now affect the planet and that in some cases are actually gaining momentum — we see that those trends will undermine the global economy. I have traveled a great deal over the last 35 years, since living in villages in India in 1956. My original interest was agriculture, so, as I traveled, I spent a great deal of time in the countryside. And I have seen over the past 35 years, over the past generation, an enormous degradation of the earth's natural capital in the form of forests, grasslands, and croplands.

We know that eventually these trends will undermine the economy. It cannot be otherwise. There are now some 23 developing countries that were once exporting forest products that now, because of deforestation, are forest product importers. In a large part of Africa the per capita grain production is declining. It has declined at least 15 percent since peaking around 1970, and it is going down at roughly 1 percent a year. That can't continue for much longer before there will be Ethiopias throughout

Africa — societies in which even in years of good weather farmers can no longer produce enough to feed themselves.

If you hike around the highlands in Ethiopia you come across villages that have been abandoned. No one lives in them any more because there is not enough topsoil left to support even subsistence farming. You see the expansion of deserts and the degradation of land. You see it in the Andean villages of Latin America. You see it in Peru where, as the soil comes down the mountain, the people inevitably follow and end up in the shanty towns around Lima. You see the degradation of land in the countryside in Mexico. People leave their villages for Mexico City — millions of them have done so in the last few decades — or they head north across the border to the United States. So, we are seeing a growing flow of environmental refugees.

One sees the same phenomenon in North Africa and Europe, where North Africans from Morocco to Turkey are migrating to Europe in search of work. You travel in the Soviet Union and you see enormous devastation of the countryside. The Aral Sea Basin is a dying ecosystem. In 1960 the Aral Sea yielded a fish catch of 100 million pounds. Today there not only is no fish catch, there are no fish left in the Aral Sea. Of the 27 commercial species, all are now dead. The fishing communities that dotted the shore are now abandoned. Just as surely as the villagers in Ethiopia had to leave their homes when the soil was gone, these fishing communities had to leave their villages when the fish were gone, because that was their only means of livelihood. We see the Aral Sea, once the fourth largest inland body of water in the world, as essentially dead.

Similarly, the Black Sea and Caspian Sea are rapidly losing their fish. I crossed the Bosphorous twice last week and the fishing industry is deteriorating there at a rapid rate. Whole species are dying off in the Mediterranean. The great lakes of Africa are in serious trouble and deteriorating rapidly. Look at what is happening to the forest in Eastern Europe that I visited two weeks ago. There are whole areas in Czechoslovakia where the coniferous trees are still standing but there are no needles left on the trees. Look at the lakes in Scandinavia that are now dead because of acidification. As one who has traveled for years watching this process unfold, I could go on and on with similar examples. Civilization is in trouble; far more trouble than most people realize.

But your point about this being the "turn-around decade" is that this process will soon become irreversible.

We have very little experience understanding this process because throughout our lifetimes, at least until recently, for most people in the world, things have been getting better. The global economy has expanded fourfold since 1950 and the average level of income in the world has probably doubled during that period. But we are now moving into a period when the world economy is not growing very fast. It did not grow very fast in the 1980s or in 1970; in the 1970s it didn't grow as fast as during the 1960s. In the 1990s, in many parts of the world, growth of the economy seems likely to fall behind population growth. And, at some point, as living conditions deteriorate, societies begin to disintegrate.

We studied the archeological sites of societies that went through this process in times past. North Africa was once the granary of the Roman Empire; today it is largely desert and countries there have to import half their grain, on average. The Fertile Crescent in the Middle East supported a very sizeable population, but salinity in the irrigation systems slowly undermined it and led to its demise. The lowlands of Guatemala supported maybe two million people in the ninth century.

But in these ancient times people could move on to another fertile area once they had destroyed the fertility of their homeland; now they can't.

Yes, they could move on and many did. The whole New World was populated with the excess from Europe. They could move on and the effects were also local. If civilization collapsed in the Fertile Crescent, the Tigris/Euphrates region of the Middle East, it really didn't affect much of the rest of the world. But today, in an integrated global economy, when the economy starts to deteriorate in one region of the world it affects the entire system to some degree. And at some point you get enough weaknesses in the global system that the whole system begins to deteriorate. The whole international financial system is based on the assumption that economic growth, as defined in terms of GNP, will continue to expand. If it begins to shrink that system will be in trouble and so will we.

You went to some pains in your book, Saving the Planet, *to describe the flip side of the problems you have just outlined. You described the chief characteristics of a sustainable world community. Would you briefly describe what changes in taxes and subsidies you think will be necessary to make it economically feasible to create this sustainable vision of the future?*

As we look at the existing economic system it seems clear to us that it is not environmentally sustainable. Indeed, the existing system is slowly self-destructing. If the system we now have doesn't work, the question is: Is there a system that will work? And the answer to that is: Yes.

One of the things my colleagues — Christopher Flavin and Sandra Postel — and I have been doing over the last couple of years is trying to apply the principles of ecology to the design of an economic system. And the exciting thing is that we can now see what an environmentally sustainable global economy would look like.

We can create such a system using only existing technologies. For example, in the realm of energy, we can now see how we can harness energy from the sun in its many forms: hydro power, wind power, photovoltaic cells, solar-thermal power plants, organic matter in various forms such as firewood, alcohol fuels, sugar cane, the use of agricultural waste to produce electricity, or rooftop solar water heaters — there is a long list of the many forms of solar energy. Solar thermal power plants of the sort being built in southern California now supply electricity to almost half a million people. These plants convert 21 percent of sunlight into electricity at a cost of 8 cents a kilowatt hour compared to 6 cents for coal and 12 cents for nuclear generated electricity. We can see how this technology, employed on a larger scale, would produce cheap solar electricity that could then be used to electrolyze water to produce hydrogen. Hydrogen then becomes a way to store sunlight so that it can be transported efficiently. We think that all these various sources of solar energy can play a role. We can see how it is now possible to create an environmentally sustainable world. That is the exciting thing.

Then the question becomes: How do we get from here to there? Governments have many policy implements they can use. One is the allocation of research and development resources. Another is the use of tax policy. A third is the use of regulation to ban certain economic activities that are environmentally destructive. Of these various policies and instruments we think tax policy is by far the most efficient. Governments now tax income because it is an easy way to acquire revenue, but it doesn't serve any particular social purpose.

In a sense the income tax is a disincentive to work.

Exactly. We are taxing work, discouraging work and encouraging environmentally destructive activities. We think we should reverse that situation and tax not work but environmentally destructive activities such as carbon emissions, the generation of hazardous waste, the use of pesticides, the use of virgin raw materials in manufacturing as opposed to recycled materials, etc. If we restructure the tax system, tax policy can be used as a steering mechanism to move the global economy in an environmentally sustainable direction.

At present the European Community is considering an environmental tax on energy, specifically on fossil fuels and nuclear power. The proposed tax, if adopted, would amount to the equivalent of about $10 per barrel of oil when fully implemented by the end of the decade. We think that will tip the scales, in many cases, away from investment in fossil fuels or nuclear power plants to investments in energy efficiency and in the development of renewable energy resources such as wind and solar thermal power. We don't think it will take very much of a shift in relative cost to bring about this transformation of the economy.

The basic weakness of the existing economic system is that we have a faulty method of accounting. We have an economic accounting system that includes depreciation of investment capital in plant equipment, but does not include the depreciation of natural capital. You can deforest a country in one year and the GNP will jump dramatically, and yet the ecological consequences would be devastating. Right now with the existing economic system we count that as progress.

What environmental taxes do is approximate the external costs — the externalities, as the economists call them — and reincorporate those costs back into the economic system as an environmental tax. We are not suggesting any change in the level of taxation, but a change in the pattern of taxation — the way in which governments collect revenue. The exciting thing is that it makes such eminent sense.

Will the environmental taxes mean that only the rich will be able to drive around in cars because only they will be able to afford highly taxed gasoline? And what effect will these taxes have in developing countries?

I would broaden the question somewhat. Can people in developing countries achieve the consumption levels that the rich countries now have? My answer is that I don't think that Third World countries will ever achieve the consumption levels that now exist in the industrial countries, nor do I think that the industrial countries themselves will be able to sustain the consumption levels that now exist.

The question is not how much can we consume. The question is how do we assure a meaningful life and the satisfaction of basic needs without destroying the earth's life-support systems. It is possible to satisfy our needs with only a fraction of the earth's natural resources that we now use, whether it is energy, land, water, or whatever. What we need to do is rethink the structure of the economic system.

Let me just use a simple example or two. If we substitute returnable glass beverage containers for the existing throw-away glass beverage containers or aluminum cans, we can reduce the energy required to provide beverage containers by close to 90 percent and the related pollution of air and water by almost as much. By using returnable glass beverage containers we can achieve a 90 percent drop in related resource use and pressure on the environment, but still have the same number of beverage containers. The only difference is that instead of throwing them away we refill them.

Look at the transportation issue. In the U.S. we have created a situation in which thousands of Americans get in a car and drive to a fitness center someplace to sit on stationary bicycles for a half hour, then take a shower, and get in a car and drive home. I am convinced that in our sedentary, health-conscious society, if we created a bicycle-friendly transportation system, in our cities in particular, millions of Americans would bike to work because they would like to. In the process, we would greatly reduce the resources used for transportation. We would also improve health in two ways: We would have cleaner air and more exercise. The quality of life would be much higher, but the level of resource consumption, the manufacturing of automobiles and the use of energy for those automobiles, would drop substantially. I could extend this analysis through every sector of the economy.

11

Coming to Washington on the train from New York I was thinking about your vision of a sustainable future while looking at the landscape rolling by. I saw six-lane highways choked with fuel-inefficient cars, rusting factories with outmoded equipment, houses with single pane windows and little insulation, and enormous oil and gas depots. Almost everything made by man that I saw out of the train window would have to be replaced in order to achieve an ecologically sustainable economy.

We call it the Environmental Revolution.

All right, but if you are going to fit that transformation into a decade or two, as you seem to suggest, it will require a staggering investment. Where will the investment money for this transformation come from?

It will come from a number of areas. First of all if you take energy, which is central, I don't know how much we spend a year on energy but it is billions and billions of dollars. We can spend that money on energy or we can begin to shift some of it, using an environmental tax on energy use. We can shift some of that investment money into efficiency, toward retrofitting some of the buildings you saw, toward increasing the energy efficiency of the transportation systems. A tax on those cars that you saw on the highway, as you were riding on the train, would encourage more people to use the rails. We need to change the pattern of expenditures, and that is where we think tax policy can play an enormous role.

We have made some progress in this country in fuel efficiency. For example, during the energy crisis in the 1970s, when prices quadrupled, the average car on the road was getting 14 miles per gallon. Now, in 1992, the average car is getting more than 20 miles per gallon; the average car sold this year will probably get 28. There are many cars being sold that get over 40 miles per gallon. All the major automobile companies have prototypes of cars that get 60 to 90 miles per gallon. So, even staying with cars, you can see the enormous potential there. When you combine that with redesigning the public transportation system, more investment in rail for both passenger and freight, and a bicycle-friendly transportation system, you can begin to see how we can transform the system. It won't all come within the next couple of years. It will take time, but a lot of it can come this decade if we get our act together with a shift in the tax policy.

We also have some resources to use if we redefine security. Over the last half century we have defined security almost exclusively in military terms. But almost any thoughtful person now realizes that the real threats to our future are much less military and much more environmental. The real threats to our future are the continued depletion of the ozone layer that protects us from ultraviolet radiation, the continued pumping of greenhouse gases into the atmosphere that is driving climate change, the loss of biological diversity, and the continued deforestation and loss of topsoil. These are the real threats to our future. If we begin to realize that, and begin to shift resources away from weapons systems and supporting an enormous military establishment, then we can invest in family planning, tree planting, soil conservation, energy efficiency, and developing renewable energy resources. If we do that we have a chance of making it.

The exciting thing is that we are now seeing a real surge of interest, particularly on the part of the superpowers, in strengthening the peace-keeping capability of the United Nations. We also see both the International Monetary Fund (IMF) and the World Bank now talking about conditioning assistance to developing countries on reductions in military expenditures, where they are considered to be bloated.

The World Bank and IMF may put that kind of pressure on Third World nations to reduce their military expenditures, but who will put pressure on the United States and other industrial nations to cut their own military expenditures?

In order to make this case credible to developing countries, we, of course, have to be engaged in the same process. I think the reason that the World Bank is beginning to think about this — and it wouldn't touch it before because military security was such a sacred national policy — is that they see that if we can't reorder priorities rather dramatically we will not be able to reverse the trends that are now converging in many Third World countries. In its *World Development Report* for 1991 the World Bank published economic data showing that incomes fell during the 1980s in more than 40 countries. These 40 countries contain over 800 million people. Almost all of these countries have three things in common: rapid population growth, rapid environmental degradation, and heavy external debt. These three trends — one demographic, one environmental, and one economic — have combined to undermine progress in more than 40 countries that contain one-sixth of humanity.

The risk is that if some bold steps are not taken, the trends in these countries will not only continue but they will spread to more and more countries facing a similar situation. Eventually the whole world will be caught in an economic down-draft as environmental degradation and economic decline begin to feed on each other. This is no longer something hypothetical: Living standards are falling now in a large number of countries around the world. I think it will take some dramatic initiatives to reverse that process. In a sense, I think that is what Rio is going to be all about.

As we in northern industrial countries ask the people in developing countries to make sacrifices in order to preserve global environmental integrity, they look to us to see what we are willing to do in return. Does "responsible global citizenship," as you have called it, require reducing per capita carbon dioxide emissions in wealthy countries to the per-capita levels in poor countries?

We have recognized for some time that those of us living in industrial countries consume a disproportionate share of the world's natural resources, whether it be energy, minerals, water, or food. What we are now beginning to see is that we are generating a level of carbon emissions that is far greater than that of the Third World, despite the fact that the earth's atmospheric system is a shared resource. It is one thing to be able to afford to consume more energy, and in the past we have assumed that if you have the economic resources you have the right to consume more energy, or food, or whatever. But when you have a common resource such as the earth's atmospheric system, the question becomes how much of it each of us can claim.

What I think we have to realize is that we have to redesign the economic system so that we reestablish a carbon balance in the world, so that carbon emissions do not exceed carbon fixation. In that process I think we will have to change and restructure the energy economy so that we are not using fossil fuels. And in that process I think we will begin to move toward a much more equitable global energy system, one based on renewable energy resources that are much more evenly distributed throughout the world.

You are suggesting that we are moving toward this more equitable balance, but are you saying that our goal should be that we in the industrialized world should live with carbon emissions similar to people in the developing world?

The question is somewhat broader than that. The question is: How do we reestablish a carbon balance, which is a precondition for a stable climatic system. And in doing that it will not be a question of how much fossil fuel we consume versus the Chinese. The question is: How do we redesign the energy system so that their basic needs can also be satisfied along with ours without disrupting the earth's climatic system? That requires a change in energy sources. The question is not: Can we continue to consume fossil fuels indefinitely, and how close to our level of consumption can the Third World come? That is not really the issue. We are in trouble even if we don't consume any more than we are consuming now. We have to change the energy system, and when we make that change away from fossil fuels toward renewable energy sources, then I think the equity issue begins to sort itself out, simply because renewable energy resources — that is, solar energy — are distributed much more equitably in the world.

So all those countries where the sun beats down on the desert will be making a lot of money selling energy.

Exactly. Those deserts will be worth something.

Al Gore:

Sustainable Development in the Post Cold War Era

l Gore, U.S. Senator (D., Tenn.) is Chairman of the Subcommittee on Science, Technology and Space of the Senate Commerce Committee and Chairman of the Congressional Energy and Environment Study Conference. He is president of Global Legislators for a Balanced Environment. Senator Gore is Chairman of the U.S. Senate delegation to the United Nations Conference on Environment and Development (UNCED), and author of *Earth in the Balance: Ecology and the Human Spirit.*

Steve Lerner: How would you rate the importance of the United Nations Conference on Environment and Development (UNCED) negotiations in the context of other environmental negotiations?

Sen. Al Gore: I think that UNCED is the designated time and place for the emergence of a new world ethic. I argue in my book, *Earth in the Balance*, that the effort to save the earth's environment must become the central organizing principle of the post Cold War era. If that is indeed to be accomplished, the Earth Summit is the first place that that basic idea will be addressed in a global forum.

However, there is now a risk that the Earth Summit will be perceived as more style than substance if several of the important negotiations going on produce no meaningful commitments. It will be labeled a success no matter what happens.

What do you think of the role the U.S. Administration and delegation has played at UNCED?

The positions the U.S. has taken at UNCED are not the delegation's fault. The delegates are quite professional and I have the deepest respect for them. But the policies of the Administration, chiefly President Bush, have much to answer for. This has been a disgraceful performance. It is the single worst failure of political leadership that I have seen in my lifetime. Even if the United States had been committed to this task, it would have been difficult to engineer the sort of agreement that the Earth Summit calls for. Without U.S. leadership the task becomes impossible. With U.S. obstructionism the world will become cynical at a time when it is ready to be inspired. The opportunity cost is immense, just immense, incalculable.

But there is still time. High-wire acts have been seen before under this big top. Twenty-four hours before the London Amendments of the Montreal Protocol were finalized, White House Chief of Staff John Sununu was still refusing to allow U.S. contributions to the fund. With 12 hours left in the conference, he changed his mind.

Now that Sununu is gone, the decisions are more nakedly evident as Bush decisions. In an election year, with environmentalism a fluid force in the election, the Administration will find it difficult to continually reassert the idiotic position that has been taken on these questions. It is embarrassing to see 139 countries lined up on one side and the United States on the other.

Of which issue?

On a whole range of issues. Now, if we were right and the whole rest of the world was wrong, I would be proud of that stance. But for us to take such a position when it is wrong is really arrogant and willful. It goes beyond the normal obsequiousness that is shown to powerful industries that don't want any new burdens placed on them. In this case some companies in the coal industry lead the charge, arguing that the evidence does not support the need for action.

On global warming?

Yes, much as scientists for tobacco companies will still pretend that the evidence is insufficient for the link between smoking and lung cancer. They make money by twisting the truth. And the same practice is underway with regard to global climate change. President Bush gives these self-interested cynics a megaphone — and portrays their views as credible.

Gus Speth at World Resources Institute points out that in 1972 at the Stockholm Convention on the Human Environment, the role of the U.S. was quite different than it has been at UNCED. At Stockholm, the U.S. took something of a leadership role.

Yes we did. And on a bipartisan basis. By the way, my predecessor, Howard Baker, played a positive role in that.

What do you think has changed in the last 20 years to take the U.S. from a leadership position to one primarily engaged in damage limitation? Why are we passing up the opportunity to make progress on international environmental issues?

Why is the U.S. taking an obstructionist position now as compared with a constructive position in 1972? There are several reasons. First, unlike then President Nixon, President Bush and President Reagan gained election with the support of a coalition much further to the right of center, a coalition that included some rather extreme elements. Some of these elements actually believe that the ozone hole is a myth perpetrated by NASA to build its budget; and that the whole global environmental crisis is a hoax designed to expand the role of government when ironically most environmentalists point the finger of blame at government as much as at any other institution.

Second, the Bush Administration is significantly more craven in its willingness to serve the short-term desires of powerful political supporters, some of whom fear the transition that will be necessary if the world confronts global climate change in any meaningful way.

Third, our civilization is in a deeper crisis than it was 20 years ago. We find it harder to devote sustained attention to the problems confronting us. The willingness of political leaders to distract the attention of the electorate with trivialities is significantly more pronounced now. The political dialogue is more compressed into shorter sound bites that encourage slogans rather than substantive communication.

On the positive side, the deeper trends among the American people are in the opposite direction. One can go into any classroom in the United States — and this would not have been true in 1972 — and ask the children what is the most important issue and they will tell you it's the environment and climate change. They know all about it. In many other countries the political dialogue is far advanced. I believe it is only a matter of time before the American people express a demand to their leaders that we face up to this issue.

Do you think President Bush will attend the Earth Summit in Rio in June, 1992?

The odds are heavily in favor of a decision by the President to change his mind and go to this conference. I don't think he knows that yet. But at some point his political advisors will notice that the California primary occurs on the second day of the Earth Summit and that he must engage the environmental issue in order to win in California in the fall. If, at the peak of political publicity in California, President Bush suffers a devastating embarrassment as a result of his willful refusal to attend the Earth Summit, it will have a very serious effect on his reelection prospects. And I think when his advisors put two and two together they will recommend that he go. I think there is at least a chance that he, being a man of principle, will change his mind and go.

The tragedy is that this reversal will come so late, if it does come, as to preclude the changing of the U.S. position on substantive issues under negotiation. And the President may end up being embarrassed if he does attend the Summit.

The Bush Administration recently announced that it would make a grant of $75 million in "environmental aid" to developing nations. The Administration says it will also announce a series of initiatives on energy efficiency instead of agreeing to set a target of stabilizing emissions of carbon dioxide at 1990 levels by the year 2000. How would you characterize this Administration initiative?

Without an agreement to set targets and timetables for reducing carbon dioxide emissions, these commitments to take actions, some of which are already included in the Energy Bill, really don't amount to very much. When we address the question of how the world would protect the stratospheric ozone layer, and eliminate the emission of chemicals that destroy ozone, the obvious approach is to set some targets and timetables for the reduction of emissions of these chemicals. How else can we measure progress; how else can we fashion a global agreement to sing from the same sheet of music?

The U.S. approach of calling for every nation just to state its good intentions and not make any commitments, not set any goals — if that approach was taken by everyone in the world, there would be no agreement, there would be no progress, and there would be no way to tell whether or not there had been any progress.

I think it is a sham just to list this series of policy changes. For example, one of the policy changes is premised on the assumption that we will build another 110 nuclear power plants. That's interesting. No utility has ordered a nuclear power plant in the last 14 years. In fact, I'm not even sure that that qualifies as a good intention.

With respect to the announcement of the $75 million grant, it is important to realize what that really involves. Twenty-five million dollars of those $75 million will fund greenhouse gas emission inventories in developing countries. But nothing was agreed to for capacity building, which is the heart of what is needed in developing countries.

The other $50 million contribution was to the core fund of a revised Global Environment Facility (GEF). The nature of the revisions to GEF is very much in negotiation. Some revisions are quite sensible and, in my view, needed. But to condition even that amount on the separate question under negotiation leaves the whole matter shrouded in uncertainty. If this contribution of $50 million turns out to be real, then it represents a tiny first step forward and is slightly better than nothing. But not much, because, if the United States is unwilling to set targets and timetables for carbon dioxide emission reductions, and if the Administration refuses to move forward in a leadership posture to make the climate change negotiations a success, then the entire process is jeopardized.

Is UNCED an appropriate forum in which to work on the problem posed by the global population explosion? What has been the position of the U.S. on the need to stabilize the global population?

It is important to note that population stabilization is not formally a part of the charter for the Earth Summit. However, it inevitably affects the approach taken to all the other issues involved. When one takes an objective look at what must be done to stabilize world population, it is apparent that we have to create three conditions around the world which, when established, lead to the stabilizing of population.

The first of the three, making birth control available, is the one where all the debate has occurred, although, in my opinion, it should not be controversial. But that is not really a part of the UNCED negotiation.

The other two conditions necessary for stabilizing population — raising child survival rates and levels of literacy — are, in fact, a part of the UNCED agenda.

How do we raise child survival rates? Julius Nyerere said 30 years ago that the most powerful contraceptive in the world is the confidence on the part of parents that their children will survive. When child survival rates go up and stay up, then family sizes begin to come down, provided that two other conditions are present. These are making birth control available and raising levels of literacy and education, especially among women so that women are empowered to participate in the choices on family size and contraception.

I personally believe that in order to solve the global ecological crisis we have to address the population explosion. How we do it internationally and domestically is critical. I have dealt with the international context: it is not formally part of the UNCED agenda, but indirectly many of these issues will inevitably be a part of the discussion.

On the domestic side, I think it is amazing that President Bush has turned his back on the rest of his political career prior to his bargain with former President Reagan. At that time he agreed to give up his convictions on the population issue and argue a case that he had previously argued against. When Bush was the Ambassador to the United Nations in the 1970s, he wrote eloquently of the need for stabilizing world population. He later made a pact with a right-of-center coalition in the United States within his political party, where a tiny minority within a minority believes that birth control is immoral. They have leveraged the rest of that coalition to make a demand that he be against international family planning programs. He directed that the U.S. policy change. He reversed his personal position. And he continues to do what this tiny minority within a minority insists upon as a price for their support.

How much worse does it have to get before there is the political will to do something about accelerating environmental degradation? The temperature is rising, the sea-level is rising, the hole in the ozone is growing larger. Do you think it is going to take some kind of further catastrophe before someone can run for President of the United States on a sustainable development platform?

I hope not. But on the other hand, we have a lot of catastrophes with us right now. For example, 37,000 children under the age of 5 die every 24 hours in the world. Isn't that a catastrophe? The Aral Sea, the fourth largest inland sea in the world, just dried up. Isn't that a catastrophe? The Arctic Ocean is now threatened with millions of curies of radiation. Isn't that a catastrophe? We have an ozone hole three times the size of the United States of America above Antarctica and a new one that may open up above heavily populated areas in the Northern Hemisphere. The air we are breathing right now has 600 percent more chlorine atoms in each breath than it did 40 years ago. We are losing living species at a rate 1000 times faster than at any time in the last 65 million years. We are losing forest land at the rate of one and a half acres per second. Dolphins are washing up dead on the beaches of the Mediterranean Sea for the fourth time in this decade. Frogs, toads, and salamanders are disappearing on every continent. Coral reefs are bleaching in every ocean. The ice is melting so rapidly on mountain glaciers that we are discovering 5,000-year-old stone age hunters who haven't been seen before because the ice hasn't melted in all that time. How many more signals do we need?

An alcoholic who has a series of drunk driving accidents will argue that each one of them is an isolated misfortune, unconnected to the other. But the family will say: "Please, stop drinking, the next accident could be fatal." There is a pattern here. These ecological catastrophes are related. They have a common cause. Our civilization is colliding violently with the ecological system of the earth. We are now threatening the integrity of that ecological system. And in the process we are threatening the integrity and stability of many societies around the world that are configured precisely to the climate balance that has persisted since the first cities appeared in Mesopotamia in the Levant 9,000 years ago. So, I think when you ask will it take a catastrophe, I would say: yes. But we have already had catastrophes. How many will it take?

The temptation to be frustrated at the lack of response to these ecological catastrophes should be resisted because the perception of no response is an illusion. Think of the way earthquakes occur. Two tectonic plates will move slowly until they oppose one another directly. Pressure builds up with very little sign on the surface until a threshold is reached and then suddenly the pressure is released when one plate moves decisively over the other sending out shock waves that knock down buildings. Ideas move the same way. The most recent example is that of Democracy and Communism opposing each other in Europe along a faultline that runs right through Berlin. Change took place beneath the surface until suddenly freedom moved over Communism, submerging it. The shock waves knocked down the Berlin Wall and all the Communist governments in Europe.

The idea that we are separate from nature, unconnected to the future, entitled to exploit the earth with impunity, alienated from the communities in which we live, and the physical world itself, this way of thinking is under enormous pressure from a new, opposing, and more powerful way of perceiving ourselves as part of the ecological system, with responsibility to each other and to the future, and as part of a civilization which is itself a force of nature more powerful than the hurricanes and the tides. Even though the older, obsolete way of thinking seems to be holding fast, and there is a temptation to assume that it will never give way, the pressure is building. And when we reach the threshold the world will change.

Maurice Strong:

Launching an Era of International Environmental Negotiations

 aurice Strong is Secretary General of the United Nations Conference on Environment and Development.

Steve Lerner: *Some critics say that the United Nations Conference on Environment and Development (UNCED) negotiations took on too many issues at once. They argue that it would have been better to select several discrete areas having to do with environment and development, and to try to make progress on them. For example, UNCED could have taken up the issue of improving energy efficiency worldwide, and using the savings to invest in sustainable development projects in the developing world. Or UNCED could have pushed for expanding mass transportation systems around the world as a way to reduce the global consumption of fossil fuels. Either of these two initiatives could have made a considerable contribution to improving the health of the planet. Looking back on this process, do you feel it has been advantageous to take on such a long list of environmental and development issues?*

Maurice Strong: First of all, I didn't make this decision. People who criticize should go back to the source: the U.N. resolution that gave UNCED its mandate. But, you either have to look at issues systemically or individually. There have been a lot of special events surrounding particular issues such as renewable energy and the population issue. But I believe that what is needed is to look at this whole series of issues in terms of the systemic set of relationships amongst them. This allows you to look at them in a different way than you would in a one- or two-issue conference. The one- or two-issue conference is a traditional way of dealing with these issues; it has its place and its merits. But within this whole environment and development relationship, there has to be an understanding of whole systems, and the place of each of these issues within its system.

Here at UNCED we are going into a reasonable amount of detail with respect to each of these issues, but not the same degree of detail we would achieve if any one of them were the sole focus of the conference.

I expect that UNCED will spawn a whole series of individual conferences. It already has. There is a special conference on industry in Copenhagen, there is one on water in Dublin, there is one on water and river basins in France, one on water resources in Turkey.

And these were brought about because of UNCED?

In quite a few cases they were; in other cases they have decided to focus on input into UNCED. The water, rivers, and industry conferences are all specifically for UNCED.

I believe the system itself is the important issue. The fact is that we have not learned how to manage the cause-and-effect system that we live in. Individual sectoral activities and policies impact on the whole cause-and-effect system in ways that we are not geared to manage. So basically I think the governments did the right thing in delineating the tasks for UNCED. They did it in a fairly conventional way by just listing the issues, but that enabled us to do what I think is needed at this time. That is, to try to put the issues in the systemic framework in which they can be dealt with. That is why the International Institute for Applied Systems Analysis is such an important part of our process, and the linkages among the issues are among the prime elements of our work.

So, the critics are right that you would get far more done on particular issues if you focused only on them. But I think that is the conventional approach that most conferences are following and I am glad that this isn't one of them.

UNCED has become a real focal point for interest in global environment/development issues. After Rio what will happen? Where will the focal point come to rest? Will there be an institution to carry on this work?

That question is being considered. That is why the institutional issues, which are at the very end of our agenda, are a prime concern. But the institutional issues — who does what and what kind of institutional changes are needed to insure the implementation of the results of UNCED — these are a major subject for the conference itself.

I think there are several dominant themes in what governments say, and in what we in the UNCED Secretariat have been saying in our documents. One thing is that there should be no new huge global authority set up to deal with these issues. Second, existing institutions need significant strengthening if they are going to be called upon to do a bigger, broader, and better job. One such institution is the United Nations Environment Program (UNEP). But also there seems to be a strong understanding, which I certainly am promoting, of the need to strengthen the environmental capacity of *all* the various agencies of the U.N., particularly in the areas that impact the most on the environment, such as energy, transport, agriculture and, industry.

The mechanisms by which these institutions work together need to be strengthened. I don't mean just coordination, but actual active collaboration. We are developing a pattern in our UNCED process that provides a good model.

Regarding the general sentiment that there should be no new big institution, does that preclude the possibility of an existing institution being changed so radically that one would not recognize it?

No it doesn't. One of the strands that is coming out of these negotiations is the need to decide on a follow-up mechanism for UNCED. I think everyone has conceded that while you don't need a new global institution — at least the world is not ready for that sort of thing yet — you cannot just leave the follow-up of this conference to "business as usual." There is a general recognition that some mechanism is needed at the intergovernmental level, and that it should be a high-level mechanism, probably at the ministerial level, with some form of supporting secretariat. There remains a question as to where that secretariat should be located. Will it be in New York, at U.N. headquarters? Will it be within one of the organizations such as UNEP? I think the general view is that it should not be in any one of the several organizations that will have to be contributing to it. To put it in just one would be difficult. But that is not decided yet. So there will be a follow-up mechanism of some kind, I think.

If you were to bet on what it would look like, what would you say?

I won't tell you how I would bet, because that would not be consistent with my role as a public servant. If I do have ideas they will come out in due course, but it would not be helpful to the process to state my position now.

On the financing of sustainable development, can you give me an idea about the amount of money that is being discussed? And does it not look as if the Global Environment Facility (GEF) within the World Bank is likely to be the big winner out of the UNCED process?

No, I don't think so. I don't know what you mean by the big winner. The amount of money handled by the GEF at present makes it a peanut stand compared with the amount of money that is needed.

My understanding is that the World Bank's GEF has started a pilot project with some $1.5 billion to be spent over a three year period to support sustainable development projects.

That is a peanut stand in terms of what is needed.

Then what is the level of funding required for the promotion of sustainable development?

I don't know that. I know it will be in the billions of dollars. One of the important things that we will be doing between now and the last Preparatory Committee session is trying to cost the proposals that have been made at UNCED. Clearly the needs of developing countries are very large. But equally clearly they cannot be met by simple increases in aid. They need to be met through a whole series of things including the redeployment of funds within developing nations. Most of their funding has to come from within. But they will also need to receive a lot more external funding. And one of the things that we will have to help them do is stop the hemorrhaging of the money flowing North. There are billions of dollars a year flowing out of the developing countries.

Is there any reason to believe that this conference will be able to do anything about those South-to-North financial flows, which are now estimated to be $50 billion dollars a year.

That is one of the central issues. UNCED is not the place where the trade negotiations will be completed. That will be done in the General Agreement on Tariffs and Trade (GATT) negotiations. UNCED won't be the place where debt is actually forgiven. But UNCED is the only summit conference in our times that can address these issues at the highest level and try to devise a political breakthrough that will permit these issues to be handled with a whole new set of perspectives and priorities. That is one of the primary purposes of the conference. It won't be the place where you negotiate the particulars, but UNCED will provide the political basis for a major reorientation in the relationships between North and South. If it doesn't it will fail. And it might.

Are you not concerned that there will be a lack of harmony between the results of UNCED and the GATT negotiations?

I am not sure there will be a lack of harmony between UNCED and GATT. The political will to make a serious effort to improve the trade relationships will be given a tremendous boost by UNCED. Even GATT is looking to us for that, to give them the high level political sanction they need to try to break the impasse that exists there. But the actual negotiating process will not be done by UNCED but by GATT. I am working with the director general of GATT and he looks to UNCED to give GATT a tremendous boost with respect to their work on environment.

Developing nation delegates see the possibility that there could be many good intentions here at UNCED, but then the GATT negotiations could do something diametrically opposed to the promotion of sustainable development.

That could happen. Of course it could happen. But I could be run over on my way to work tomorrow morning. Or an asteroid could strike our planet and everything would be over. The fact is that if UNCED remains a summit-level conference, and nothing happens to change the commitment to that, UNCED can provide the maximum potential for mobilizing political will on these issues. If we get a commitment, it is certainly possible for nations to renege, but it should be politically very difficult for them to do so. None of us can guarantee anything. I cannot guarantee that the Earth Summit in Rio will do anything useful.

In other words, if various governments try to renege on the commitments made in Rio, the international community can embarrass them by pointing out what they agreed to in Rio, and emphasize that they are not

living up to the terms of the agreement. It could be pointed out, for ex-
ample, that the leaders of the Group of Seven (G-7) nations agreed to
one set of principles at UNCED and a different arrangement at GATT,
if that should happen.

It happens that governments renege on agreements, and it could happen again. But it is unlikely to happen when these commitments are
made so visibly. UNCED will be a highly visible conference where
heads of government will commit themselves in a very public manner.
There is nothing above nation states. You can't put them in jail. You
can't shoot them. But international agreements are the highest level on
which you can apply political will. Of course it doesn't guarantee anything to sign an international agreement, but it is the best guarantee you
can get.

In the area of financial mechanisms, what do you see as the viable
options?

It is all set out in the UNCED paper on finances. I talk about the
Green Fund and the pluses and minuses of that. Some say that the GEF
cannot remain as it is because its governance mechanisms are not suit-
able. We in the UNCED Secretariat do not have any feeling as to
whether the GEF should or should not be the ultimate funding mechanism. We are only saying that it is a pilot project now, and if it is going to
be the ultimate funding mechanism it will have to have a lot more
money. Secondly, it will have to have changed very significantly in its
terms of reference and governance.

From listening to the debate so far, do you feel there is movement in
terms of changing the way the GEF would be administered?

Yes. That is not the primary focus at the moment; however, that position is brought out. The industrialized countries like the GEF because it
is World Bank oriented. They have disproportionate voting rights in the
World Bank and they have confidence in it. The developing countries
are not anti-Bank, but they are less committed to the Bank as the primary institutional mechanism. So these positions are being set out now.
The developing countries have said they don't like the present arrangements for the GEF. The industrialized countries say that they do like
them, but might be willing to change them a bit. But that isn't the primary subject yet, although it is becoming an important subject. The issue isn't joined finally here at this meeting. It will be debated further in
New York.

In trying to communicate about what is at issue at UNCED, most
people I talk to grasp what is happening with the climate change and
biodiversity conventions, and with the Earth Charter. They see that if
these are signed, UNCED will have achieved something significant. It
is harder for them to grasp what will be the real achievement of the
Agenda 21 documents.

A charter without a program for its implementation would not mean much. Agenda 21 is a tightly negotiated series of very specific actions. Some of them are still at the stage of simply enunciating policies, but a great many of them are at the stage of actually detailing the actions for dealing with toxic and hazardous wastes, and forestry issues. There is a whole series and they are laid out there in very concrete terms under our options in each of those areas.

Yes, but what I would like to know is, if these are all signed at Rio, do you feel that constitutes a commitment to do all the things listed in Agenda 21? After all it is a very long and ambitious list.

That is because it is an agenda for the world community; it has got to be a long list. It is only one item on the UNCED agenda, but as you can see, it accounts for vast of amounts of negotiations on the individual issues. In Rio it will be listed as a single item, Agenda 21; the delegates will approve that. But the contents will have to have been approved in advance.

I believe all of these things are part of a package: the principles, the Earth Charter, the actual program of action that will be endorsed at the highest political level. I believe we carry a high degree of commitment, which will have to be enforced by parallel decisions in each of the governing bodies concerned with the implementation of Agenda 21. But then you need commitment on the means to carry out Agenda 21. That is why commitment on finances is important, and commitment on how to make the technologies available, and then the necessary institutional arrangements. I see these as part of a package: principles, action program, and the means to implement it through finance, technology, and institutions.

The conventions on climate change and biodiversity are separate things. They are being negotiated on separate tracks. And they will be signed, not negotiated, in Rio. So it is a fairly simple package, although difficult to come by. That whole package should be subject to the same comment I made to you earlier: that we will get the highest level of political commitment possible. And that should mean that the prospects for these proposals being carried out are very high. There will be some slippage, but then there will be some nations that will do a little better than their commitments. But if we don't get a high level of commitment on these agreements, then UNCED will be a failure. Even if we do get this high level of commitment and if subsequently governments don't live up to it, UNCED will have been a failure. I can't guarantee anything.

The implication I get in questions like the one you posed, although not necessarily from you, is that because nations might not live up to their commitments under UNCED, because it might fail, why bother attempting it. Then I ask, OK, what would *you* do? Just because we might lose the basketball game next week, should we not have it? Is there any other set of issues more important than those that impact on the future of our planet? All these doubts are quite in order; it is your business to have them. I have them also. But operationally, what do you do about them? You do the best you can. You cannot say that one of the heads of state will be shot if he or she reneges on the agreement. What you can do, and this is what we have done, is get these negotiations to the point at which they will take place at the highest political level. That maximizes the prospect that the commitments will be real, but we can never guarantee it. In fact, there is no way to guarantee it. If someone could tell me how, please do.

How do these quite elaborate documents in Agenda 21 fit into the legal process as we understand it in the West? "Soft law" has been used as a buzzword to describe it. Some of these papers that form part of Agenda 21 are very promising, the intentions are very promising, but it is hard to know how they will be used if you are outside the process.

If you are going to have a conference, you have to get governments committed to take some actions. Agenda 21 is the putting together of all those actions. The thing that is different from other conferences is that they are not just a list of items. They are put together in a systemic framework that permits you to see that there is an interactive relationship amongst these issues. We hope that out of this conference will come a much better set of tools for understanding and dealing with complex systemic issues. Our process is designed to do that. One of the things that should come out of the conference is a much better means by which governments can actually exercise the levers on issues that don't fall into the neat sectoral and disciplinary compartments of most governments.

It is a new way for the "world brain" to be thinking.

And it has to. You have to think at a certain level of detail in each area, but you have to also provide the context and framework in which each issue can be seen in terms of its impact on the total cause-and-effect system, and the reciprocal impact of that system on it.

The delegates from the developing world say that it strains their resources to deal with all these issues at the same time.

It does, but you do have to begin thinking about these things in systemic terms. It is like your body. You can't say "There is a pinprick in my toe, so I am going to draw a line and it will not affect the rest of my body." You can draw a line around a nation and say: "That is my border, so I am going to ordain that nothing that happens outside it is going to have any effect on me." That is not the way it works in real life, and we have to devise real-life methods of governance that recognize that. And we haven't. One of the important products of this conference is to get people thinking about these complex issues as something more than just single problems to be dealt with. They do have to be dealt with individually, but they also have to be dealt with as part of a system. That systemic way of operating needs to be devised.

You have taken on a herculean task.

No one forced me to. I am not complaining. I am enjoying it.

You were a very successful businessman before you turned your hand to this work. What made you interested in environmental and development issues?

This is the most important business of all: trying to provide maintenance and amortization for planet earth. It is like taking over a company that is going down the drain. You have to put it on a sound basis. And that is what we are trying to do with the planet. Right now we are under liquidation. Planet Earth Inc. is in Chapter 11 (bankruptcy). So we are trying to put it on a sustainable course. This is not a personal effort. When I say we I mean the larger we — the whole world community.

This is not new to me. I started with the United Nations a year after it was founded. I have been involved in the environment and economic issues a good part of my life. What I am doing now seems to me a logical extension of what I have been doing for many years.

Do you see other parts of the business community getting seriously interested in becoming part of the solution to the global environmental and development problems that UNCED is tackling?

Yes. Some of the most enlightened business leaders I know are very concerned and active on these issues. They are still a minority, but they are a very influential minority. A good illustration of that is the Business Council for Sustainable Development. It is headed by a very able and enterprising Swiss who has a foundation devoted to sustainable development. There are about 50 of the world's chief executive officers who have made a special commitment to the Business Council on Sustainable Development as a means of making a major input into the UNCED Conference. Now, of course, 50 CEOs is not the entire business community. There are many business people who still look at the environment issue in a negative way. They see at it as an additional nuisance and cost. But, on the whole, I see a shift in the real leadership of the business community.

I have not seen representatives of the major transnational corporations participating in the negotiations. Is that by design?

A lot of our work takes place in working committees and in our own little working groups. We call them working parties at the Secretariat level and working groups at the governmental level. The 50 CEOs have a $10 million budget to do nothing but contribute to our conference. We met over the weekend with them. We have had special meetings of our Preparatory Committee with the representatives of the Business Council, and they are making significant, substantive inputs. They don't sit in and negotiate with governments, but they do have their input. At a certain point they can make their voice heard again in the actual Preparatory Committee meetings, but they don't sit down and negotiate the wording of all the resolutions.

28

There is also the World International Conference on Environmental Management in Rotterdam. They adopted a major Business Charter for Sustainable Development. There is the World Economic Forum, which represents something like 1000 of the leading corporations of the world. It has special groups of CEOs in nine major industry sectors as part of its Eco-Industry Initiative for the UNCED '92 Conference. Three weeks ago I met with representatives of some of the world's major automobile companies right here in Geneva. So, there is a lot of engagement.

Let me ask a central question about the North/South confrontation. In your opinion, have the major industrialized nations offered to make any real sacrifices to show developing nations that they are serious about sustainable development? And if they have, can you give me some examples of concessions they are ready to make?

If you look at it strictly in terms of this conference, the position of the North is not homogeneous: There is no broad agreement among the nations of the North about how to respond to developing country requirements. The U.S. has taken a strong position, which you are familiar with, that there will be no additional resources as far as they are concerned. The European Community has taken a much more positive attitude. It has recognized in its statement the need for new and additional resources, and has crossed the bridge, at least in principle. That is encouraging.

That is on the funding side of the equation. But I am also asking about sacrifices the North might be willing to make in energy policy, for example.

Some have. For instance, Europe and Japan have made substantial progress in improving energy efficiency. Japan now uses half the energy per unit of GNP that the U.S. does. Even the U.S. has made some progress, but it has a relatively long way to go. If you look at what the North has done more broadly, as distinct from the position it has taken at this Preparatory Committee, there has been a lot of evidence that it is possible for the North to move. Again, if every country were to do what the best performing country has done, we would have a very significant diminishing of greenhouse gases. In my view, based on what it has done domestically, Japan is headed for leadership in the environmental field equivalent to the leadership it has in the economic field. And the two things are related.

You just came from there, did you not?

Yes. I have probably spent more time in Japan than in any single country, other than Switzerland. I am very impressed with what the Japanese are doing. I believe they are way ahead of the Western business community in recognizing both the necessity of accommodating to a more environmentally-oriented economic scene and the way in which that necessity can be turned into a new opportunity.

But at these Preparatory Committee meetings that has not been as evident in the positions that Japan has taken.

True, they have been very cautious here in the positions they take. They are conscious of the fact that they have performed well in their own country. They feel that has not been adequately recognized. They contest the idea that you simply accept targets on greenhouse gas emissions lower than where you currently are. They contend, and I think rightly, that some account should be taken of what you have already done.

Certainly, on energy efficiency they are way ahead of the U.S. and a number of other countries. However, in the area of logging in developing nations, or over fishing certain areas, one could argue that the Japanese also have a long way to go.

Yes. Internationally they have not demonstrated the same degree of commitment that they have shown domestically. But their domestic performance is not confined simply to air and water pollution, where they have done better than any of the other industrialized countries. It is also a question of energy use, and raw materials use per unit of production. Across the board, domestically, they have turned in an impressive performance.

Internationally, on fishing issues, yes, that is a special kind of cultural problem. They have a hard time making transitions like that, just as they do on agricultural subsidies for their rice farmers. They move slowly on those. But what impresses me is that the Japanese do recognize, now, that they have to make the same kind of shifts in their international performance that they have made domestically. They have not done that yet, although there are signs that they are doing it.

There is some comment in the press that the Japanese are thinking of funding significant environmental initiatives around the world, and that they are considering this as a major area of investment. Can you confirm that?

Yes, I am hopeful. To my knowledge, they have not yet made any decisions on that,. My strong message to Japan is exactly that: Japan needs to take some major international area and make it their issue. This is one that is looking for leadership; their interest and experience make it ideal for them. That message seems to be getting quite a good response in Japan. The Japanese are moving cautiously, but I believe that there is a real opportunity, and that they will give primary emphasis to this area.

I just attended a meeting hosted by the World Resources Institute in which they put forward an initiative. It calls on Canada and the U.S. to reduce carbon dioxide emissions by 30 percent by 2005, and Canada and the U.S. to levy a $60 per ton carbon tax phased in over 15 years. It also calls for an Eco Fund financed by a $1 per barrel oil tax. These kinds of initiatives, if they came from the U.S. and Canada, would change the dynamic of the UNCED conference entirely. In your opin-

ion, why hasn't that happened? What are the prospects for some kind of real movement on these issues?

The very reason that you have a special conference like UNCED is because it is recognized that there are fundamental changes needed that go beyond the normal evolution of events. We need to bring to bear special political energies and focus in order to develop the political will to make changes like this. It should not surprise people that these issues are difficult. We wouldn't need a conference if everything had fallen into place without it. One of the primary purposes of the conference is to try to provide the political impetus that will in fact move important governments on these issues. It should not be surprising at all that the U.S. has not agreed up until now. The U.S. recognizes, perhaps more than others, the fundamental nature of the changes being negotiated. The U.S. will be affected more than others by these changes. That very fact means that the changes are more difficult for the U.S. So it should not be surprising that movement for the U.S. takes some time. On the other hand, the fact that it is taking time doesn't mean that the whole process is wasted. Some of us believe that these changes are imperative, and therefore inevitable.

You speak about using the conference to create the political will necessary to bring about some of these changes. Do you get the sense that we are generating that political will? If I took a poll of government delegations to the Preparatory Committee negotiation sessions, I don't think it would be terribly impressive in terms of their status in their own government hierarchies. Even among the non-government organiza tions, we don't have Gus Speth or Lester Brown here, or some of the other major spokespersons for the environmental movement. If we are going to generate the level of political will necessary to bring about real change, where are the people who have the political clout to bring it off?

You are dealing with the sherpas here. They are making the bullets. They are doing all the nitty-gritty work. They are not going to be the people who will generate the breakthroughs. They are the people who are preparing the ground and staking out positions for their governments. Ultimately, they will narrow down those positions to the larger issues. Then you will get the more senior teams coming in. As you say, if you were to take a survey you would find that most of the people here who come and spend four weeks are in the middle levels in their governments or organizations. But you also get quite a number at the ministerial and senior official levels, who come for a shorter period of time. They are the ones who send the signals to their teams at home. That is normal. After all, you have more than a two-year process of negotiation. The fact that UNCED is a summit-level conference means that the preparatory process itself is elevated within each government. For example, in Germany, Chancellor Kohl's office has now set up a unit focused on these negotiations. Don't judge the level of government interest in the UNCED negotiations solely by the number of people they send here for four weeks of negotiations.

I take your point that the higher levels will come in later.

The higher levels are engaged already, even in the United States. Frankly, the major signals on the big issues for UNCED are being called from the White House.

Do you mean the major signals that our delegates should downplay the whole UNCED process and not do much with it?

Or is the U.S. position changing? You will notice that the U.S. delegation has come out in favor of Agenda 21 now. There is no change in the basic U.S. position and I would not expect that yet, but there is a change in their acceptance of the process. Before, they were standing back from it; now they are in it in every issue. Sometimes one wonders about their introduction of positions that they know are difficult for other governments. Nevertheless, they are doing their homework; they are engaged, which they weren't before to the same extent.

President Bush came back from the G-7 conference and recounted that he was quite surprised by the interest of the other G-7 leaders in UNCED. Apparently, he is now beginning to receive signals from people other than those who control access to him within the U.S. Government.

If you were to guess today about the major outcomes of the Rio conference, do you expect that there will be a climate change convention, a biodiversity convention, forestry principles, an Earth Charter, and Agenda 21?

I would put them in a different order than you have. I see a process that moves from principles to the program to Agenda 21 to the means of implementing the program through agreement about financial resources, technology, and institutions. The conventions are in a separate category. I think we will get agreement on all of those things. We are going to get an Agenda 21 and an Earth Charter. What is in them is still in doubt. Whether they will really be the historic commitments that I believe must be made, I don't know. In fact, if they are not, I would rather see them fail. I don't want to see failure, but I don't want to see a soft success — a real failure that pretends to be a success.

Do you mean by a soft success an empty climate change convention with no real commitments?

That's right. Now the conventions will not be empty, but they will not be as full as we would have wanted. They will be simply framework conventions with as much meat on them as possible. But again, on climate change, you are dealing with a very fundamental issue. Take the Law of the Sea: look how long it took. We are going to get a major first step; I think that is almost certain. And we will also get political impetus for the continued negotiating process on climate and, I hope, on biodiversity.

Forestry has not been preceded by the same amount of preparatory work that, say, climate was. To reach the stage of a framework convention on climate change it took several years, two climate conferences, and the work of the Inter-Governmental Panel on Climate Change (IPCC). Negotiators have been working on biodiversity, but not for quite as long. The forest principles are moving forward; negotiators have decided not to have a convention on forestry for Rio, but the very fact that they are using this process to negotiate principles is, in fact, the first phase of the negotiating process.

James MacNeill, former Secretary General of the World Commission on Environment and Development, argues quite persuasively that it would be better not to have any convention on climate change if it is essentially an empty convention, as he calls it — one that does not have any real commitments or targets for reductions of greenhouse gas emissions. Others argue that it would be better to pass a reasonably vague framework convention, the type that the U.S. has been pushing for, with no protocols. They say: look at the history of the Law of the Sea. It tried to achieve everything at once, and then they didn't get enough signatures to bring it into force. But MacNeill points out that if you sign an empty convention it takes the pressure off to really do anything. How do you feel about that?

I think it depends on how it comes out in the end. If a framework convention is seen as, and is used as, a means of absorbing the pressure to do something while not in fact doing anything, then it would be a setback. If it is in fact a major first step in a process that is going to produce binding commitments, then I think that you could say that is useful. Maybe it will not be as much as we would like to see, but at least Rio should produce not only a signature but a strong political commitment to move ahead. It will not be possible to judge that progress absolutely, but it will be feasible to judge within certain limits at Rio itself. So I don't think it is only exactly what is in the conventions that is so important. What accompanies the conventions, in terms of decisions in Rio that relate to the ongoing process, will also be important. There remains a danger that a framework convention can be used as a means of delaying real action and commitments. I share MacNeill's concern, but I think the outcome is still an open question.

James Gustave Speth:

Environmental Progress Requires Improving Conditions in Developing Nations

 ames Gustave Speth is President of the World Resources Institute.

Steve Lerner: How would you rate the importance of the Earth Summit?

James Gustave Speth: The Earth Summit is critically important, but it's easy for otherwise well-informed people not to see that. The event is officially called the U.N. Conference on Environment and Development (UNCED), but the word "conference" is a misnomer. UNCED is in fact a major international negotiating process, potentially the most important multi-party negotiation since the ones that set up the United Nations and the World Bank. Its importance is more apparent in the informal name, "Earth Summit."

For nearly two years, Earth Summit negotiators have been grappling with two of the world's most crucial needs: how to protect the environment and how to spur economic development in developing countries. This dual thrust is right on target because there's so much feedback and synergy between environmental degradation and underdevelopment that they can only be solved together. And they can't be solved at all without unprecedented, sustained, international cooperation — which is why so many have been pushing so hard for progress at Rio.

What role has the U.S. played at UNCED?

Thus far, U.S. policy has been widely seen as the main obstacle to the North/South agreements needed at UNCED. As I travel around and talk to people, I hear repeatedly that it will be mostly the U.S. Government's fault if UNCED fails. I think that's a fair assessment. At the moment, though, there appears to be some softening of the Administration's hardline stance, at least on climate change. If there's more movement over the next several months, the United States can still play a constructive role. U.S. leadership was crucial to the successful outcome of the Stockholm conference 20 years ago, and it's not too late for that to happen again — if the President and enough people in the Congress recognize soon enough that our country cannot afford to fritter away this once-in-a-generation opportunity.

What have been the chief problems with the U.S. position — and how do you see things changing?

The two areas where U.S. policy is most misguided are climate change and financing. How can we expect developing countries to take the need for a global climate accord seriously unless we're willing to curtail our own wasteful use of fossil fuels — and unless we're willing to support their efforts to deal with global environmental problems not of their making?

On climate change, we're out of step with our European allies and Japan. They've all committed to specific targets and timetables for stabilizing or reducing carbon dioxide emissions. Now, as I understand it, the U.S. Government, while still intractable on the question of goals and timetables, has come around somewhat by suggesting a compromise — that the United States enact some measures to promote energy efficiency, while taking a "wait and see" approach as to what effect these measures will have on carbon dioxide emissions.

On financing, the United States has been refusing to even talk about offering any additional aid to developing countries. In February, though, the Administration apparently began to see the light and promised $75 million to developing countries to address climate change. That's not much, of course, and it's too soon to tell whether it's "new and additional" funding or a shell game. Agenda 21 — the Earth Summit's action plan — is probably going to require that the wealthy countries double their overall development assistance, so I hope the $75 million is only the beginning of a sea change in the U.S. stance. It's clearly unreasonable to expect developing countries — most of them in dire financial straits already — to take on a host of new obligations without substantial amounts of new development assistance.

In your testimony before the U.S. Senate Committee on Foreign Relations you said that the Earth Summit "comes not a moment too soon, for while the earth's geopolitical systems may be faring better, its ecological systems are in deep trouble." You set three litmus tests to ascertain whether or not the Earth Summit lives up to its promise. UNCED must advance concrete initiatives that (1) are capable of having an impact on global problems, (2) are amenable to intergovernmental adoption and implementation, and (3) can be ready by the time of the Earth Summit in June, 1992. Given this basis for judging UNCED, how would you say we are doing thus far, and how would you characterize the role of the United States at UNCED?

I think we are doing pretty well on the first two of the three. I think exciting ideas are being proposed. A lot of new people in government are having to grapple with issues that they have not grappled with before. The momentum is being developed to do something. What has changed since I gave that testimony is that progress has been slow. It is not that it is not happening. But now I think we have to see the Earth Summit as the beginning of a period of international cooperation that might extend for two or three years after the conference with a lot of churning on different subjects, and a lot of continuing effort to reach additional agreements and put new programs in place. In my optimism, I am looking forward to a fertile period that starts with UNCED.

But that presumes that the event does not turn out to be a demoralizing, souring experience for people. That gets to your last question about U.S. policy. Unless U.S. policy changes between now and June, there is a real risk of the event turning sour. There is a lot of interest around the world in increasing development assistance. Numerous industrial countries and many panels of international leaders have called for a doubling of the development assistance that rich countries make available. That doubling would bring development assistance into the ballpark of the price tag that has been put on Agenda 21. There is a general recognition that we have to make both public and private investments in our common future. But, right now, our Government is feeling broke and taking a very hard line about "new and additional resources."

Given that we are in a recession and have a huge budget deficit and given that this is an election year when the electorate is demanding that politicians turn inward to cope with our domestic problems, is it realistic to expect that the U.S. will provide new and additional resources for sustainable development?

There are two ways of looking at that question. Is it wise for the U.S. to do that, is it prudent, is it far-sighted, is it a good investment both politically and economically? The answer is: yes. Is it going to happen between now and June? I fear not, for all the reasons you listed.

The best we might be able to accomplish right now is to indicate an openness and understanding of the need for new and additional resources. We could signal to the rest of the world that we realize there will have to be further bargaining to reach a compact, but that right now, while the U.S. may be willing to commit to some new and additional financial resources, it will take more time to raise the larger resources that will be needed.

We can't expect the developing world to attend to their own domestic environmental problems until some of their economic problems are under better control. And we cannot expect them to attend to global environmental problems if they are not able to attend to their own domestic environmental problems. These issues all have to be taken up together and it is not going to be easy or cheap.

What should the U.S. be trying to achieve at UNCED?

I would put four goals at the top of the list: First, an international agreement on protecting global climate and controlling cross-boundary pollution. Second, initiatives to protect world forests and biodiversity. Third, agreement on the goal of population stabilization and the means to achieve it. And, fourth, effective international programs to address the problems of underdevelopment, poverty, and hunger.

These are hard economic times. Hard-nosed reporters and tough-minded politicians will ask: What is in this negotiation for the United States?

The short answer is: plenty. Some may disagree, arguing that environment and development goals are "soft," that they don't advance our country's economic and political interests in the world. But they're wrong.

Developing countries make up a third of our export markets, so our trade balance is affected by how well these countries are doing. So is our workforce: An estimated 1.8 million American workers lost their jobs when exports to developing countries sagged during the international debt crisis of the 1980s. If we get in on the ground floor in helping these countries develop — through capacity building and technology cooperation — that will lay the foundation for expanding U.S. investments and trade in the future.

What relation do the UNCED negotiations have to the stalled Uruguay Round of the General Agreement on Tariffs and Trade (GATT) negotiations?

UNCED presents another opportunity for the U.S. to raise issues that it's already raised in the GATT negotiations — the need to eliminate agricultural subsidies, for instance. We're at loggerheads with the European Community over this in GATT, but protecting the environment requires eliminating all kinds of subsidies that encourage misuse and overuse of natural resources all over the world — so the U.S. should pursue it at UNCED. Then there's the free-trade question. I'm all for the trade liberalization the United States is pursuing through several channels. But if freer trade merely accelerates today's environmentally unsustainable and socially imbalanced growth patterns, it can't deliver on its promise of lasting economic progress. Earth Summit agreements can help provide a larger framework in which international trade can prosper.

How much does it matter whether or not the U.S. seizes the opportunity UNCED offers to improve our relationship with developing nations?

A lot rides on this. Our country has overarching political interests that depend on the friendship and stability of Latin American, Asian, and African nations. But the large and growing North/South gap — the divide between the haves and the have nots — is threatening our relationships with these nations. GNP per capita in the developing world is only 6 percent of that in the wealthy countries. Couple that disparity with widespread hunger and poverty and the international debt crisis, and it's easy to see how international equity issues can undermine our long-term interests in the world. If our country takes advantage of the opportunity UNCED offers to promote sustainable progress in underdeveloped countries, that can open the door to friendship and cooperation on many issues.

Is the failure of the U.S. to take advantage of this opportunity to promote sustainable progress in developing countries a consequence of near-sighted leadership?

I'd say that's accurate. Our leaders aren't keeping up with a changing world. Environmental security and international equity are two important new areas where the U.S. should be exercising leadership, but Europe and Japan seem more far-sighted than we in recognizing the significance of these changes. UNCED gives us a second chance to catch up: Many of the right issues are being raised, and the UNCED Secretariat is framing many proposals to address them. A new generation of government officials is having to grapple with all these issues. If the U.S. adopts an attitude more like the one it brought to Stockholm in 1972, our country can help steer the transition from the postwar world we're leaving behind to the multipolar world we're entering.

The World Resources Institute (WRI) has produced a model agreement on a wide range of environment and development issues that you call "Compact for a New World." This agreement was worked out among experts from North, South, and Central America on issues such as global climate change, deforestation, biodiversity, population, and debt relief. Reading the Compact it becomes clear that agreements between the North and South can be shaped when the North is willing to admit that it must make progress on improving energy efficiency, reducing emissions of greenhouse gases, and helping the developing countries with debt relief. Once the North signals the South that it is willing to make sacrifices in an effort to create a partnership on sustainable development, people from developing nations are much more willing to address issues such as population control and deforestation. The Compact appears to be a model for cooperation between North and South America on how to overcome some of the impasses that have paralyzed the UNCED negotiation.

When you submitted the "Compact for a New World" to the UNCED Secretariat, how was it received? Do you get the sense that any of the formulas that you worked out for making a North/South deal in the Americas have been adopted by the UNCED process?

In one sense the response has been very positive. I participated in a meeting that UNCED convened in the Hague, a sort of North/South dialogue, that was one of the preludes to UNCED. There were repeated statements during the meeting that the Compact is a good model and that we have to begin a partnership between North and South. They saw the Compact as an innovative and attractive part of the answer of how to do that. We also presented the Compact to the Organization of American States (OAS) ambassadors. There have been about 150 additional signatures to the Compact since its release.

On the other hand, there are some problems. One is that for this kind of bargain to take place you have to be willing to accept that these problems — whether priority problems of the South or priority problems of the North — are real. That is the prelude to a bargain. And I am afraid that right now the U.S. Government does not accept that many of these problems are real. The U.S. Government is just on the verge of admitting that the global warming issue is a real problem rather than a scientific curiosity that needs to be studied further. In other areas it is not clear that our Government has focused on these problems, even though it may concede that these are substantive concerns. We have not heard a willingness from the U.S. Government to approach these issues with the seriousness they deserve and that is reflected in the Compact.

A second obstacle in using the Compact in the UNCED negotiations is that our Compact dealt with the issues in an integrated way.

Isn't that what UNCED is supposed to be doing?

Unfortunately, UNCED has been negotiating issues in a segmented way. There have been discussions about forestry, about atmosphere, and about 20 other things. There have been separate negotiations on the side on climate change and biodiversity. As a result, there has been a kind of segmentation of the UNCED process.

The cross-cutting issues that should pull UNCED together, especially the issues of funding and institutional reform, are being debated last. These issues don't get looked at in an integrated way until the costing analysis is done. That is when a price tag is put on Agenda 21. Also looked at late in the negotiation is the question of what type of institutions will be needed within the U.N. system to implement Agenda 21. It is only when the negotiators debate what Agenda 21 is going to cost that the real bargain is struck. At UNCED they are getting to that debate late in the process, whereas that is the stage we started at with the Compact.

Whether the UNCED process with all those governments, so many issues, and so many debates can pull an agreement together is in question. The industrial countries are unlikely to come up with $125 billion in concessional finance, which is what Agenda 21 is calling for. The industrialized countries won't come up with any large amount unless there is some reciprocity. A bargain will require people saying: "If you will do this, we will do this; it doesn't make sense for us to do this, unless you do that; but if we both do x and y and z, we will all be better off." That kind of discussion has been extremely hard to accomplish within the UNCED context so far.

So, while the Compact is a good model for UNCED, it remains to be seen if it is going to be used. My guess is that, whether or not it is used between now and Rio, at some point, either on a regional basis or on a global basis, countries will take the kind of approach we took in the Compact, although perhaps not as comprehensive an approach. What is crucial is that we have a real understanding and sympathy for each other's aspirations. While we must recognize that our priorities are not the same, nevertheless, we can agree that "if you help us pursue our priorities, we can help you pursue your priorities and we will both benefit." That kind of discussion must occur at some point but it may not occur until after Rio.

You criticize UNCED for taking a segmented, sectoral approach, and for waiting until the end of the process to begin the financial negotiation. How could UNCED have done a better job?

I don't really mean to be critical of UNCED in that sense. I am not sure that there was any alternative. UNCED has been ambitious and impressive in the scope and seriousness with which the issues have been tackled. I think that there will be a process with more limited numbers of negotiators sitting down and discussing these critical issues after UNCED. I can envision working groups coming together out of UNCED around specific issues and a major, long-term follow-up effort being put in place, both public and private.

For the Western Hemisphere, I can envision, at some point, a session establishing the intergovernmental panel that we called for in the Compact. As soon as enough of the major governments in the Hemisphere recognize that these problems deserve attention, we could easily see some type of negotiations that either are combined with or complement the negotiations on trade. There is going to be momentum for trade liberalization in this hemisphere; that needs to be complemented by discussions on environmental and equity issues.

WRI has suggested that "economic and environmental conditions imposed on debtor countries should be replaced by symmetric commitments for sustainable development in developed and developing countries alike." That sounds only fair to me. But who is going to force the wealthier nations to be more energy efficient and use fewer resources? The North has economic leverage with the South: Industrialized countries can say to developing countries that unless they do various things to promote sustainable development — such as halting deforestation — they will not receive aid. But what leverage do the developing countries have with the North?

One of the reasons for helping developing countries stop deforestation is because we know we have a global warming problem. That implies that we should also start doing something at home about global warming. If we can get to the point where we are talking seriously about helping the developing countries, I think it will be in part because we know that we have got to make some changes at home.

Second, developing countries definitely have some leverage with the industrial countries because there is no way to solve the global problems of the environment without developing country leadership. But the general point you make is quite right: we have got to move toward a sustainable economy and life style in our country. And the most powerful thing we can do — not merely to save the global environment, but also to affect developing country behavior — is to clean up our own act. We are not doing that. Right now we don't even have a vision of what it means for the United States of America to have an environmentally sustainable economy and environmentally sustainable life styles.

We are underdeveloped in that respect.

We are setting exactly the wrong example during a period when the world is adopting our model. And that is frightening because we are not offering the world a model that can be safely replicated or adopted by other countries. To put more meaning on that, the consumption of resources and the generation of pollution per dollar of GNP in this country is intolerably high. We live in a country that produces a huge amount of waste and pollution for every unit of output that we produce and consume. Yet the possibilities of using technologies to become more efficient and less polluting per unit of output are dramatic. I don't buy the argument that we have to lower our standard of living in the U.S. Obviously we have to change our life style. Driving an electric vehicle is not going to be the same experience as driving a Porsche. But still I don't think we have to go to the American public and say that it is time to adopt drastically lower standards of living.

The fact is that there are opportunities to reduce our resource consumption and pollution by dramatic percentages without lowering our standard of living. These are the opportunities that we should be rapidly exploiting. The rest of the world is moving in that direction, not in the sense that the train is leaving the station but there are examples of other countries that are ahead of us in becoming "eco-efficient." We are behind in that sense. I don't think the leaders of the United States realize that there are new values that will be dominant in the years ahead, new sources of national strength and national prestige.

What are you referring to?

Basically, issues of equity and environment.

Do you mean that the United States is going to be criticized for being the world's most selfish consumer of resources and energy?

You bet. I already hear that as I travel around the world. I hear that Organization of Economic Cooperation and Development (OECD), which account for 25 percent of the world's population, countries are consuming 75 to 80 percent of virtually every resource you can list. And the U.S. is the number one offender. The same holds true for pollution loadings. We are beginning to hear talk about the lack of replicable lifestyles and a demand on the part of developing countries for living space and for room to grow. They feel as if we, in the industrialized world, have co-opted the planet's resources and assimilative capacity for environmental insults. People in developing countries feel as if there is nothing left for them. This is a real, deep, legitimate fear.

And there is anger about it.

Right: anger and fear. There is an issue of equity and an issue of environment and they are linked. Japan and some countries in Europe are ahead of us in responding to this concern in part because this "living space" concept (for lack of a better phrase) applies at home as well. If the economy is going to grow domestically, then the amount of environmental insults per unit of output will have to shrink. The public is not going to accept or legitimize companies that are transgressing those limits. That is another way of saying that in the future environmental concerns are going to increasingly drive and effect the nature of economic activity. The Japanese and the Europeans understand that to a larger degree than we do in the U.S. and they are getting the jump on us.

Are you saying that the United States may be forced to become more energy efficient and careful in its use of virgin resources as a result of economic competition from those countries that are recycling materials and becoming energy efficient?

Absolutely. Our products might make sense in an economy where energy prices are at an all-time low. But those products don't make a bit of sense in an economy where energy prices are several times higher than they are here, and certainly not if those products involve as much use of energy as ours do. We're missing out on economic opportunities here, because the acceptability of products and processes is going to increasingly depend on environmental considerations. Meanwhile, countries like Japan are investing in the "green" technological innovations that will be in demand worldwide. I think the Government is doing American industry a real disservice by not leading the way in recognizing this new reality. Having an energy-efficient economy here at home would give us a competitive advantage abroad.

We are beginning to see that in California. The California energy policy is now factoring in the environmental and health costs of producing energy. That makes alternatives to nuclear and fossil fuel energy generation economically viable. But if you look at what is happening with the U.S. energy policy it is a dramatically different vision.

You are right that there have been facilities such as Southern California Edison, Pacific Gas and Electric, and New England Electric that have adopted far-sighted policies on energy. And you are right that our own Department of Energy and the President's National Energy Strategy have adopted basically business-as-usual strategies. Those business-as-usual strategies are going to lead us into an unacceptable future in terms of both the environment and our competitive position internationally.

The only answer is to change national policy. That can be accomplished either by changing the hearts and minds of the people who are in power or by putting new people in power. There is going to have to be a realization that energy policy in the U.S. has to change in a major way. I think it can be done, but it has to be done with great sensitivity. It is politically difficult to do because there are winners and losers and there are problems of equity that have to be dealt with. But there is no reason in principle why they can't be dealt with. It is just that our political system is a problem unless you have really strong leadership from the President.

Why do we not hear the environmental issue being raised in the U.S. Presidential primary contest? Is that significant to you?

I think it will increase. It started increasing with the last debate in New Hampshire and my guess is that by the time of the general election in November these issues will be rather prominent. But even the discussions that have occurred in the political arena haven't really dealt with the most basic need, which is to straighten out energy prices. People are more willing to talk about new fuel-efficiency standards for automobiles than they are about higher gasoline prices. Part of the answer to that dilemma is to guarantee to the public that funds that are raised through environmental taxes are not intended to be revenue raising taxes, but rather to be price rationalization taxes and environmental policy rationalization taxes. All of the money raised through these taxes will be given back by reducing some other tax, or otherwise refunding or rebating it to consumers and the public. So we would be changing relative prices, but not taking money out of people's pockets.

You call for a $60 per ton carbon tax and a $1 per barrel tax on oil. When I bring up this approach with developing country non-government organization activists, their response is that these taxes would mean that only the wealthy will have access to gasoline and other resources on which environmental taxes have been levied. They argue that solving these problems by raising prices through taxes is going to hurt the poor.

In my mind we have to subsidize people not commodities. Right now we are subsidizing commodities. If you are concerned about the loss of farm income and farmers in the United States, we ought to have a program that deals directly with those human needs, rather than indirectly supporting commodity production in agriculture. That same principle can be applied more generally. I don't think that an economy with environmentally honest prices will discriminate against the poor. My guess is that, in the end, an economy where prices are environmentally honest will be a lot fairer socially, although I don't think that is the automatic result. It will require attentive policies. You have to have environmental policies and social policies to complement the economic policies.

In the Compact, you call for promoting sustainable agricultural practices among farmers in rural Latin America. If we adopt the theory that these conditions should be symmetrically applied both in the North and the South, we would have to promote sustainable agricultural practices in the United States as well.

Absolutely.

That is quite a radical suggestion when you consider the massive mechanized farms in the Middle West of the United States that use large amounts of pesticides and chemical fertilizers. Are you advocating a move away from the large-scale mechanized farming that has fed us and many people in other parts of the world?

No. I don't think so. We have done studies at WRI based on field experience, real data, that looked at regions in two states: Nebraska and Pennsylvania. We assessed the effect on farm incomes, and on production, of moving to sustainable techniques in agriculture. The result is that there is no long-term diminution in farm incomes or production. This is admittedly a controversial area where a lot of folks will argue the other side. We also looked at the effects of rather dramatic changes in our agricultural subsidy program — the types of changes the U.S. would have to undertake if our own proposals were adopted in the Uruguay Round of GATT. We found that there was a complementary relationship between changing those commodity programs and moving toward sustainability. The current structure of U.S. agricultural programs militates against sustainable practices in agriculture.

A lot of the changes in Federal policy that are needed to move toward sustainable agriculture have been debated in Congress and made it into agricultural laws as experimental activities and satellite programs that Congress sponsors in limited ways. But we have not really moved dramatically in that direction. We are talking about a shift here at home toward sustainable agriculture as well. But that does not mean going back to 19th century approaches.

In the last series of interviews I did, I spoke with a young Norwegian who made a good case that liberalization of trade can cause sustainable life styles to be wiped out. He said that by eliminating trade barriers, Norwegians living along the coast who had made a living by growing apples, fishing, and raising cattle, could not compete with imports. Do you think that liberalizing trade may eliminate sustainable life styles?

In general, the Compact is very supportive of trade liberalization. But trade policies and trade liberalization have to be complemented with other initiatives. On the first page of the Compact is a powerful statement that says that unless the trade proposals in the Western Hemisphere are complemented by social and environmental initiatives that are equally powerful, the trade initiatives could lead to short-term gains and long-term disaster. I think that is a fair way of putting it. The question of how you do that on a micro-level, and how you bring trade and environmental protection together, is a subject that we and a lot of other people are going to be working on intensively in the years ahead.

Section II:

The Search for a Sustainable Future

Wangari Maathai:

The Green Belt Movement in Kenya

Professor Wangari Maathai is Coordinator of the Green Belt Movement in Kenya and a former professor of microbiology at the University of Nairobi.

Maathai recently found herself in the forefront of a struggle for democracy in Kenya. She was arrested at her home on January 13, 1992 and charged with "publishing a false rumor which is likely to cause fear and alarm to the public" after she and eight other members of the Forum for the Restoration of Democracy (FORD) held a press conference at which they announced they had evidence proving that the current administration in Kenya intended to hand over power to the army.

More recently, on March 5, 1992, Maathai was beaten unconscious when, according to *The New York Times,* "police fired tear gas cannisters and clubbed demonstrators protesting the forceful eviction of women on a hunger strike from a city park."

An ardent environmentalist, Maathai's work as head of the Green Belt Movement involves the promotion of planting of trees. This activity not only serves to increase Kenya's forest cover and stay erosion, it also provides shade, firewood, fence posts, and fruit for those who plant the trees. The Green Belt Movement, now deeply rooted in the soil of Kenya, takes a very practical approach: those who plant and nurture trees are part of the Movement; those whose trees die are no longer part of the Movement.

Yet Maathai dared to go beyond planting trees. She insists that sustainable development in Kenya, as elsewhere, must be accompanied by democratic reforms that allow the people to hold their leaders accountable. In particular, she is concerned that not all the aid directed to Kenya or other countries ends up being invested in projects that help the people. Some of the aid, she asserts, is being

locked away in private bank accounts in the North. Only democratic reforms, Maathai argues, will allow the people to hold their
leaders accountable and permit them to pursue a path of sustainable development.

Steve Lerner: *How did you get involved in planting trees?*

Wangari Maathai: I was at the University of Nairobi teaching vet-
erinary anatomy. In the course of my research I observed that degradation of the environment was probably more important for the livestock
industry in our country than the diseases I was studying.

At the time I was studying a disease called East Coast Fever caused
by a parasite that is transmitted to the cow by a tick. When the tick bites
the cow, it transmits the parasite. For indigenous cattle and the cattle-
like animals we call buffalos there is a certain amount of acquired im-
munity. But when you try to improve your livestock industry by bringing in exotic species, especially from temperate zones like Europe, then
the disease is 100 percent fatal. So it is a very important disease. And I
was trying to do my part in contributing to a cure by studying the
anatomy of the parasite. I wanted to observe the cycle of the parasite,
how it moved from the salivary glands of the tick into the cattle.

I used to go out into the field to collect the ticks from the cows to see
how many of the ticks were infected. It was in the course of this exercise
that I realized that environmental degradation was a threat to the livestock industry, and I started getting interested in environmental issues.
This was in the early 1970s, so there was not much of an environmental
movement yet in Kenya.

At the same time I was interested in women's issues. I joined the
Kenya Association of University Women, and that organization sponsored me to become an executive committee member of the National
Council of Women, an umbrella organization of many women's groups
in the country.

I started hearing reports about the problems that women were en-
countering, especially in rural areas. One of the reports that struck me
was a report that there was a lot of kwashiorkor in central Kenya, which
is comparatively affluent by Kenyan standards. (Kwashiorkor means
literally 'red boy,' severe malnutrition in children and infants caused by
a diet low in protein and high in carbohydrates.) I was shocked to hear
that children in this region were suffering from kwashiorkor. So I in-
quired into why that was the case and I discovered two things that led
me further into an interest in ecology.

First, I found that because coffee and tea are major cash crops in this
part of the country, many people do not produce food. Instead, they depend on buying food with the money they earn from their cash crops.
Also, because they have money, they tend to buy highly refined carbohydrates, which they consider "affluent food". Combined with that was

the fact that clearing the land to make way for these cash crops had eliminated trees, so there was very little firewood in the area. As a result, the tendency for women was to prepare meals that did not require much firewood. The combination of being comparatively affluent, wanting to eat highly refined carbohydrate diets — such as white bread, wheat flour, sugar, butter — and the fact that women had very little firewood, meant that they were actually undernourished. They were not eating traditional foods, and there was not an underlying awareness of what people should eat. Since they had money they ate what they thought rich people ate. And that was the reason that children were suffering from kwashiorkor.

That started me thinking that maybe we should do a project with the women. But for some reason, and I don't really know why, I identified tree planting as the tool we should use to attack these problems. It was quite clear to me that it would not help these women to give them food, or give them lectures about what to eat. Somehow I identified tree planting as one way of solving the problem of firewood, as well as showing these women the importance of growing food.

In the National Council of Women I suggested that we make tree planting a vehicle to reach women and to discuss with them some of the problems they have. It would solve the problem of firewood, give them fencing and building materials, protect their soil from erosion, and encourage them to grow the food that they needed to eat, rather than relying on purchasing food. That is how my path started. It started from different paths, but they all converged in the realization that the environment is an important issue.

My understanding of the Green Belt Movement in Kenya is that the planting of trees is encouraged to improve the livelihood of the people who plant and nourish them, not just for conservation purposes.

The whole theme of the United Nations Conference on Environment and Development (UNCED) is to be able to live in harmony with nature. That was the way of life of our people, the way of life of my grandparents. But by the time my own mother was raising children, this harmony with nature began to be disrupted because we opened our land for new agricultural fields, for commercial farms.

It was the time of the settlement of Africa, clearing of the bushes, cutting down of the jungle, and clearing the savannah for agriculture. There was little awareness that you needed to preserve vegetation in order to maintain the fertility of the soil. That jungle, savannah, and bush were part and parcel of what made life possible in subtropical Africa.

What has happened now, after almost 80 years of clearing, and cutting, and not planting? People did not cut and plant at the same time to maintain the balance. We just cut. To many people, especially the Westerners coming into Africa, this bush, jungle, and savannah needed to be exploited. They just cleared everything.

And we believed them. We thought that they knew. We came to appreciate open lands as if that was the good thing. We came to believe that good agriculture was monoculture, not the intercropping with trees, bananas, and several layers of crops. A typical traditional African farm has several layers of crops from the highest trees, which have a wide canopy, to the higher crops like bananas, to the very low crops like beans, and sweet vines, and potatoes, and such. That method of farming was associated with primitive farming and foreign to the white man.

The Europeans were accustomed to monocultures grown in summer and maximizing the exposure to the sun. But in Africa they had come to a land where the sun shines every day for 12 hours. As a result, it did not pay to maximize exposure to the sun; if anything, we try to cut down the amount of sun that hits the ground.

What I am trying to emphasize is that no one knew that we needed to retain some vegetation. So this is now being learned anew. We are learning all over again that intercropping — which is now being popularized as agroforestry — was always the best way of farming in that part of Africa. Since the people do not have alternative sources of energy, and they have to burn wood, we encourage them to plant more than they cut. The message is: You need the wood, but you have to plant more than you cut.

Where the Green Belt movement is successful people are indeed planting more than they cut. The problem is that in some areas, especially among the pastoral (nomad) communities, among the people who are always on the move, they do not settle down to plant trees and take care of the land and then move on. Unfortunately, it takes more than a campaign such as the Green Belt Movement to heal the afforested areas, because they are, ironically, the most eroded. And that is where you need a lot of tree planting and restoration of grass. But unless you can settle down and plant, unless you fence off big areas and plant, it is very difficult. We have been unsuccessful among the pastoral communities.

Does that suggest to you that the Green Belt Movement and these nomadic people are incompatible, or is there a solution?

There is an answer. One answer is to fence off small patches, so that wherever the people are, they can fence off and plant grass and trees and allow that area to regenerate while they move into another area.

That sounds similar to leaving a field fallow.

That's right, but here you have to fence it. That takes a lot of money.

But are nomadic people going to take the time to plant trees and grass? Does that work in their economy?

They would. They would keep moving, but they would leave that area protected. And by the time they came around again it would have regenerated. The problem is that we do not have the money. It also takes political will, because many of these pastoral communities just move from one area to another. In the past they had huge tracts of land to use. Now they don't, because of the boundaries between countries. For example the Masai in East Africa do not move the way they used to in the past. There is not the room any longer. Settlers come in and cultivate land is meant for grazing. So, the pastoral communities are no longer able to migrate with their animals. As a result, they concentrate in some areas, and this causes the land to degenerate.

There is also the pressure of national parks. In the past, wild animals and domestic animals moved harmoniously from one place to another. These days there is a lot of pressure, whether it be from people or animals. And these days people fence their lands, and this prevents the animals from moving from one place to another and sometimes completely wipes them out. So while we have been very successful among farming communities in promoting tree planting, we have not registered as much success among the pastoral communities. But this is an issue that requires political decisions and economic resources that are beyond a non-government organization (NGO).

You mentioned in your book that after more than 10 years in operation the Green Belt Movement has some seven million trees growing and some 600 tree nurseries in operation. Is this the number of trees that survived after planting? Have some of these been harvested?

In 1988 we did a count and by then we had 10 million trees growing and 1500 tree nurseries. But these tree nurseries are very small in small communities. The 10 million trees are trees that people planted and then reported as having survived. I'm sure that some of these that were planted in the early 1970s have been harvested for firewood, or for fencing to meet the needs of the people. So, it is not as if they are all standing. However, if you go to areas where the planting has been going on, you can hardly notice that some have been cut, because more are being planted all the time.

Have you looked at your survival rate?

You must bear in mind that we are dealing here with people who are comparatively illiterate and their record keeping is not perfect. There is a certain amount of estimation here. The survival rate on private farms can be as much as 90 to 100 percent. These are the mini-green belts planted by private farmers. When the trees are planted in school compounds, or on public land, the survival rate may go down to 50 to 60 percent. But our survival rate has been good because we have tended to concentrate on the private farms and on school compounds. We have not ventured much into public lands. First, people do not want to plant trees on public land because that is public work and who wants to do work for nothing? Second, there would not be proper follow-up on public lands. One would have to use the equivalent of the forestry service to plant trees that way.

The philosophy behind the movement was to try to make people plant trees because they saw the need for it. We started with helping people plant trees to meet their immediate needs. As we continue to enlighten ourselves, we hope that one day we will be able to go on public lands because we see that our needs go beyond our immediate needs. It is like starting with a very local concern, and then moving to the community level, national level, and then global level. There are many of us who plant trees because we are concerned about the global changes, but it has to start from personal needs. And we are still very much at the personal level.

You mentioned that there is the question of whether people have enough land on which to plant trees. Some people may have very little land or none at all to which they have real title, or because the land is owned by the men and it is the women who are doing the tree planting. You have suggested that in this case it is sometimes possible to plant them along roadways or along pathways. How does that work? If a woman plants a tree along a path or a road, is this her tree? Won't other people claim that the tree isn't hers because it is planted on public land?

We have not had any problem with that because traditionally, people were there before the roads. The roads were developed just the other day and they passed through people's land. The policy of the Government is, quite often: Don't plant anything on public land that the Government claims. I think that is very negative. But the public land that is next to your land is often seen as the land belonging to whomever's land adjoins it. So, no one would dare come to cut a tree there. At the moment, a lot of people graze their animals along the road on public lands. But in principle, if a woman plants on public land, the Government can still decide that whatever is on public land is public property. Usually what happens is that people plant trees on Government land adjoining their land, and it is quite clear to everyone who owns the trees.

Does the Green Belt Movement confront the problem of land distribution with the Government and the big land owners who plant the land for export crops?

No, we have not gotten into that. Kenya has a policy of private ownership of land, so anyone can own it. It is true that a few people have large tracts of land as compared with many who are landless. And this is a bone of contention between the two parties. The Government continues to advocate a system of "willing seller, willing buyer." But of course if you are poor you cannot buy. Some politicians urge that the landless should be provided with land, and urge that people with too much land should give it up. But the Government has not done it.

What to me is even more important is that the land that was confiscated by the British and declared "Crown Land" then became state land. That land includes national parks, forest lands, river banks, etc. When the national parks and forest reserves are called state lands, then they should be seen as belonging to the people. Originally these lands belonged to the people who lived there. They belonged to the tribes that lived there. I think it is extremely unjust for the Government to use those lands as it pleases, especially when they are used in ways that do not benefit the people.

People who lived near forests traditionally used the forests either for firewood, food, or honey. When the land is declared public land and is fenced off and people are not allowed to go into the forest because the Government is using the forest in other ways, then I think the Government is overstepping its mandate and is usurping the land and taking it away from the people.

When the land is usurped in this fashion by the Government, it may be very difficult to protect those forests from the people who live near it, because they do not see it as their forest anymore. They see it as a resource that now belongs to the Government, so they do not take care of it. We have had examples in Kenya where the animals attack people who live near the forest, or their animals, and then the people set the forest on fire because they want the wild animals to move farther away. Huge tracts of land are destroyed in this fashion. I think this is because the Government has kept the people away from these forests and now it seems as if the forest belongs to someone else.

What is the relationship between the Government and the Green Belt Movement? Has the Government helped start nurseries or given you access to public lands on which to plant woodlots? Or is it often a more adversarial relationship?

We started with the objective of encouraging women, particularly, to grow trees to meet their own needs. We encouraged them to establish tree nurseries on public lands, and for them to inform the Administration about what they were doing to get whatever support they needed. For example, if they wanted to start a tree nursery near a river, it might be that the only land near the river is public land. The Administrator, therefore should be willing to allow the women to use this land. For a long time we worked like that with the Government and it was a very good relationship.

But recently the Green Belt movement has criticized Government policies. Of particular significance has been the acquisition of land in the cities for public parks. In some cases the Government has allowed this land to be used as if it were private property. The Green Belt Movement, as part of its campaign for the environment, has been criticizing the obliteration of public parks and open spaces particularly in Nairobi where we are headquartered.

How does the Government use the parks for private purposes?

This hinges on the unspoken phenomenon in Africa, which is called corruption. Of course, we are not supposed to talk about or even know about corruption. It seems to me that once a public park has been identified in a city — and there is ample evidence these days that open space is very much needed in the city — that park should not be transferred from public hands and given to a private developer. For an individual person or private company to acquire such land is inexcusable.

The Green Belt Movement has occasionally found itself in a position where it was opposing interference with these parks. Now because the Government was involved, or had given its OK, or some Government leaders were involved, Government officials did not take our intervention lightly. In recent months the Green Belt Movement has been seen in a bad light by the Government. But I know for certain that it is partly because the Government leaders, some politicians, perhaps many politicians, did not realize how important the environmental agenda is today. And that such an issue, once it is raised by environmentalists, suddenly becomes a big issue not only nationally, but also internationally. I am quite sure that in months to come, not only politicians but many people in Nairobi will be happy that the Green Belt Movement was there to stand up against the private acquisition of public open spaces.

Have you been successful in protecting some of these open spaces from development?

Fortunately, we have been successful; but I don't know if we have been completely successful, because politicians can always turn around and do it again. But so far we have been able to save the park. In one way that experience has helped explain to the people what the environment is all about, that it is not just about planting trees, but that when we talk about planting trees, this is only a vehicle. There are many other issues that affect the environment: development, poor planning of cities, soil erosion, and non-accountability of leaders. A lot of issues get discussed, but we prefer to do something positive, instead of just talking about it.

The tree has been a miraculous symbol of the ability to do something so that we are not completely incapacitated by the huge problems confronting us in our part of the world. We can always feel that at least we can plant a tree and help take care of it. And that tree can meet some of one's needs: food, firewood, building materials. In this way you don't feel completely helpless.

That is why we call ourselves a movement, not a society or an association. It is only a society for the purpose of registration. But it is supposed to have very loose membership. You become a member by planting a tree. If your tree dies you are no longer a member. You have to replant. So it is like a personal commitment to do what needs to be done, rather than a membership organization.

Tell me about the subsidies for tree planting. You point out that in order to make this movement work, people have to see some short-term gains. You write that if nurseries are started and seedlings are grown that can be sold, that gives the women who have done this work a reward in the short term. You also mention that some of this money comes from abroad. How much does the Green Belt Movement pay per tree; and what is the size of the budget to keep this movement going?

It is important that people have short-term gains especially because we are dealing with poor people, rural populations, which often have no cash income, and who would not do this work if it were completely unpaid. Even though they know that it is good for them to plant a tree, I don't think in the beginning they would have done it without being paid. Sometimes when we can't raise funds and don't have enough money to pay them, they will say that they cannot do this work for free. We have to keep reminding them that it is not for free, because these are trees that you are planting on your own farm.

Nevertheless, these are poor people and their problems have to be met now. They are not going to wait for 20 or 30 years so that they can harvest the trees. We pay them very little, partly because we have no intention of making this a money minting program. First, we don't have that kind of money; but also it would probably lose the dimension that we are planting trees because we need to do it for our own survival, not because we are being paid by the movement. We pay them the equivalent of about four cents U.S. per tree that survives. It is not much money, but the women will still do it because they need the money badly. And also because they see the second stage of benefit when those trees grow on their farm. But it is very little money by any standard. Our budget is about $200,000 a year at the moment. But when we started we did not have a budget.

With the other countries we are forming a Green Belt network of organizations that are interested in initiating tree planting. We have about $50,000 from a Finnish organization to reach out to other countries in Africa. But what happens is that once the movement is started in a country it is often helped out by donor agencies in that country. The important thing is for people to realize that this is work that has to be done by the people themselves, that it should not be an outsider coming to do it, that it must be an indigenous effort.

Can you give an example of a case in which you have uncovered some traditional knowledge about tree planting?

One of the best things the movement does is to make people feel that they are OK and that they can do it. I found that one of the biggest disadvantages that we have is that our people have been bombarded with the idea that "you don't know, you don't know, you don't know" for so long that they are constantly waiting for other people to come and do the simplest things for them. They need to be encouraged to believe that they can do it. You don't need an expert to look for seeds, for example. This is mentioned by Gilbert Arum from the Kenya Energy and Environment Organization (KENGO).

These are women who cultivate crops; they know how to make seeds germinate. Unlike KENGO, we don't give people seeds. We believe that the women should go look for seeds wherever they find them and experiment with them. And we find that they know a lot of different ways in which they can make seeds germinate, especially the older women, who know a lot.

One group I visited told me that they knew of a certain plant that they would collect because they knew that birds ate the fruits of that plant. So whenever birds went and "did their own thing" (defecated), the seeds would germinate. The women knew that. We have not yet recorded all the experiences that are to be found among the women, but it would be an astonishing list. They know how to go around collecting wildlings — as they are called by foresters — the seeds that are carried by the winds and germinate when the rains come. And they are able to differentiate the tree seedlings from the weeds. They collect them, and preserve them, and then go to the nursery and plant them.

They also do simple technologies that they develop themselves. The ordinary method of preparing a seed bed can be very complicated, if you ask a forester. But if you ask a woman, she just takes a piece of a broken pot, puts good soil in it, and places it on an elevated place so the chickens don't eat it. This way, when the seeds germinate she knows what they are. Then all she has to learn is to transplant them into bags and containers to nurse them. But they have lots of ways of managing nurseries. It is not like what you would expect a forester to do, but then who wanted that? All we wanted were trees to be planted. And the foresters are now the first to admit that they are amazed by the ability of these ordinary women to grow trees.

The Green Belt Movement is dealing with people who have no training whatsoever. They can't tell you the botanical names of the trees they are planting, but they know their local names. The nurseries are very small and serve small communities. The nurseries must be close enough to the people so that they can collect the plants with wheelbarrows, or in baskets, or just carry them in their hands. This is in contrast to Government nurseries, which are usually huge, and professionally run, and contain mostly exotics, despite the fact that the Government now says we should plant indigenous trees. If you go to Government tree nurseries they are still filled with exotic species because those are much easier to harvest. But having said that, I should note that the Government has begun to change its policy, and it has decentralized a lot of these formerly huge nurseries, because it has seen the need to take the trees to the people.

In terms of scale, the Government releases many millions of trees — more than we could ever release ourselves. But I don't believe a lot of them survive. During the beginning of the Green Belt Movement the foresters would not believe our records of survival rates, because they said the survival rate should not be more than 20 percent. So a lot of the trees planted out of Government nurseries die. I think it is partly because of the amount of trees they produce, the method they use, and the method of distribution. Their poor survival rates induced them to change and decentralize. They also work very closely with the women. They go around to the nurseries run by the women and provide advice and technical know-how. And that is greatly encouraged, because they have information that they should give to the women.

The only problem that we have had is that because of the criticism of the Government by the Green Belt Movement that I mentioned earlier, there has been some intimidation of women. But when we have good relations, the foresters are most welcome to our nurseries. And in fact, many of them are very enthusiastic because they can see that what the women are doing is what they themselves are being paid to do. So there is some collaboration.

The general population is very fond of the Green Belt Movement and very supportive of its activities, not only in rural areas but also in its advocacy role. Although our advocacy role puts us in a very dangerous position, it is a position that one sometimes has to take. The people are happy that the Green Belt Movement can stand up and advocate good environmental management. Of course, sometimes that means that we become the enemy, rather than the friend, of the Government.

Other than the example you gave of the campaign in the city over open space and park lands, are there other examples of confrontation with the Government?

No. The thing I have discovered in Kenya is that the power of the Government is very centralized, particularly around the presidency. If the President says something, it is as if the whole machinery has been advised that you are a bad guy. So, in the countryside, where women are doing nothing but good, they may be punished because their leader in Nairobi has said something that the President doesn't like. That is why I keep emphasizing the need to democratize the Government and the need to make leaders accountable. You can not have sustainable development unless the leaders can be questioned. To question is not bad; we should be credited for questioning the Government, and not punished.

Does the President have some disagreement with the Green Belt Movement?

I think when we criticized the Government's activities in the city, he didn't like it because he was associated with one of the companies involved. He was in favor of part of the park being developed; we were against that. He didn't think that anybody should be against him. But I'm sure one day he will realize that we were not against him as a person, we were just against bad environmental management.

What is the connection between the very practical tree planting work you are doing in Kenya and your presence here at the UNCED negotiations?

I came to UNCED to be part of the process. At home we are going through a process with the women. (When I say women, the Green Belt Movement is associated with women, but it is actually a community development project. It is what you would call a sustainable development movement.) I want to see if the decisions being made here are sufficiently sensitive for us to apply them at the local level because, in the final analysis, everything that is decided here has to be transmitted into action. And unless it can be applied at the local level it will really remain nothing but a piece of paper.

Trying to implement the Green Belt Movement does not just involve the planting of trees. Our concern is not just forests. Many of our indigenous species were destroyed in the process of modernization. Only about 3 percent of our old forest is left in Kenya, and even that is being interfered with by people who want to plant exotic species for the development side of the agenda. These are people who want paper mills for pulp, people who want fast growing trees for timber, people who want to establish more tea and coffee plantations so we can earn more foreign exchange, so that we can pay our debts.

So we are deeply affected by the discussions going on through the International Monetary Fund (IMF) and the General Agreement on Tariffs and Trade (GATT). We are also interested in the discussions about oceans taking place here at UNCED, because most of our coastal areas and marine life have been destroyed by soil erosion. Unless we stop soil erosion we are going to destroy the marine life off our coast. So, the Green Belt Movement is involved with many of the issues being discussed at UNCED. Even the climate change issue. We have to plant more trees, because we want to contribute toward the sink for carbon dioxide. We have a positive role to play in helping to halt global warming by planting more trees. But if we are going to play that role, does the world owe us anything for contributing toward the solving of this problem? We do not have cash. Many of our constituents are poor. We are not contributing to the destruction of the ozone or the accumulation of carbon dioxide in the atmosphere. So why should we contribute toward solving these problems and not be paid what is due us?

When our Government is negotiating abouf more financial resources for the South, it makes a lot of sense to us. But, for me personally, I want to know whether those resources will be used properly. So I want to hear the word "accountability" put into the documents of agreement. I want an understanding that accountability should be spoken about. We should not continue to pretend that we are helping African countries when we know that the financial aid given to African nations is often retained right here in the North in private bank accounts. I want people to understand the relationship between financial transfers, non-democratization of our governance in Africa, non-accountability of many of our leaders, and the worsening situation of poverty in the South.

The issue of poverty has been discussed a lot. I know something

---

about this because I work with poor people. But I also know that much of that poverty is perpetrated by our own people. They are part of the problem. But here, at UNCED, the Government is the negotiating party. Some of the issues I am talking about you can't get to the floor because they are considered embarrassing to the Government. Yet, to me, I feel that they are very important issues that must be brought to the fore.

I know it is only a matter of time before the people will tell it as it is. They will say: "You African leaders, stop being corrupt, be accountable to your people, invest in your own country. When you get aid, use it. And if you don't use it, don't hide it in some northern country and then wait until you are overthrown so you can come live comfortably in the North. Therefore democratize." Sometimes when I say democratize, I am reminded that there is very little democracy anywhere. Even in the U.N. system there is very little democracy. But there has to be a beginning somewhere.

Can you imagine an international, legally binding treaty on forestry that would be useful to the Green Belt Movement and to the women with whom you work? Or would you like to see no international instrument on deforestation, and instead community control of the forest? Or is it possible to have some combination of those?

Although the picture is still very blurred and one cannot see where the negotiations will end, I would consider that a combination of both would be desirable. People at the local level must be able to control the forestry resources in order for them to protect them.

Even if they use them foolishly and selfishly?

What does that mean? I am assuming that we have governments and mechanisms at the national level that are interested in protecting the forest. I am assuming that we are past the stage where we look at forests as trees that should be cut, and that there will be an understanding about how important forests are.

You are assuming a lot.

Maybe. But without that understanding I do not think we can protect the forest.

In some parts of the U.S. and Canada, the local communities are so alienated from nature and good environmental management that their main interest is in the short-term gain of cutting the trees down to get the money for the logs. National regulation should prevent overcutting, but very often it doesn't. What happens when you have local communities that want to exploit a local resource until it is ruined?

That is why I say that you have the combination of both local control and international agreements. One reason I feel that the communities must be involved is that the reverse could also be true. You could have a central government that misuses the resources because it wants to make some money. And in some countries, especially today in Africa, if you have a corrupt government, you may have a government that at that

59

particular time just wants to enrich itself and completely deforests the country. So, you need some kind of control of the forests by the local people.

Coming back to my point about democratization, governance, and popular participation, that allows you to elect people who understand that the forest is a very important resource both locally and internationally. I guess we need to put on an intensive public education campaign. Governments have enormous capacity, which we see when they go to war. If the forests are that important to the survival of the planet, the governments could do something to protect them. It is important for the people themselves to be involved, because they have to be able to protect the forest both from themselves and from governments that might also become non-accountable. And the reverse is also true. You might have communities which, if left without government control, would destroy the forest.

Internationally, I think we need to have certain conventions to prohibit irresponsible governments from coming in and destroying other peoples' forests.

Is it not the transnational corporations that come in and do the most damage?

In many ways those transnational corporations work very closely with the governments. It is two sides of the same coin. The governments provide the political protection that these transnational corporations require when they are operating abroad. So the convention would have to look at all these interests.

What is important here is the issue of sovereignty. We must avoid a situation where a powerful government can decide what to do with the forests of smaller countries. We must avoid a situation where a powerful government like the U.S. can tell other countries not to cut their forests because of the impact that will have on the climate. At that point the smaller country would lose its sovereignty and we would get into a situation where smaller nations are at the mercy of bigger nations. So I think that if climate change turns out to be a big threat, as we are informed it is, I can imagine that some people will be very interested in their own survival. And since you cannot survive without the trees that make the oxygen, we may have to fight over these resources in the future. We need conventions that will not leave the powerful with all the might and all the right.

We have heard at the third Preparatory Committee meeting of UNCED that the Global Environment Facility (GEF) has $1.5 billion to use for funds for sustainable development. You have said you want to see a certain level of accountability in the use of such funds. And you are also interested in seeing local people have some control in this process. Can you imagine a reformed GEF that would provide accountability and real input from the community level?

The $1.5 billion is not much money compared to all the work that needs to be done. Perhaps they want to use that money for an experiment to see how it works. I have a problem with the World Bank. The World Bank has not done much for the environment, nor has it encouraged accountability. It has allowed a lot of non-accountability and therefore destruction of the environment in many parts of the world. So I wonder whether it has changed its attitude and will promote accountability. The current proposal is that money can go to NGOs, but that the local government must endorse the grant. But, it is not true that the most effective environmental organizations are the "pets" of their government. Sometimes being effective means standing up when the government would rather that you sat down. The very organizations that are actually doing a good job and have been pushing a sustainable development agenda may be the ones barred by their governments from receiving funds. Therefore I am not sure how accountable this process will be.

I am very worried about this. For the last 30 years Africa has received masses of dollars for development, and yet Africa today is poorer than it was 30 years ago. We all know that a lot of that money has been stolen by our leaders and has been hidden in some banks in northern countries. And this has been done with full knowledge of leaders in the North. And certainly with the full knowledge of the World Bank and IMF. I cannot believe that their intelligence units do not know that. The fact that this has been allowed to go on to the point where we now have millions of poor people struggling to pay a debt for money that they never received is to me immoral. My question is: Is this a new leaf we are turning over; or is this the old game that we are going to run through all over again? In another 10 years will we evaluate UNCED and come to see how much we have failed?

There will be a meeting in Miami in November, 1991 where successful stories of programs mainly run by women from all over the world will be presented to a group of women who advise the executive director of United Nations Environment Program (UNEP). That is where I would like to see representatives of the World Bank and GEF come and shop for small, successful projects that have been launched with little money, but with a lot of commitment and accountability. Unless we are going to have more of that commitment and accountability, I really don't think things will change much at all

Certainly, listening to discussions here at UNCED it sounds like the good old game all over again. It does not look to me as if people see an emergency ahead of us with which we should be dealing. I get more the sense that people feel there is a problem with the environment, but it is not that bad. But if it is as bad as scientists tell us it is, we should be concerned. I believe the scientists. They tell me that there is a hole in the ozone and I am scared. If the temperature is rising, then that is an emergency. But I don't see that sense of urgency among the politicians in the UNCED process. This makes me wonder if these problems are real, if they are exaggerated, or if the delegates to UNCED just don't want to confront these problems.

If the World Bank gave money directly to non-government organizations (NGOs) would that not interfere with the sovereignty of a nation?

The World Bank should not waste a lot of time and money on experimenting. That experimenting has been done and success stories have already been identified. So the money should go to support these success stories. The governments that have not democratized their governance should do so. If they did it would allow genuine and effective NGOs to approach their government and say: "Give me one good reason why this work should not be funded." For sustainable development to take place we really must have democratized institutions. It is not as if I am looking for utopia, but we really cannot work in a dictatorial situation.

Do you see anything coming out of UNCED that would help the democratization process? Do you find useful some of the "rights and responsibilities of states and individuals" that are being considered for inclusion in the Earth Charter? Or are they just well-intentioned words that are unenforceable?

Sometimes words can have quite concrete effects. The democratization process is going on all the time. We just witnessed history rewriting itself in the East. In Africa there is a lot of lumbering and kicking, and this will continue. But I think many people in the North, confronted by the poverty that is prevalent, especially in Africa, unless they are inhuman, must ask themselves certain questions. It is not as if they can say that everything has been done and still these people are not emerging from poverty. At UNCED there are some people who will have their consciences touched, and who may feel, especially in the case of Africa, that the democratization process must be hastened. It is moving, but it is moving too slowly to prevent further degradation.

Look at what happened in the East. Development in the East completely ignored the environment. And part of the reason that no one raised the issue is that these nations were so strictly controlled. But now, with democratization, people are talking about the environmental problems. This is the same kind of thing we are trying to say about Africa. We have to talk about these problems. Our leaders have to be accountable. They have to stop treating their people with such contempt. Otherwise the issue of poverty becomes partly a self-inflicted disease.

Have you examined macro-economic issues such as the GATT negotiations and the impact of commodity pricing on the Green Belt Movement? Can people working at the community level have an impact on these international trade and development issues?

I am not an expert on these issues, but I know superficially the implications of these activities. I know, for example, as long as Kenya keeps producing so many cash crops, and they are purchased at the price the North wants to pay, the result will be that more and more of our land will have to be planted with cash crops in order to service our debt. And as a result, more trees will be cut down and more brush cleared.

Do the Kenyan people decide how much of their land is devoted to cash crops? Or is it decided by people outside Kenya?

I think some of the pressure from outside is changing. I think debt relief is possible. But we should not get rid of some of our debts and then borrow more. And that brings us to the question of our leaders wanting to borrow in order to create "white elephant" projects, prestigious projects that try to copy the Western development model that has done so much damage to the world. Some decisions have to be made at the level of the IMF, World Bank, and GATT. But other decisions have to be made at home by our own Government, and others have to be made by the very women with whom we work. But at the moment the law in Kenya says that if you uproot coffee, or tea, or any of these cash crops you will be arrested. This enslaves the people. The Government can arrest you and take you to court if you uproot cash crops.

Let me get this straight. If you are a farmer and part of your land is planted in cash crops and part in subsistence food, and you decide to uproot some cash crops and plant more vegetables, are you telling me that the Government can arrest you for that?

Yes. That is the kind of enslavement people are under these days.

Is it because of Kenya's debt that this is the law?

Partly. The Kenyan Government does not want people to uproot coffee because Kenya wants more coffee and tea for export. The only way they can guarantee so many tons of export is if every Dick and Harry continues to plant these crops. We export some of the best tea and coffee in the world, but we are not even allowed to intercrop things like beans and potatoes among them. However, in the last few years, because farmers have not gotten paid regularly for their cash crops by the Kenyan Government, people have just disobeyed this rule and intercropped — beans especially. But, legally, they are not allowed to do that.

Let me go back to the concept that the people should be able to question their government about why they should continue to pay for these loans, what were these loans given for, what did the government do with the aid money, and where is that money. If the government of the day was corrupt and misused it — as many African leaders have — and then the government tells a farmer that he cannot intercrop because a lot of coffee is needed to pay the debt, and all the time that money is lying in some bank in Switzerland, that is madness.

That is why these UNCED negotiations are very important because the delegates eventually must agree on what to do with all these debts. At the national level, governments must choose between feeding their people and continuing to pay huge debts. At the local level in which we in the Green Belt Movement operate, our people also have to make a decision about what is good for them. That is why popular participation and democratization is necessary, otherwise you enslave your people.

Can you think of the story of a woman whose life has been changed by the Green Belt Movement?

Well I know one woman who in 1981 came to a meeting where I was talking to women. I did not know her but she was among the women. She heard me talk about the need for women to plant trees in order to protect the soil and all of the things that are stipulated in our pamphlet. And she caught it. She then went home. She was the chairman of a religious group of women. And she told her group about the Green Belt Movement and her group decided to establish a tree nursery in its area. I was invited and I was there when they launched it in 1982. In that area there were very, very few trees. It is a highly populated area where there was a lot of soil erosion and no firewood.

In this women's group there were 80 members but only about 50 agreed to be involved in the tree planting. They started a nursery and subdivided the work. To cut a long story short, today that area has been completely transformed. That woman was already a leader of this religious group. But since then she has become a very important person in that community and she is highly respected. On her own land she has planted mangoes and firewood trees, fruit trees, food crops, and bananas. So she now has food, fruit from her trees, and firewood, and she has prevented soil erosion. Her land is completely protected. That community has a lot of respect for the Green Belt Movement and it sees her as the person who brought this development-oriented program to the community. This story represents what the Green Belt Movement is trying to promote through an individual who becomes responsive to a good idea, carries it to the community, and literally transforms her community and herself.

It seems incredible to me that it did not occur to people in this community to plant trees and crops before this woman came to your lecture. Why did she not plant before she heard you? Wasn't it logical to plant trees for shade from the sun, for fruit, for firewood?

I think it is part of our heritage. We came from a community which did not plant trees. The trees just grew. In the old days we were very few and our community lived in the highlands and we had a lot of trees until commercial agriculture was introduced. So, she had to be told that we need to plant because we have evolved into a culture that thought that open land and monocultures were desirable.

And now, I listen to her tell the story of what Africa was like before the Europeans arrived. At that time we were very few, she says, we had a lot of jungle and trees and bushes and grasslands. At that time we did not have to plant. God did it for us. But now God needs a little help.

64

Martin Rocholl:

European Environmental Activists

 artin Rocholl works with European Youth Forest Action (EYFA) and Action for Solidarity, Equality, Environment and Development campaign (A SEED) in Freiburg, West Germany.

Steve Lerner: Please describe the student and youth groups that you work with and what they do.

Martin Rocholl: I work with the European Youth Forest Action (EYFA). EYFA is a loose network mainly of environmental youth action groups from all the countries in Eastern and Western Europe. EYFA evolved out of a European-wide action against the causes of forest dieback. The main purpose of EYFA is to give groups around Europe the chance to do environmental actions together. We provide help with contacts, organizing, and fund-raising. We do not have a formal membership or membership fees, and only very basic nonbureaucratic structures, which allows young people to come up with crazy ideas and realize them. The activities are carried out by the groups themselves with support from EYFA.

For example, let's say a group is concerned with the growing truck and car traffic in Europe. It finds out that decision-making in this field is done on the European level and it wants to do a European-wide action. This group comes to EYFA and asks for help. We keep about 6000 addresses of groups and individuals in our computer address file so we can assist the group in finding others to join with them. They can also use our newsletter to find interested groups. On November 15, 1991, for example, we conducted a European Traffic Action and blocked streets for 15 minutes simultaneously at about 100 places in 15 different European countries.

What was the point of that?

Car and truck traffic is one of Europe's biggest environmental problems. Growing road traffic adds to the greenhouse effect substantially, causes acid rain, destroys landscapes, etc. There is no question that cars and trucks are the most destructive means of transport, while trains can do the same amount of transporting with about 5 percent of the environmental destruction and only 30 percent of the energy cost.

Transportation is a very hot issue at the moment in Europe because with the coming of the European Common Market we are expecting an increase in truck traffic of about 40 percent, which will cause a collapse of the highway system. But there are no steps being taken to ensure that transportation is planned in the most environmentally sound way, such as the expansion of the train system. And there will be a lot of unnecessary transport taking place as well. One of the best examples is the apple juice made in Italy, bottled in Sweden or Denmark, with labels from Portugal and drunk in Germany (where we of course have apples). This insanity is only possible because the trucks don't have to pay for the destruction they do to society and the environment on their way through Europe.

The issue of traffic will also be part of the Action for Solidarity, Equality, Environment and Development (A SEED) campaign. A SEED is a global youth campaign that developed parallel to the United Nations Conference on Environment and Development (UNCED) process. It was initiated by EYFA and Student Environmental Action Coalition USA (SEAC) and has now spread to all continents.

We see the European transportation issue as a major example of how our governments in the North talk about sustainability a lot, but don't really do anything. We believe that all the talk about sustainable development is only lip service as long as the rich North refuses to change its own destructive development path.

A sustainable traffic policy in Europe would make major investments in the train system. But actually the opposite is happening today. Train prices are rising, railroad lines are closed down, and road traffic is indirectly subsidized. Serious estimates say that the gasoline prices should be at least three times as high to pay for all the environmental and social destruction caused by car and truck traffic.

In Germany we are concerned at the moment with what we call a traffic collapse. Already now, during holiday times, we have traffic jams some 50 kilometers long on the highways. This is totally crazy, and still road traffic is increasing. But at the same time we have a rather ignorant transportation minister in Germany, who comes from a generation that still believes that driving around in your own car means freedom. We had a talk with him about the upcoming traffic collapse and he gave us a 15-minute speech on how people in Germany, and especially East Germany, want to be free to drive wherever they want. He held really old-fashioned views that are totally opposed to sustainability. At the same time Chancellor Kohl is making a big fuss about UNCED and saying that Germany is number one among nations in pursuing sustainability.

The situation in Eastern Europe is certainly more complicated. Eastern Europe needs better transportation systems in general, which might in some limited cases also mean more trucks. But here as well, it is sad to see that the main emphasis is on building new roads rather than modernizing a train system that so far has satisfied most of the transportation needs.

How long has EYFA existed? How big are the groups?

EYFA is a network and not an organization. We have about 300 affiliated organizations, of which about 100 are active. We have no stiff structures and no big leaders. The whole idea is to have a tool for European-wide actions. Someone has an idea and then we start thinking of how to do it.

EYFA was founded in 1985. It started with a bus tour through Europe with actions, seminars, discussions and meetings focused on acid rain and forest die-back. These tours, which we still do today, have an educational and a publicity aspect. The variety of subjects grew. In 1988 we organized a bus tour through the Soviet Union and to Chernobyl. We were probably the first Western/Eastern European group to go out on the streets there and protest. We saw industrial cities with coal mines, and steel mills, and burning factories where there was not a single healthy tree within a circle of 100 kilometers around the factories, and in a circle of 20 kilometers everything was dead.

In 1990, we conducted our first European-wide bike tour with 100 participants traveling 4000 kilometers. The topics were traffic and alternative tourism. We started in Bergen in Norway, where the European and North American Environmental Ministers were meeting for UNCED. In Bergen, we joined other grassroots organizations and held our own parallel meeting. This meeting was initiated because we were dissatisfied with the official process. We talked about the subjects that were left out by the ministers. For example, they did not talk about development issues and the destructive effects of Western Europe's and North America's overconsumption. We also engaged in actions outside the meeting place.

The Bike Tour 1990 that started in Bergen went all the way to Hungary, where we had EYFA's annual meeting and summer camp, called Ecotopia. For two and a half months we were greeted every day by a local environmental group, which would give us free food and lodging. With each of these local groups we would organize a small local action, using the international support from the bike tour. We demonstrated for bicycle paths, against road-building projects, for alternative types of tourism, against polluting power plants, etc.

The best things we do happen spontaneously. On July 2, 1990, the first day the West German mark was introduced into East Germany, we held an "unpacking action" in front of a new supermarket offering all these shiny new Western products. You have to understand that in East Germany they recycled 90 percent of their bottles, paper, and plastic before western products came in. They only had three types of bottles and only one kind of plastic so that their recycling was perfect. Now all these shiny western products come in wrapped 5,000 times. So we went in and bought the food for the bike tour for one day. We unwrapped it directly in front of the store entrance to show people how much unnecessary waste was produced when they bought these western products. We put it up like an exhibition. It was an enormous amount of waste. We spread it out and made some signs with it. We had a very positive reaction from the people.

That is our strength. We try to make our actions concrete and direct. In Geneva, at PrepCom Three, we were upset that the southern non-government organizations (NGOs), and also groups like us who don't have a lot of money, don't have a chance to participate. These sessions are held in Geneva, one of the most expensive cities in the world. At the same time the U.N. does not give sufficient grants to NGOs, especially from the South, to stand up to its promise to involve NGOs in the UNCED process. So on one day we conducted what we called a "cooking action" where we cooked a very low-cost vegetarian meal for NGO participants. We wanted to continue doing it throughout the session but got in trouble with the U.N. cafeteria, which sells very expensive food.

In Geneva we were a group of 30 young persons from five different continents. We stayed in a bomb shelter, which the city of Geneva rented to us cheaply, and cooked vegetarian meals for ourselves. We managed to live on approximately $5 per person per day. Still, we had to pay that small amount of money ourselves, because we were told that the U.N. had no money for us. This is hard to believe when you see the incredibly opulent surroundings the PrepComs are held in. It is even more difficult to understand because our activities were very much welcomed by U.N. officials. Sometimes one gets the feeling that we are only wanted because it looks good to have some young people around when one talks about the future. But whenever we have some demands, be they political or financial, we are ignored.

I take it you are vegetarians not just for health reasons but also because you believe that eating lower on the food chain will lead to a greater food surplus and better distribution of food.

Certainly. It is outrageous that we import food to feed our cattle from countries where there is starvation, when at the same time eating too much meat is a health problem in Western Europe. But besides that, industrial meat production in Europe is also an environmental problem.

Europe imports grain and soybeans from Third World countries to feed cattle in big farms. The manure that the cattle produce, which normally could be used as fertilizer, is produced in quantities too great to be used properly. It washes into the ground water, and the nitrates from the manure get into drinking water and cause a health problem. It also ends up in rivers and eventually the Baltic Sea. There the nitrates and phosphates are causing algae to bloom, which endangers life in that sea.

What we have here is a typical example of a broken cycle. Normally the manure should go back on the fields where the grain was produced and serve as fertilizer. But these fields are thousands of kilometers away in the South. Instead, this potential fertilizer ends up in our drinking water and in the rivers and the sea, where it doesn't belong. This "export" of fertilizer at the same time causes soil degradation in the South where the cattle fodder is produced.

Coming back to EYFA's activities, where do you get the money to fund your projects?

We are in debt most of the time. Most of our members are youth organizations and many of them come from Eastern Europe. None of them has surplus money. Therefore all our money comes from grants we get for certain actions. We apply at environmental and youth ministries as well as private foundations and European institutions. This is always high risk because most of the government grants only arrive shortly before or even after the start of an action. Our office receives a small regular grant from the European Community, which just keeps it alive.

All of our activities are done on a very low budget. We expect a lot of personal involvement from our participants and organizers. EYFA, for example, normally does not reimburse for travel.

In EYFA we have our own currency system, which is another financial risk but a very important part of our network. The idea behind it is that a person, let's say from Russia, coming to France could not buy anything and could not pay any participation fee because of the official exchange rates. (For a person from Russia to pay a participation fee in France amounts to about a month's salary.) Therefore, we created our own currency system, called ECO (not to be confused with the ECU, the unit of the European Currency). The ECO is based on a socially fair exchange rate. We calculate the normal amount of money that a student needs to survive in his country and from that we calculate the exchange rates. For example, on the free market one West German mark is worth about 50 rubles now. But in fact, when we go to Russia with this exchange rate I can buy a drink for a tenth of a mark, which is about 7 cents. In the ECO system one ECO is one mark and one and a half rubles. So when we conduct any activity, each person pays in his own currency according to that exchange rate. Of course this gives us money problems because when we do things in the West we have to subsidize the participants from the East. But on the other hand we recouped some of this money when we held our summer camp last year in the Soviet Union. In the East, at our camp bar, a German student pays as much for a beer as he or she pays at home. So does the Russian person. So if we buy the beer in rubles we take in some money to offset the subsidies we have to pay when activities happen in the West.

Are you making plans for the Brazil Summit?

In reaction to UNCED we started the global youth campaign A SEED with the U.S. student environmental group SEAC, which has spread now to all continents. We are working together with groups like the

Asian Student Association and many other youth networks. A SEED developed out of our experiences in Bergen in May, 1990, where the European and North American environmental ministers met to prepare for UNCED. The main idea of A SEED is a decentralized but interconnected approach.

What experiences did you have in Bergen and what were the consequences?

First of all, we found out how little success there is when we try to influence the official process. We spent a lot of time trying to change a word in the documents here and there, but when it came to decision making we were ignored. Since we were shiny nice young people we were used as a photo opportunity, but in the end they did not give a damn about what we were saying. Secondly, we noticed how important it is to do direct actions during these conferences not only to influence the delegates directly, but also to build up public pressure through the media. I don't mean to be arrogant, but I think these delegates need a push from young people because it is our future that is at stake.

In Bergen we surrounded the hotel where all the environmental ministers were staying. They wanted to go out to dinner on a bus. We decided to let them travel to dinner as fast as they had been moving on the issues at the conference. So we surrounded the building and let their bus go one meter every 10 minutes. They spent about three hours on this bus going to dinner. We had 4,000 signs saying "blah." So they looked out on a sea of signs saying, "blah, blah, blah, blah."

Protesting is important because it gives young people a chance to let out their anger and say: "This is not the way they should talk about our future. This is a very serious subject but they are avoiding the most important questions like the debt crisis and trying to sneak away from the difficult questions. They are leaving us very little hope that something will be achieved!" But protesting is not all. It is important that we develop our own agenda and start working on solutions. In Bergen we had a parallel conference, the A SEED Popular Forum, with very serious and constructive discussions. The ideas developed at this meeting still live on in the A SEED campaign.

How do you picture the UNCED process today?

We are rather disappointed. It is already questionable whether any real conventions will be signed at the Earth Summit. The delegates are not talking about the real issues, such as the debt crisis. The real issue is the exploitation of the South by the rich North. Instead, they are talking about forest management. The North is talking about how to teach the South to exploit its tropical rain forests in a better way, so the North can still get the timber exports but the forest is not completely destroyed.

The U.S. delegation is blocking the climate convention, because they are questioning whether global warming is in fact happening. The background is of course that this is the convention that would need the biggest commitment from the rich countries in the North, which produce most of the greenhouse gases and waste most of the energy. I believe that global warming is a very serious threat and find it very ignorant of the U.S. delegation to hide behind unclear scientific statements.

But let's suppose global warming is not a danger yet. There are many other good reasons to stop the over-consumption of energy by the North. We are using up an unfair share of the world's resources, which leaves little or nothing for the poorer countries in the South. To keep the stream of resources flowing from the South to the North, we have built up post-colonial structures, like the so-called debt crisis or the General Agreement on Tariffs and Trade (GATT), which serve as modern tools for exploitation. This needs to be stopped and a first step is to stop energy waste and over-consumption in the North.

A commitment to produce less CO_2 and work on higher energy efficiency in the U.S. would have positive effects on the U.S. economy and the environment in the long run.

But we have had a number of things to say about other delegations as well. The Scandinavian delegation on UNCED, for example, has been very outspoken on saving the tropical rain forest. At the same time, for several years we have been fighting to save the last virgin mountain forests in Sweden. Only after we threatened the Swedish Government with a boycott of Swedish wood products (a major export item) did we have success. In the fall of 1991 the Swedish Government decided to halt the clear cutting for a year.

What are your plans for the Earth Summit?

When we first heard about UNCED, our spontaneous reaction was: Let's go to Rio and do the same as we did in Bergen in 1990. But we gave that idea up very quickly. We would have to fly thousands of young people to Rio, which is environmentally very destructive and also unaffordable for us.

So what to do? We chose a decentralized global campaign, with three parts.

The first is finalizing a discussion among young people about our UNCED demands during regional meetings taking place simultaneously in 20 countries on all continents during one weekend in March, 1992, and connected by fax and e-mail. We will also discuss direct solidarity actions (like chain letters of protest to multinational companies) and plan further activities.

The second is bringing our ideas to the public during an action period in April and May. We will present our demands and comments to the politicians going to UNCED. We hope to build up public pressure and influence UNCED that way.

The action period will bring the global issues down to the local level. We want to point out the policies in our own countries that go against the concept of sustainability. In Europe an action will take place in the harbor at Rotterdam, where a lot of resources from the South arrive, including soybeans and other cattle fodder. But this could also be just a local action for recycling on a university campus, or for better public transportation, or against an additional parking lot in the center of a city. It is these small-scale political decisions that cause or solve global environmental problems like the greenhouse effect.

The third is that during UNCED, on several continents, international Youth Festivals will take place. We will call them UNSAID. UNSAID is the festival about what is not said at UNCED. We will discuss our own agenda and try to find solutions to the global crisis. At the same time we will watch what the politicians at UNCED are doing and how they react to our demands. We believe that the fact that the participants at Rio will feel watched by thousands of young people around the world could have a positive effect on the Earth Summit. So far UNSAID festivals are planned for Germany, Kenya, Malaysia, Brazil and the U.S.A., all of them expecting participants from their respective continents.

Do you really think that you can have an influence on UNCED?

To be honest, I don't know. We wish to be able to. It will depend on how clever our publicity is. But it has been one of our principles in EYFA that a campaign always has two aims: a political goal and a personal goal. In this case our political goal is to influence UNCED and what comes after it, and our personal goal is to learn and understand on a global level.

If we send our participants home with new ideas, with inspiration for further cooperation and with the hopeful feeling that they are not alone with their struggles, I think we will have already achieved a lot. There is still a lot to learn. Environmental groups in Europe still have to understand more about the connections between poverty, exploitation and environmental issues. If a youth group in the Netherlands talks with another group in Kenya and they start understanding each other and promise to support each other in the future, we will have made an important first step.

We will have a small office in Rio for the A SEED campaign, which will provide all UNSAID festivals with updated information. Every day, this delegation will send the festivals 10 quotations from politicians in Rio — some ignorant, some positive. They will also provide background information on why we believe this statement is stupid or positive. The young activists at the UNSAID festivals will vote every day on a hit list of the most ignorant and the most positive politicians. This politician hit list will be given to the press. I believe this will be a powerful tool in our media campaign. The UNSAID festivals aim to provide a voice for young people who are most affected by the global crisis but are the last to be heard. This is especially true for our partners in the South.

You said that you came to the third Preparatory Committee meeting directly from an Ecotopia camp in Estonia. Tell me about that.

Twenty of us took a bus directly from Estonia to Geneva. For those of us who spent two weeks at our summer camp, known as Ecotopia, in Estonia, it was quite a change to come to this PrepCom in Geneva, with all its cocktail parties, receptions and the whole wealthy atmosphere.

Ecotopia is EYFA's annual meeting, held every summer from August 1st to 21st. But it's much more than just that. It's an alternative summer university, a place to try out new ways of living, conduct actions, play music, have a lot of fun, and attend workshops on a large variety of subjects such as biotechnology, water pollution, Yoga, political movements, UNCED, and sexuality and politics. At this point we don't invite speakers to Ecotopia anymore. All the speaking is done by the participants for the participants. There is enough knowledge now among the participants. Ecotopia has taken place in Germany, Hungary, and Estonia and will be held in Bulgaria in 1992.

Is this held in the countryside?

Yes. In Estonia it was held out on a small farm. We were all camping. The workshops take place in tents. One of the ideas of Ecotopia is that we should live a very simple life. There are only cold water showers and biodegradable soap. And we eat very simple vegetarian food. People live a much less materialistic life during their time at Ecotopia. It is very much down to the basics. Yet at the same time they experience for perhaps the only time during the year that this could be a more joyful life, a more fulfilled life, and a more satisfactory way of life.

It is part of the Ecotopia idea, I think, to teach people that a life that is based on limited use of materials is possible. This can also be a life where you are involved in politics. Normally young people would not think that it would be fun to engage in politics on their holiday. But here we have people engaging in difficult political discussions for 10 hours a day and yet they enjoy themselves. This is part of a learning experience that teaches young people that they can be involved in politics and have a good time. It also teaches young people that they don't need to take their VW Rabbit down to the Côte d'Azur and spend thousands of dollars to be happy. We are teaching that by practicing it.

Another part of Ecotopia is to enjoy the different cultures of Europe and beyond. If you think of what is happening in Yugoslavia at the moment, where people are killing each other because of different backgrounds, I believe this is very important. EYFA is strong as a network because there is an international group of 100 to 200 people who are deeply involved. You could locate Ecotopia in Antarctica and they would show up because they want to see their friends. The network is strong because people have learned to enjoy doing things together. Enjoying what we are doing is not seen as an extra. It is not like holding a rock concert so people will come to a political event. The fun is integrated into the work.

Do you have to be a student to be part of this group? Is there an age limit?

No, but EYFA comes out of the youth movement. Our definition of youth is anyone who has stayed young in their mind. This definition can cause problems because other organizations define youth as being up to 25 years old. EYFA has a budget of 250,000 to 500,000 marks every year. So you really have to know what you are doing to avoid screwing that up. So, in the core organizing group, people are in the 23- to 30-year-old range, some even older.

Gunnar Album made the point that the North has further to go to achieve a sustainable life-style than do people in the South. Do you see a real movement evolving in Europe away from conspicuous consumption which, if not going to the extremes of living in tents and taking cold showers, at least involves a simpler way of life?

Well, we don't live the whole year in tents and use cold showers. I am happy to return to my little apartment and have a warm shower after two weeks of Ecotopia. We do not feel that we have to suffer to have a better way of life. I don't see this transformation to a simpler life happening in Europe yet. But I keep asking myself why, with all the financial difficulties EYFA has had, why is it still going strong? We hold a meeting in Estonia and we just expect young people to scrape their money together to come, and even pay to participate. No political organization could do that. Why is there so much willingness among these people to invest themselves in this organization? I think the reason is that people are slowly beginning to realize that this non-materialistic life-style is a better way to live.

I think it is obvious that SEAC is one of the fastest growing environmental movements the U.S. has ever seen. It has spread to several hundred universities within a year and a half. When I was in the U.S. I really got the sense that this is a new movement. People are sick of the Yuppie Age and the materialistic way of life. They want to have a reason for their lives. The environmental issue is a very good reason for them because it is directly related to our survival. For example, having a clean river to swim in is something very basic. If it is true that the U.S. experiences movements two or three years before Europe, we might see that happening in Europe soon.

It is interesting that you see this happening in the U.S. I see increased interest in environmental issues, but it is still very cerebral. It is not a movement that is yet dedicated to a sustainable life-style. The exceptions are some of the people who were involved in the back-to-the-land movement in the 1960s and the growing interest in organic farming and alternative energy.

I was expecting an environmental movement in the U.S. that focused on putting catalyzers in cars but then living the California way of life: cruising around the streets with a can of Coke. I was amazed to see that people involved with SEAC were talking about issues such as racism, the problems of indigenous people, uranium mining, and toxic waste dumps in poor neighborhoods. They were integrating a lot of social issues. They had enormous interest in international issues. They had come to the point of saying that we have to change our life-style if we really want to do something for the environment. The U.S. has to stop exploiting the world's resources for its own wealth. I was surprised to see that the young environmental movement in the U.S. is open to this change of life-style.

The North has been exploiting the South for centuries. If we agree that we have about 40 years to make a transition to a sustainable life-style, do you think it is possible that we in the North will give up our trade advantage with the South and that we will stop importing their raw materials at bargain basement prices? Do you think we can change the economic order of the world in the next 40 years?

I think it is necessary and possible but also not very likely. For myself I have found a way of sustainable lobbying and being an environmentalist while ceasing to care about the question of whether or not we totally succeed. There will never be paradise nor will this world collapse. But there will be a better or a worse life for many people and that's what politics should be about.

For me being involved is a very good way of life. The process of trying to do something is what is important. With EYFA and A SEED I had the chance to work for my ideas and meet some of the most fantastic people at the same time. I feel very fortunate.

Last summer we succeeded in having 400 young people come to our Ecotopia camp. I believe they go home more open-minded than before. Maybe now the young people from Germany who went to Ecotopia will not join others who attack foreigners on the streets. Maybe they even have the courage to speak out against it, because they experienced being in an international group in Ecotopia. That would be a step in the right direction. What makes EYFA strong is that we have always been proud that we are involving young people in a positive experience.

There was a girl on our bike tour who had had a plane ticket to the U.S. She was going to pass her holiday touring in a car. But after she read about our bike tour she cashed in her plane ticket, bought herself a bike and went on the tour instead. This two and a half months with an international group has really changed her life. She will not let go of these environmental issues. She will never believe this bull that it is the foreigners who are making all the trouble. She will always be open to new ideas and new developments in politics.

I hope our campaign will have an impact on international politics. I hope that if we elect George Bush as one of the most ignorant politicians during UNCED it will have an impact and even make him think. I believe that lobbying can be a very effective way to do politics without having to be a politician myself. And as long as it can be done with an organization like EYFA or SEAC one can even have a good time with it.

I can not be a politician myself. I can not bring myself to spend 80 percent of my time supporting things I don't really believe in to get 20 percent freedom to change something in the right direction. I admire politicians who are willing to do that and have still kept their idealism. But at the moment that is too much for me.

We hope to influence politics in the long run by changing the public's mind. A group passing out leaflets somewhere in a small town participates in that just as much as an organization conducting an international campaign. I believe it is underestimated how much the environmental movement has already achieved. It is my hope that we can make big changes in the next decades. The necessity for them is so obvious that we will have a good chance of convincing people.

One problem with the environmental movement in the past, especially in Germany but also in the rest of Europe, was that we did too much moralizing, became too serious, and gave the impression of being people who are so caught up in wanting to save the world that we forget to enjoy our lives. I call that the ideology of sacrifice. That is why we are teaching young people that it's possible to live a more joyful, more satisfactory way of life if you get involved. For our last Ecotopia camp we had the motto: "All he wanted to do was to save the world, but he was against everything."

Being an environmentalist or activist I sometimes get sick of all the organizational work that dominates my life. I get tired of writing yet another application for funding, running after people, trying to bring things together. But in the end it is my way of life and I am enjoying it very much. It is much better than having a lot of money and a big car. I have my experiences and my joy when I do this. If we want to have a sustainable way of life in the world, we have to make people understand that having fun does not have to come from buying a Mercedes. It can be something very different.

Vandana Shiva:

Village Women Fight Deforestation in India

andana Shiva is Founder and Director of the Research Foundation for Science, Technology, and Natural Resource Policy located in Dehra Dun, India. For the past 10 years she has focused on assessing new technologies and conflicts over natural resources. She is author of a number of books including *Staying Alive: Women, Ecology, and Development.*

Steve Lerner: *What kind of work do you do in India?*

Vandana Shiva: Initially I did research at the Indian Institute of Science before I shifted to the Indian Institute of Management where I was engaged in science policy research. My work in the area of science policy and my involvement with the Chipko Movement caused me to embark on a ten year period during which I have focused on conflicts over natural resources.

When new technologies are introduced in India they often have the effect of taking control of other people's resources. Through this robbery of resources it can appear as if the new technologies are smart and others are inferior. By doing science and technology assessments I saw huge fishing trawlers displace traditional catamarans, the green revolution crops displace traditional strains of crops, and imported Eucalyptus trees displace indigenous trees.

Each time this happened a scientific evaluation would show a decline in productivity and efficiency. These new technologies were really only "improvements" in terms of the interests of the powerful: a paper mill in the case of the introduction of Eucalyptus trees; the international seed and chemical business and food commodity distribution companies in the case of agriculture; and, in the case of the trawlers, the big fishery interests.

In doing this work assessing new technologies one had to recognize, sooner or later, that there was a conflict between the interests of the new technologies and the interests of the people. My heart was with the people and I wanted to keep it there.

But your background was academic.

Yes, my background was in physics. I have a doctorate in foundations of physics, which is an inter-disciplinary degree.

It must have been quite a long journey from physics to working with the Chipko Movement.

It is a very long journey if one goes through new degrees, retrains, and starts fresh building a new career. It would have been quite an impossible journey as a career move. But I just followed by heart, my soul, and my mind. I followed where my thinking took me. In 1981 it became quite clear that to do the kind of work I wanted to do in ecology research, the first thing I needed was independence, so I left Bangalore to set up an independent research program.

Since I wanted to be independent, I couldn't be tied to other people's money. So I went back home to where I was born and where my family owned property in Dehra Dun in the foothills of the Himalayas. My mother loved cows and had four cows and a huge cowshed, so I used the cowshed to house the new research institute. My research team was made up of research assistants or research associates who had worked with me in the past.

What did you call this independent research institute?

For a very small institute in a cowshed we have a very heavy name. It is called the Research Foundation for Science, Technology, and Natural Resource Policy. We began this in 1981. But my real affiliation from then onward was with an informal research group associated with the environmental movements of the ordinary people of India, including tribal and rural people.

How did you become involved in the Chipko Movement? I understand it is a grassroots movement of people who are attempting to arrest the deforestation of the Himalayas.

For me it was kind of inevitable. The Himalayas are home for me. I grew up there. I grew up in the forest of the Himalayas where my father was a forester. I have walked those hills in the central Himalayas. It is in my blood. I was away from the Himalayas for higher studies when I was doing my undergraduate and graduate degrees, but just before I left for Canada to do my Ph.D. work I decided to go back home to one of my favorite spots. I knew I was leaving the country and it was an uncertain time for me because many foreign students who come to study in North America prefer to stay on. So, while I planned to return to India, I didn't know how life would go. My trip home was like a pilgrimage to what was the most important part of my life. I didn't calculate it too much; it just had an immense draw.

At the time I made that pilgrimage, I had already been away from home for about seven years, and the change I saw when I returned was unbelievable. The old forests were not there any more. The area had been converted to apple orchards. "Growth centers", as they call them in the vocabulary of development, had been established in a beautiful area. They put up a few shops and turn an area into an urban slum and call it a growth center. They pour lots of money into banking systems and call it a growth center. It tells you a bit about the patriarchal mindset, which thinks you can pour money into a few buildings and growth will take place.

This beautiful spot of mine was totally transformed. At the one place I had chosen to return to, the stream was as good as dead because the forests had gone. I talked to people in the surrounding villages to ask them what had happened. They described how the orchards were introduced as planned development, and they were placed exactly where the forests had been, which fed the streams. The villagers knew exactly what the ecological processes of destruction had been.

One of the older men told me that it was not too bad now because of the Chipko. So, of course, I asked him what was that? I asked: "What is this Chipko, which is a counter to this development destruction?" He gave me a little information about how the local villagers had been involved in actions to stop further deforestation. Just hearing that sent a charge through me. So, when I came back for my first vacation from my Ph.D. studies, I made a trip to visit the Chipko.

Chipko means to physically embrace (as in embracing a tree to prevent logging). It also means to embrace philosophically so that you make your links to nature known; and you are making it quite clear also that there is something for which you are willing to lay down your life.

Where did you find the Chipko Movement?

The Chipko Movement is all over; it is dispersed and you can't find it. But there is an address for the Chipko Information Center which is an old ashram run by Sunderlal Bahuguna and his wife Vimla Bahuguna who are basically the elders of the Movement.

In 1952 they started this ashram to serve the hill communities. In the late 1960s and early 1970s the ashram became a center for planning strategy and information on Chipko. It has a library, and archives of the Movement, and it is where the young activists gathered before moving out to do their thing in different parts of the hill region. The ashram was the point of contact. From then onward you enter the dispersed, invisible Chipko, which you cannot see because it has no sign board.

Where is the Chipko Center located?

It is not in a town. It is upstream from a place called Tehri, which is now to be submerged as a result of this Tehri dam. Recently Sunderlal Bahuguna and all the Chipko colleagues, who had been on a new Chipko action to stop this dam, were arrested. But they have now been released.

The evolution of Chipko is important to understand. Chipko started as a movement of direct action to protect the earth. The first thing they did was to protect the forest because that is where the first onslaught occurred. A commitment was made to save the forests in 1968 at a place called Tilari.

Tilari is of historic importance because people had been massacred there in 1930 for protesting British rules designed to take forests away from the local people and turn them into Reserve Forests. It was like the Indian Enclosure Movement, the counterpart of the British Enclosure Movement. Communities were, of course, up in arms. People don't let their vital resources slip out of their hands without a struggle. So, there was a huge protest that took place in 1930 in the Himalayas at this place called Tilari.

This movement to protect the forests from the British had been inspired by Gandhi's famous salt march, which also took place at that time. In 1930 Gandhi said that the British should not be allowed to privatize salt. He said that salt is as vital to life as earth and water. He pointed out that Indians had always made salt freely and that they would continue to make it freely, and would violate immoral laws that tried to put a tax on it to finance the army. So, you might remember, he walked to Dandee and picked salt from the beach. Tens of thousands were arrested for making free salt with him.

Gandhi's salt march is an example of the kind of innovation that the ordinary Indian community is capable of. It tells you how democratically alive the Indian civilization is. I feel privileged to be part of it. When I come to America and hear democracy being talked about at a time when every community in the United States is being crippled, I feel that this is not democracy. Democracy is when every individual and community is able to find innovative ways to regain control over his or her life, and have the space to do it, and know that he or she can.

In the Himalayas in 1930 they turned the salt march or salt satyagraha, the fight for truth, into a forest satyagraha. They said that there was no way that they would permit the British to place boundaries on Indian forests and claim territorial rights. These forests are common property and they will stay common property, the people said. They belong to the villages and they will stay with the villages; they cannot be claimed by the British state. In the conflict that followed at Tilari there were shootings and people were killed.

In 1968, on the anniversary of the Tilari massacre, many people gathered on the same spot and said that if people could die fighting for our forests in the past, we had better be ready to do the same once again. Otherwise the forests wouldn't survive.

What was threatening the forests in 1968?

The new threat was posed by increased logging prescribed by international agencies. These international agencies said that the forests of the Himalayas were underexploited in remote regions, hill areas, and tribal areas. They gave money for road building, improved access, and heavy machinery. The second factor was that during the war between India and China in 1962, India built a huge road network through the Himalayas for its defense. That network of roads was soon turned into a resource exploitation network because it permitted trucks to reach areas they had never reached before. As a result forests could be logged that had never been touched before.

Were these transnational corporations that came into India to exploit these forests or were they Indian-owned logging ventures?

The technical expertise came from the Food and Agriculture Organization (FAO); the financial aid came from other international organizations. But it was the Indian Government that gave contracts to private loggers. These loggers were often the families that had been set up in the logging business by the British. They go back two or three generations in this business. Since my father was a forester I knew many of them personally.

To counter this, the Chipko women just went from forest to forest embracing trees, not letting the logging take place. They would say: "our bodies before the trees." They told the loggers: "You will have to hit us with your ax before you touch the tree." And all kinds of very beautiful and powerful slogans emerged. One of the slogans was: "The forests do not bear timber and revenue; what the forests bear is soil water and pure air." This totally changes the paradigm of what forestry is about. And the struggle goes on and on.

In 1981 the Prime Minister of India was forced to make a decree announcing a logging ban in this region. So, the Chipko Movement enjoyed some real success. After more than 10 years of direct action, they were able to get the Government to recognize that, as a policy, for hill forests, mountain forests, and catchment forests, it made better sense to conserve than to exploit them. The reason for this is that the costs of logging were much higher — ecologically, economically and socially — than any benefits the state could derive from it. That realization came about because floods and landslides had started to increase, and productivity was falling.

In 1983 I was called in with a team of other people to do an evaluation for the Indian Ministry of Environment on the impact of mining on our valley, the Dun Valley. It was very clear that this mining was a devastating, uneconomic activity going on under the garb of economic development. By the time the study had been done, a public interest legal case had been launched. The Supreme Court of India, on the basis of this public-interest case, brought by the citizens, made a judgment on the basis of ecology for the first time in the history of India. The Supreme Court ruled that the fundamental right to life of the people of the valley was being destroyed by the ecological impact of mining. The ruling said that the right to life is a constitutional and basic right, therefore the mining had to stop.

From what I have seen of the Indian judicial system, it often issues very progressive judgments that are not necessarily carried out in the real world.

In this case it was carried out except that they had been misled a bit.

And I had been misled in the sense that I had not been given full maps of the mining area. There was one corner of the valley where the mining continued and we had not been informed. The people of this village instantly geared up. They contacted the Chipko Information Center and they contacted me. Then they announced that they were going to do a Chipko action to stop this mining. They said they were not second class citizens: "If the right to life of other people can be preserved, surely ours should be, too," they said. The women set up a blockade. They put up a tent in the middle of the road that goes up to the mine and they stopped the bulldozers from working.

What is a Chipko action really like? These confrontations must get very dicey. These women set up a blockade in an isolated area. A bunch of men come in with bulldozers and equipment and they have a job to do. Does it not get violent?

It has always been dicey. There have been arrests and attacks. The initial action can never be carefully planned because the activists never know where or when the loggers will come. So, it is often just one or two women who hear the loggers. Then these women do their little bit in trying to make sure that they don't log. I remember one instance very clearly. An activist named Doomsun Nagi was alone in a forest when the loggers came. He ran from tree to tree fighting them off.

What does that mean exactly?

When they tried to cut the tree he would embrace it. He would physically embrace the tree.

Activists have been arrested and attacked. They were attacked very badly in a particular action in Dun Valley. I had to bring them to the hospital. In that case the miner had hired goons, armed them, put them in a truck, and sent them off to attack the site. Another time they attacked and this one woman lay in front of the truck to stop it. They could, of course, have driven over her, but they didn't. It is this level of commitment that provides the power to stop the loggers.

Now, in the case of Tehri dam the violence is very clear. The Tehri dam has been under construction since the 1970s. Tehri is the capital of the Kingdom of Gahrwal, which is the central Himalaya region. Tehri is one of the biggest towns of the area and is surrounded by the most fertile valley, which is why it became the capital. In the Himalayas the only real agricultural land is down in the valleys. This bottomland, which is really the granary of this entire region, is to be submerged by the dam that is being built at Tehri. It will submerge a flourishing town.

People have been resisting this and there has been an anti-Tehri-dam movement for years. The case has been before the Supreme Court. But in October of last year the whole situation changed when a very severe earthquake occurred. One of the reasons the Tehri dam has been resisted by people is that 80,000 people would be displaced. But, in addition, the dam is being built on an earthquake fault. There has been a lot of scientific information available on the danger posed by earthquakes, but the engineers have always said that the danger is exaggerated and it is in the imagination. That is what they argue in the courts. But that imagination turned into reality on October 20th, 1991. After that the protests against the dam increased. No one wants to live next to a dam on an earthquake fault.

You keep referring to the people involved in these actions as being mostly women. Was it always the case that the Chipko Movement was primarily a women's movement?

There are three kinds of people in the Chipko Movement. First, there are villagers. Most of the people involved at that level are women. The second group is made up of the local activists who came out of the Gandhian tradition, and the Independence struggle, or other aspects of the post-Independence Gandhian Movement. In the third group are people like me and others who form support groups and give whatever professional, economic, emotional, or political support they can to make the Movement have an impact on the political system. That support role is played by an informal and unstructured network called Friends of Chipko.

Do you find it significant that most of the people involved in the Chipko Movement are women?

Yes, women and their children.

What do you think it means that this movement is largely constituted by women?

That is the question I tried to answer in my book, *Staying Alive*. I tried to make sense of this process, because this is not unique to the Chipko Movement; it is true anywhere that there is ecological action. It is as if women somehow are able to see and act on the fact that there is another economy that we are leaving out of our analysis, which is the economy of nature. Women seem to realize that there is another world from which different values come, which is the ecological world. Women are able to maintain contact with that world even after the society, the economy, science, and technology have tried to make us think that the only economy that matters is the one in which we earn money through markets; and that the only science and technology that matters is the one we have built. So we build huge artifacts, mega-systems, big dams, and big power plants.

I am able to explain the number of women in the Chipko Movement on the grounds that women in India are still providing subsistence: the water, food, and fuel. On a day-to-day basis they are interacting with this other natural economy. They are in fact the main participants in it, because men have been sucked out into the formal economy or the cash economy, while women have continued to provide water, food, and fuel.

But it is not just in India that women play a predominant role in environmental actions. Even in the U.S. most actions against toxic dumps are started by women. I think the issue is deeper. I think so-called "development" or "progress" often fragments human beings into atomistic entities.

The sexual division of labor and the role women have been forced to play has, over time, left women to worry about relationships while men worry about jobs. As a result, it is the women who see the child ill, who get a sense that something is wrong with the local area. They begin to say: "Something is wrong because my child is falling ill too often." In the Third World, because women have remained in intimate contact with nature, they often give the early warning signals that something is wrong with the environment.

How do you define Eco-Feminism? Does it just describe the fact that many women are involved in environmental actions? Or is there a philosophy behind it?

I think it is deeper than that. Eco-Feminism is not one philosophy: It is plural. Eco-Feminism is an alternative to the dominant paradigm which is patriarchal, capitalist, anti-nature, and anti-women. The common thread is that we need something that is not anti-nature and not anti-women. We need a world view that does not build on the destruction of women and nature. That is a shared premise. I would say there are Eco-Feminisms. They are a group of philosophies that are creating some of the deepest and most vital insights of our times.

Do you see Eco-Feminism taking off as a movement in India and elsewhere around the world?

Not under a label. I believe the era is over where people rallied behind party labels. That era is quite dead. But people will rally around ideas that are close to what they hold dear. In that sense Eco-Feminism, the link between women and the environment, is a growing movement. This became very clear to me last year when many of us set up the World Women's Congress for a Healthy Planet, in Miami. That was the counterpart for women of the United Nations Conference on Environment and Development (UNCED). There has been nothing more exciting that I have participated in on an international level in the last decade. One thousand five hundred women from 83 countries came. Each of them was brilliant, sensitive, an had a dynamism of her own.

It was very different from UNCED, where 99 percent of the delegations just sit there without any commitment to do anything. They are 99 percent men and 99 percent of them have orders not to do anything.

At the official level, UNCED delegates seem bent on killing a global environmental commitment . That is the reading I am getting. And the U.S. position is the best example of that.

You have been critical of the Enlightenment for having launched a certain kind of development that has devastated nature and women. If you are critical of the Western model of progress and development, what is your alternative vision?

The Enlightenment derived its power, at one level, from the power of man over nature and woman. The alternative vision, for me, is quite simply bringing it all back into balance. We need politics, economics, and technologies that do not derive power for one aspect of interrelated systems by crushing the other aspects. Power should come from empowering the other aspects of the integrated system.

In my view, a sophisticated science and technology is one that understands what keeps ecosystems alive and then, on the basis of that knowledge, finds out the interventions human beings can make without violating those linkages. That is not the kind of sophistication we have in our science and technology. Our science and technology comes out of the Enlightenment stream and is now reaching its final stage with genetic engineering. In genetic engineering we are intervening in a system before we know how it ticks. We disrupt it and then claim we have created something new.

Who should decide what we should tinker with or not tinker with? Would it be the state? And would that not lead to a state-controlled system of development and away from a market-based approach?

There is a third entity, which is forgotten in the dichotomy made between the market system and the state system. That is real living communities of people who are in contact with the environment, be it polluted or pure. Those communities have systems of knowing the state of their ecosystem and how ecosystems hang together or get destroyed. We should be listening to those communities. Listening to those communities is the primary political issue, in my view, that UNCED is bypassing.

Both market and state systems need limits in order to keep them from doing damage. Those limits can only be grasped by listening to what people have to say. People realize long before governments do that toxic dumps cause hazards.

It sounds as if you place a great deal of faith in the wisdom of local communities. But are there not communities that do not have the best interests of their ecosystem at heart?

It is only when livelihoods are linked to the survival of the ecosystem that protection of the ecosystem becomes the economic logic of a community. That is why, in my view, the kind of mobility that is part of development is the biggest hazard, because uprooted people have no stake in the environment and development creates displacement and uprootment. The more you create social and cultural conditions that lead to displacement, the less chance there is that there will be communities that have knowledge, wisdom, or values that lend themselves to protecting the environment.

I believe that if you don't have communities that retain their roots, no government and no market can protect the ecosystems. The markets will always need to be told that they are overstepping boundaries. Markets work on maximizing profits, which means forgetting about what you are destroying. Growth is premised on creating markets where they should not exist, creating addiction so that people will want, and need, and desire the things they don't really need and desire.

Does not this logic lead to the inability of a society to engage in any large-scale construction such as the building of an airport?

If enough people say no to the wrong thing then we will be able to create the right thing. By having enough nos we will be able to create systems of living and human settlements where people don't have to spend four hours a day sitting like zombies in cars. I think enough nos will create the alternative structures that are more peaceable. I believe we need more nos than we are getting just now for the destruction that is around us.

Do you think that northern industrialized nations owe compensatory aid to the developing nations? Some have described this as an "ecological debt" owed by developed nations to developing nations for having taken up the lion's share of resources and most of the absorptive capacity of the global commons.

I think the ecological debt is very important in the biological domain. This is not just an issue of the past; it is an issue of the future. This is not just a North/South issue, it is also an issue for the North itself.

We have grown up with the paradigm that made us believe that, for the industrialized world, wealth came out of machines. But machines do not create wealth. Machines process raw materials that create wealth. The raw materials came from usurping other peoples resources, many of which were biological in nature, such as the cotton and indigo. All our independence movements are linked to this resource conflict at one level.

But the industrial system has had a convenient way of avoiding a calculation of what is owed to the larger social, political, and ecological system. The mechanization of textiles makes it look as if growth started in Lancaster and Manchester, while it actually started in the indigo plains of Champara; it started in the villages of Africa where all the slaves were being picked up and brought to North America; it started in the colonization of the Americas. That is where value was being created for one system by creating disvalue for others through robbery and theft. This analysis can be applied to cotton, tea, or opium, the sources upon which the British Empire built its wealth.

Now that we are in the era of biotechnology, an identical process of discounting the part of the biological wealth that has been taken from the South and brought to the North is underway again. This phenomenon is captured in the American attitude that insists biological diversity is the common heritage of mankind. That is a neat way to say that those in industrialized nations are allowed to steal without it being called stealing.

The calculation is made by developed nations that once they have touched that global common heritage — by identifying genes, manipulating them, or transferring them into biological commodities — they can then turn around and sell these new products to people in developing countries at high prices to cover their property rights and patents.

So, there are two religions emerging. One religion says that the resources of the South have no value and belong to all mankind. The second religion says that anything we have touched, once we have stolen it from you, becomes private property. This private property treats man as god and creator, and as god and creator he has every right to be totally free of scrutiny as to how the value is obtained and whether or not it is the right value. This also allows industrialized nations to avoid the question of whether creating genetically engineered organisms of certain kinds is good for the health of the planet or will create new hazards.

I personally feel the ecological debt issue is crucial because in the future the world is going to be standing on its head if we do not settle the ecological issue right.

In your view does the ecological debt owed by the North to the South cancel out the debt of the South to the northern banks?

Yes. This is something that the North cannot run away from, although the U.S. is trying very hard. The U.S. is arguing that ecological debt has to do with something that occurred in the past; I insist that it is something for the future. And paying that debt is the only way to build an ecological civilization.

Charles Abugre:

Sustainable Development in Uganda

 harles Abugre is Program Coordinator at the Agency for Cooperation and Research in Development (ACORD), Kampala, Uganda.

Steve Lerner: What do you do for ACORD and how does it relate to the UNCED negotiations?

Charles Abugre: ACORD is a consortium of some Western European and Canadian non-government organizations (NGOs). ACORD is currently working in about 12 African countries. Whilst ACORD is an international consortium, its management in Africa is almost entirely African.

I work in northern Uganda doing community building work and also in the research and policy program of ACORD, which tries to pull together the thinking behind our interventions from dispatches and analysis.

What are some of the programs that you work on? What do you actually do?

The program that I work on in northern Uganda involves assisting people to organize in small groups so that they can pool their savings. These group savings schemes can involve cash, material, or labor. They provide a pool from which individuals can borrow to make small investments. There are hundreds of these small groups of 10 to 25 individuals. We don't like the groups to be larger than that because it is very difficult to build cohesion and democracy in a larger group. What we do to promote democratic practices is to provide training on leadership for small groups. We emphasize rotational leadership so there is no one leader. We train them in simple bookkeeping and accounting. After this training, whether or not you have been to school, you will know how to count and keep track of the savings. We call this approach "transparent accounting." In transparent accounting the group funds are not only presented in the form of a paper report. In addition, everything is brought to the group meetings so that everyone can see their pooled resources. This is a confidence-building process.

You mean they literally bring the pooled money to each meeting?

Yes. They bring the money to the meeting. Or if there are goats and cattle, they will announce where the goats and cattle are and who is keeping them. Usually, since these people all live in the same area, everyone knows where the goats and cattle are and who is keeping them. But if it is cash, it has to be brought to the meeting and people can borrow it.

The second part of it is when people start mobilizing savings, and the savings grow, and you need to do bigger things. These groups are usually in isolated areas. We are faced with the question of how to generate a business or businesses. That involves small technology training or building upon existing technologies: blacksmithing programs, food processing, basic textile weaving, small beekeeping and wax extraction programs, textile dying at the household level, and things like that.

We have a training center, which is a very informal place in northern Uganda in a very poor, isolated district. This is where I live. We look for people within Uganda or outside Uganda who can run practical training sessions.

We also work with a fishing community along the river Nile where we help to develop alternative fishing methods instead of just fishing with nets. Fishing with nets has caused the stock of fish in the river to become more and more depleted. So we are looking at promoting the use of fish hooks because the blacksmiths can produce the fish hooks.

But these fishermen will catch fewer fish with hooks than with nets. Won't they resist this change?

You catch fewer fish this way, but you catch bigger fish, you catch the predators, which are often the largest fish. And in this way you allow the smaller fish to become bigger.

Do you teach various environmental concepts to these people?

The main concept we promote is that whatever you depend on for a livelihood, make sure that you do not destroy the basis of it. So if it is farming, beekeeping, or fishing, make sure that your "golden pot" doesn't break so that you have nothing to dip into any longer. That is the main message; it is a very concrete thing. If you are farming, make sure that you are not farming the same place all the time or planting casaba into the same hole year after year. It is very basic concept. Or, if you are a farmer, you may have to maintain your soil structure through agroforestry, i.e., the integration of crop and tree production on the same land. They don't grow very big, but they are nitrogen fixing.

Are these indigenous trees?

Most of them are indigenous trees, but one or two are exotics brought in because they are nitrogen fixing and don't need so much water. They are not plantation trees.

Do you work with other environmental and development groups in Uganda and in the region?

Environmental groups have been dealing with rather narrow issues. For example, movements have grown up around tree planting, like the Green Belt Movement. It is only very recently that people have realized that there is more to environmental management than tree planting; and that where sufficient care is not taken, tree planting may cause more harm than good. For example, where exotic trees are made to replace indigenous ones, or where exotic trees are promoted monoculturally, a resilient ecosystem may be inadvertently damaged or hitherto unknown diseases may be introduced into an ecosystem least capable of resisting. Therefore, rather than simply encourage people to plant only trees, it may be wise to encourage them to pay attention to other aspects of land management (e.g. terracing on slopes) as well. Rather than encourage people to plant trees, you have to teach them to terrace their land so that they can maintain soil structure better than by planting trees.

There was a network of environmental non-government organizations (NGOs), the African NGOs on Environmental Networking, but it became a focus of scandals and confusion and later broke down. The Green Belt Movement is trying to pull together tree planters as a network. What we do with most of these groups is to help people understand in a reflective way their own roles in society, and the deeper causes of poverty and environmental degradation. We try to help people analyze what is going on in their own village to look at the deeper causes of the problems they have, without using a lot of big terminology.

As you circulate among the small groups, do you also involve them in discussions that analyze these larger forces?

In very simple ways. Let me give you some examples. An individual wants to borrow money from his own group or from the larger association of groups. (Our small groups get together and pool their money in a larger association.) In either case the individual is borrowing money to plant, say, cotton. He wants to plant cotton as a cash crop because the cost of school fees has increased, and the cost of health care has increased. With a cotton crop the Government guarantees a price, so the individual is assured of having some pot of money at the end of the season.

In our groups we discuss the question: if you borrow money and you have to pay back interest to the group or association are you sure that in three months time, when you start paying the interest, you will be able to get the money for your cotton from the Government? If the Government doesn't pay on time, should the group or association waive payment of the interest, or will the individual take responsibility for another six months of accumulated interest because the Government hasn't paid him the money for the cotton? For cotton there is only one buyer. The Government may explain that the mill to gin the cotton is broken down, or the ginnery will say that the Lint Marketing Board, which should have bought the ginned cotton for lint, has not yet paid them their cash. Or, the Lint Marketing Board will say that they haven't managed to sell the lint. And the chain goes on. So we can analyze that whole chain towards broader international forces without saying anything explicitly about international trade. But at the base is the question of whether to borrow money to grow cotton, and what the effects might be.

There is also the question of whether cotton is an appropriate crop to be growing in that area.

That is a very important question we always ask. We used to grow cotton in the early 1960s. We ask the members of our groups: "Do you remember the 1960s when we used to grow cotton all the time? And they say: "Yes, it was very good and we got a lot of money." Then we ask them: "How often did you plant on your land before you moved?" And they answered, "Usually two or three years before we moved because otherwise there were too many insects." That means that in order to grow cotton they had to be able to move every few years. But the population has grown and there are not so many opportunities to move any longer.

Then there is another question. The women point out that if the men take all the land to grow cotton they cannot grow what they call simsim (sesame seeds) any longer. In the past, simsim was the only cash crop that a man kept his hands off. It is a taboo that a man should peek into a simsim granary. A woman can cultivate the household food and then also cultivate sesame for herself, and then she can sell it and do whatever she wants with the cash. So if the men grow cotton on a large scale, this takes up land that the women would have had for sesame seeds. This may have several consequences. First, a male-dominated cash economy will be entrenched, with far-reaching consequences for the lot of women and children. Secondly, a hitherto effective traditional income distribution mechanism will be damaged. Third, the degree of dependency on the cash economy will be enhanced, with possible negative consequences on food self-sufficiency. Those types of analyses grow up from the very practical question of how people earn their income. So, you can show the trade-offs in terms of the environment, fertility of the land, and income distribution between men and women.

How does the policy research help the staff that carries out these community-based projects?

Again, it fits in a very practical way. First we run training sessions for our own staff. One concept is poverty. We say that we are all working to eradicate poverty in our own area. But who is poor? Everybody in the village? What is the mechanism of poverty? How do we intend to intervene? Why do we chose to intervene this way? What is the effect on other people? So we say, OK, we will carry on with the credit and savings program, but who is bringing money into the savings pool? Obviously, it is those who have a cash surplus. So, in fact, we have already started to work with the cream of the people who have a surplus. That means that those without a cash surplus, a time surplus, or a surplus in goods can't be part of the savings and credit group. They are already out of it.

So what do you do about that?

Through this we have seen that we have left out the poorest of the poor. Why? Because we believe that, because of the nature of their family relationships, those people who have a little more income, those who are capable of earning a little more income, will be able to provide food for their extended family. You never allow your relative to starve.

When your relative is sick, you will be able to pay the medical fees. So, the social system allows a sharing.

Ronald Reagan and George Bush call that the trickle-down theory.

No, I wouldn't call this trickle-down but a traditional social security mechanism. In traditional African societies, people don't just share prosperity, they share poverty as well. You share what you have, happiness and pain alike. You demand a share, almost as a right, of an extended family's circumstances. But since you bring in the question of trickle-down, I might as well comment on it. I know the endless debate that this concept has generated. Indisputably, increasing a country's overall income (even if among the rich) improves the chances of spillover to others in due time. But increasing the lot of the rich is no guarantee of redistribution. That has been proven. That is why some people say that if you want an effective distribution with growth effect, a two-pronged approach is required. The two approaches might be the income-generating approach that is distributed by trickle-down mechanisms; or a direct social welfare approach through community organization and support that helps the poor provide themselves with water, health care, and education. The community-based approach or social service approach can impact the poorest more directly and provide services for them. So we used this kind of analysis to write a document called "Understanding Poverty."

Does some of your research and analysis involve both environment and development issues?

We have produced several documents relating to development and the environment. There is one on "Poverty and Vulnerability." There is another on "Food Security and the Environment," and a third on "Conflict and Famines." All of these draw lessons from our programming experiences and challenges in the field. Conflict, security and environmental vulnerability are particularly relevant to areas in the Horn of Africa (Sudan, Ethiopia and Somalia), to Rwanda and Uganda in East Africa, and Angola and Mozambique in the South. We work in all these areas.

In all these areas, we have understood that the relationships between the environment, development, and security are complex. Wars, for instance, create dislocations and displacements. For displaced people in refugee camps, or whatever, immediate survival is the paramount concern. Usually, refugees are confined to areas not large enough for sustainable land use. In some camps there are conflicts between herders and crop farmers, in competition for land. Herders like to increase their flock and to graze their cattle freely. Two different production systems are superimposed on one another and on an ecosystem probably incapable of accommodating both. In addition, land rights are either undefined or transitory, creating a disincentive for investment into regeneration. It is not inconceivable that many will discount the future heavily and therefore exploit as much as possible today, for the future is unknown. This is a survival mechanism. As you can see, the solution cannot simply be found in promoting better land husbandry programs. We have had experiences of attempting to discourage herders from indiscriminate opening of water holes, and encouraging them instead to reduce flocks whilst concentrating on quality. This is neither an easy task nor the total solution.

Yes, I was going to ask about that. In some of these societies wealth is counted in terms of the size of the herd, is it not?

Yes, though people do understand that aiming at large herds in marginal areas is damaging in the long run. That is why pastoralists have always moved, in order to spread the pressure more thinly. That is why conflicts are environmentally disruptive, because they upset the balance by narrowing down the area over which populations can distribute environmental pressures. For example, suppose we have a conflict situation where people move from one place to another. They end up in environmentally marginal areas with all their cattle, which drain the water holes and eat up all the plants. And the people, who expect to move soon, exploit the area. But then they end up living there for 5, 10, or 20 years because of the conflict. This happened in southwestern Uganda with the Rwandese refugees. And in the Horn of Africa. So we see how conflict creates poverty and also degrades the environment. But it must be emphasized that the cause and effect relationship between environmental resource degradation and conflict is not as clear. For example, it has been shown that historically conflicts have correlated positively with drought, for instance, and the paucity of environmental resources in general. One of the causes of the conflict in Somalia or Mali (involving the Tuaregs) has something to do with control over smaller and smaller natural resources.

What are some of the practical applications of this analysis?

This analysis, first and foremost, enables us (ACORD) to monitor and evaluate the impact of our interventions and the methods we employ. Secondly, it enables us, in dialogue with communities in conflict, to draw attention to the long-term, probably incalculable, effect of the conflict once the power question is settled. As I said earlier, we also use the environmental impact information to help us intervene in refugee settlements. It helps answer the question: what type of refugee settlement units are environmentally and economically sustainable? How do you handle the balance between people, animals and land/water resources?

How about giving people a sense that they are responsible for maintaining the ecosystem in their area, even if they are refugees?

You can tell people: "Since you are here and you don't know how long the conflict will go on, you actually belong to this place. Even if it is only for the next five years you have to be sure that your animals can survive here for that long. So, consider that if you ask us to help you drill more wells so that your cattle can graze, and drink, and we support you in doing that and dry up the aquifer, after five years all the water might be gone."

How does your work fit in with the United Nations Conference on Environment and Development (UNCED)? And what are you trying to achieve at UNCED that will help you in your work in Uganda?

The local situation I work in is impacted by the broader situation. We saw how the actions of the national Government affect what we do in a small marginalized place like the district in which I work. We analyzed what happens when the Government tells the Lint Marketing Board that they don't have the money to pay them. So the Lint Marketing Board ends up with Government bonds but no money. That situation affects the whole trading system right back to the people we work with.

At the same time, the Government says that there will be money if Uganda earns more from its exports. As a result, the whole cotton growing district is diving into crisis. Before, we didn't seem to get anything for coffee, and cotton seemed to be a little better, so we diversified from coffee to cotton, and then to tobacco because it has a better export market today. We are trapped into this situation. We know that the British American Tobacco Company, Ltd. (BAT) has support from the Government because they pay taxes and they provide export earnings. But the problem is that we have to cut massive amounts of wood to cure the tobacco. So the linkages are very clear, the signs are clear that we are going into a suicidal dive.

But can't the people in the local communities decide that instead of growing an export crop for cash they will grow something that is valued locally?

That is an interesting concept. That is what the analysis about the dangers of growing cotton leads us to. We must grow something that we can exchange among ourselves. And we have the ability to grow matoke, which is a kind of a plantain or banana that we eat, and casaba as well. But we have been driven into a cash economy where we have to pay education fees.

Unless you pay your teachers with something local. Besides, it seems to me that you ought to be able to earn cash by providing goods and services that people need locally.

If we paid the teachers with something local the teachers would have to change that into something to be able to buy paper and books.

Then maybe you should make paper. But I see your point that you cannot make everything and you need to be part of the cash economy.

To make paper we need some machinery. I agree that you can reduce the need for exports. But you cannot eliminate the need for exchange because you are in a cash economy. You have to understand that there have been 150 years of tying small societies into a broader market. It is not a new experience. This creates an orientation in domestic investment patterns that takes much to reverse. It creates a reliance on the market.

Do you think you can change the global economy and improve the terms of trade through the UNCED negotiations?

I think that is what these negotiations are about: to save the global environment. Apparently the global environment is taking a deep dive. Now, the main engine is consumption, which leads to the exploitation of resources. If we continue at this rate of consumption there is no way in which you can save the environment, because the resources are finite. There are things we can do. Already people in developing countries have reduced consumption in various ways to very basic levels. If it is desirable for us to save the global environment for our great grandchildren, then the question is how do we reduce consumption and/or redistribute global incomes radically. And that is a question for the wealthy nations and the members of the Organization of Economic Cooperation and Development (OECD).

Do you hear in the UNCED negotiations any suggestion that the North will really reduce consumption in an effort to help save the global environment?

Not that I can see. Most of the agreements over resources are about assigning the right price to them.

Do you mean including in the price of a given resource its environmental value?

That is the most progressive talk so far. But what does that mean? It is not a statement about the reduction of consumption, the need to go easy on the world's resources. Instead it suggests increasing the price so that those who are capable of consuming it will pay more. Apparently if you live in an economic system that is lopsided in terms of income distribution and power, and you raise the price, and I control the market, and I have the mechanisms for transferring resources, I can bid over the price because I can pay for it. What that means in terms of a finite amount of goods is that others who cannot afford the higher price have to reduce their consumption even further, because they can't pay for it. The poor get poorer, the rich at the worst merely retain their riches.

Or consume something else.

Yes. But that says nothing about reducing overall consumption.

Let me give you an example of how increasing the cost of gasoline in the United States might actually help. If we increased the cost of gasoline, it is true that it would make it more difficult for poor people to afford it. On the other hand, it would make mass transportation more attractive and as a result might reorient our transportation system in the direction of a more sustainable model. Does that not make any sense?

At the local level it makes some sense, but at a global level it doesn't make sense. It makes sense at the local level because there is sufficient capability, in terms of overall resources, technology, production, infra-structure etc. to switch from the production of one good to another. In your example, automobile firms will simply switch production to more buses and trains rather than limousines, once they have the market for them. Overall welfare does not suffer. In the case of Mali, in West Africa, higher gasoline prices mean that the rural poor will probably have to walk tens of kilometers to market. The rich will increase taxes on the poor to sustain the higher cost of living. That is why the questions of technology access, and resource and power redistribution are central to global environmental protection. Otherwise the poor will continue to subsidize the rich in the name of the environment.

Let me pursue this further with you. There is a theory that if you raise the price of fuel it will create a new market for an alternative technology that does not use fossil fuels. So instead of just selling cars that guzzle gasoline, there will be an economic incentive for many people to buy cars that use less gasoline, or an alternative fuel, or to use mass transit. What this suggests is that one of the ways of controlling behavior destructive of the environment is to increase its cost so that people will begin to seek alternatives. Is this not a useful tool?

It is a useful tool for you within your domestic economy. It is not a useful tool if it is possible for you to pass that cost generally on to some other people. By passing the cost on you increase your overall national income once more, and redistribute it into increased personal income.

There are several problems with extending the tool to trade. First is the core problem that trade, especially in the goods produced by the South, is not free but controlled by a few global firms. Commodity producers are simply price takers. Price takers, by definition, have limited control over prices. They cannot pass the environmental value of their commodities on to the price. They can only depend on the benevolence of the buyers and their regulatory institutions (northern governments). Secondly, besides the unfair market, and perhaps some surrogate arrangements, nobody knows any acceptable mechanism for attaching universally accepted weights to costs and benefits of environmental resources. What an indigenous forest dweller attaches as value to the loss of a forest cover cannot be the same as that of a timber merchant or an American consumer. Value, in this case, is a cultural and political phenomenon. It is the one whose power prevails who can enforce the concept of value.

Are you suggesting that we don't have free trade because the major trade decisions are being made by the wealthy nations and the transnational corporations?

Right. We have a very narrow market controlled by a smaller and smaller sector of all the many economic units of the world. That is not what free trade was supposed to be. Free trade was supposed to be a mechanism by which numerous individuals in the market would interact and exchange. And those individual decisions could harmonize into a non-discrimination against any individual. But once you bring in discriminatory mechanisms, then we don't have free trade.

But throughout history have there not always been unequal situations where there are some in a position of advantage and some in a position of disadvantage. Over time the groups on top change, strong regions become poor, mighty empires crumble. But it sounds as if what you are saying is that we can no longer afford to have these vast differences in the distribution of wealth. History teaches us that there have always been rich and poor; what makes you think that will change?

What has changed is the globalization of inequality, the institutionalization of it, and giving to it a momentum to build and concentrate power. In the past you had disconnected units where there was inequality. But there was also a lot of room; you could move out of this society if you wished, and set up a new system. But now we have globalized power and concentrated decision making — and nowhere to move.

Are you suggesting that the UNCED negotiations are not addressing this imbalance and that until we address these equity issues we will not have significant progress on the environment and development problems?

Absolutely.

Rodolfo Rendon:

The Debt for Nature Swap in Ecuador

 odolfo Rendon is National President
of the Nature Foundation, Quito,
Ecuador.

Steve Lerner: *How old is the Nature Foundation?*

Rodolfo Rendon: We are in our 13th year. We are a non-governmental, non-profit organization in Ecuador. We have a national board, which covers the entire country with three regional chapters. One is in Quito, which deals with the metropolitan area; one covers Guayaquil, which is our largest city, and the coastal area; and the third is in the South of the country in Azogues.

Do you have a large membership?

We have around 6,000 members. We have about 40 volunteers who have their own paying jobs outside the foundation and a technical staff of 120 people most of whom are working on a specific project. We believe in the concept of private enterprise with social obligation, so we are very careful about our efficiency. Only 17 percent of our budget is used for administrative costs while all the rest is spent on projects. We are now running some 80 projects around the country.

What are some examples of these projects?

We cover four areas: (1) education at the formal and informal level; (2) conservation, particularly in protected areas; (3) urban environmental problems in general; and, (4) specific projects with grassroots organizations. We also try to formulate national policy about the environment and remain in touch with what the people think and what the people need.

Could you describe some of the projects in the area of education?

We have finished a curriculum of environmental education for one year of preschool, the six grades of primary school, and two years of high school. We have trained 8,000 teachers to teach that curriculum. We are now in the second stage where we will train 25,000 teachers throughout Ecuador. We carried out this project in conjunction with the Government.

Do you mean that you initiated the project but the Government is helping to fund it?

In this case we provide most of the funds, and we organize the seminars to instruct the teachers, but the Government sends the teachers to our seminars. That is the way we work together.

In addition to training these teachers to introduce environmental issues into their classrooms, do the teachers take the students out on field trips to study local environmental problems?

Yes. That is part of the curriculum we have developed. We even printed books for the students and teachers. The curriculum includes everything, even how the teacher has to carry out the program. It is a complete curriculum of environmental education.

Do you find that you get into conflicts with local industries over some of these educational activities? Do some industries feel that as a result of this educational project someone will blame them for pollution?

Not in this program. But in some of our other programs we do come into conflict with industry. We have a general policy about environmental problems. Usually when we see problems we try to talk with the sources of the problems in a very friendly way so that they will understand the problems and solve them by themselves. Later on, if they don't do anything, we provide them with information, or make suggestions about how they might solve the problems. If they still do not do anything we put pressure on them. If it is an industry, the pressure might come from a campaign against their products, or we might apply legal measures. So, it varies according to the situation. But, yes, especially in the urban areas, we have sometimes had opposition, but we also get cooperation with industries, or with the Chamber of Industry.

Can you give me an example of when industry cooperated with you?

In Quito we had an area that was originally set up as an industrial neighborhood by the municipality. Later the same municipality allowed a large residential area to be built in the same neighborhood for people of the lower-middle class. There are a number of industries that emit pollution near the residential section: the textile industry, the soap businesses, the printing businesses and others. We talked with these industries one by one and some of them didn't pay any attention to us. We helped the community get organized and introduced them to city officials so that they could have a dialogue. We also talked with the Chamber of Industry of Quito and organized a joint effort with them to do an expert study of the pollution problem. Those industries that did not want to cooperate we took to court to see if we could close them. The result is that the community organization has worked out an accord with the city and the city is making a deeper study of the problems. We are waiting to see if anything practical will come of it.

How long has this taken?

About a year and a half by now.

How would you describe the conservation work that you do?

In conservation we have around 200 actions grouped in several projects. For example, we train park rangers and give them their equipment — clothes, tools, etc. We give the government some vehicles for patrolling the parks — boats, and motorcycles, and things like that. Sometimes we put up signs in national parks. This is done in collaboration with the Government.

So these are things that the Government would not be able to afford if you were not funding them; your donations are supplementary to the Government budget.

That is right. So that is what we do on the practical side in the field of conservation. We educate people about why it is important to have these national parks. We provide brochures for the visitors to the parks. And we also conduct studies in the parks. We sponsor research in the parks by students studying for degrees in biology.

Are these baseline studies to find out what kinds of plants and animals are in a certain area?

Right. Or it could be like the one we did in Quito last year where we compared the actual situation in protected urban areas with the municipal plan that established these areas eight years ago. For that study we used satellite images of the city and then compared them with the official plan for the protected areas. We showed them what they had planned and what the reality was. Then we showed them some ways of keeping control over how the city was developing. Then we gave the satellite images of the city and the findings of our study to the municipality so they could start monitoring the city to see how those protected areas were affected by the growth of the city.

We also provide funds to other non-government organizations (NGOs) to carry out other projects because we do not want to grow too large. We think that it will be good for our country if there are more NGO organizations. There are two or three cases in which we have provided funds to other NGOs for conservation programs. For one organization called Maqui-Pucuna we provided funds so that it could acquire an area that was already classified as protected, and manage the area in a sustainable way. We also established a conservation data center with another organization.

What is an example of projects you are doing on urban environmental problems?

This is a new area for us to which we have been giving more emphasis in the last three years. Ecuador is becoming an urban country. Now 65 percent of our population lives in cities. Those cities have big problems with slums and sanitation. We are doing a study of the relationship of health to environmental quality in urban areas. We are looking at the six most populated cities of Ecuador. That will give us a better picture of which urban areas to work in during the next five years.

Does that study include occupational health issues?
Yes.
That sounds like a very complicated study to do. Do you have a basis

of comparison for this study?

There are some international standards for Latin America. That would be our main basis for comparison. We will also use the national standards that were set up by our Government many years ago.

So, again, you are helping the Government see the difference between what they put on paper and the actual situation; you think this study will be a useful tool for the Government in terms of future policies and planning.

Right. Another example of our work in urban areas is that we made a 10-year plan for planting trees in Quito. This includes plans for nurseries and tree maintenance. We also set up a data base for the whole city, street by street, to keep a record of where and when trees were planted and when they would require maintenance. But this is more than a tree-planting program. It is also a community program tailored to the needs of specific neighborhoods. For instance, if you go to a slum you cannot ask a family to take care of a tree when they don't have enough to eat. So, in that case, we might try to get the family interested in planting and maintaining a fruit tree so that they could get some fruit from it.

Do volunteers from the Nature Foundation actually plant the trees, or are you just involved in planning this project?

Well, we are not interested in just making plans that will sit on a bookshelf. We try to be very practical in all our work. We helped the municipality establish a tree-planting pilot project with a neighborhood, and we placed a volunteer of ours to work with them for six months. But, we insisted that at some point members of the neighborhood have to do the work. We don't think that the Fundacion Natura should do the work for them.

What is an example of your work on national environmental policy?

We are working with members of our National Congress on the final draft of an environmental law for Ecuador. We hope to finish this draft in the next two or three months.

What kind of a law is this?

We believe that Ecuador needs not an environmental protection law but rather a law that establishes an environmental management system. The law will cover the executive area, the legislative area, and the judicial area, and also establish some mechanism of control or enforcement. It will be an umbrella type of law under which a lot of regulations could be generated.

What kind of support are you getting for this from the Congress? Is there much opposition?

The Congress has an environmental commission with which we work.

Is it a powerful or effective commission?

Not very, but they are enthusiastic about the idea of having such a law. So, we are working together with them. Later on we will have to lobby members of Congress to get it passed.

If it is anything like the process in the United States, when this legislation is proposed, lobbyists from industry, agriculture, transportation, building trades, timber interests, miners, and many other groups will try to dilute the law.

It is the same in Ecuador. It is on a different scale, but the process is much the same.

Is there a reasonably powerful environmental lobby in Ecuador?

We have a lot of work to do on that. We environmental people have a presence in Ecuador, but it is not big enough yet. We have to work very hard at it.

In many countries, environmentalism appears to be a concern largely of the upper economic classes — the people who have the luxury of having time to think about the environment. However, in some developing countries some of the most powerful environmental movements seem to be grassroots groups, people who depend most immediately on the bounty of nature. These are people who depend on fishing from the river, they depend on the topsoil and would be devastated if it was washed away. So there seem to be two different levels of society interested in the environment. Are both of those levels operating in Ecuador? Do they communicate with each other?

I don't think they communicate with each other very much. There are some environmental organizations in which you can find both levels. But I would say in Ecuador that it is the middle class that is more aware of the problem. Fundacion Natura's membership is largely middle class. Of course there are some members who come from the upper economic class and some members from the lower economic class. Usually in the Third World countries or the southern countries it is very hard to expect people in the lower economic class to even think about environmental problems because their basic needs are so pressing.

That seems true except when the environmental problem directly threatens the source of their livelihood.

There may be a few cases. But in Ecuador I can tell you of cases where people's situation is so desperate that they don't care if they face a future danger. They care about what they are going to eat today, or possibly tomorrow.

Are most of the people in Fundacion Natura business people or professionals who are giving some of their time to work on environmental issues?

At the directory level, yes. The staff are all professional people.

Where do you get your money?

Several sources. We believe that the local people should be aware that they have to put their efforts into solving these problems. So we have a fee for the membership, but it is not much. Then we have many Ecuadorian organizations that give donations to our work. We also have fund-raising activities, like TV programs. We have some projects with international organizations. We also were the first country in South America to do a "swap for nature." And that allowed us to cover about 60 percent of our project budget. Funds for the swap were done with World Wildlife Fund and The Nature Conservancy.

When did this "swap" take place, how was it organized, and what did you get out of it?

It was planned about five years ago, and we finished the process about two and a half years ago.

How large an area is covered by the swap?

We have a program that covers all of Ecuador. The swap covers several projects.

Then this debt-for-nature swap is not a swap of debt for a park, but rather a swap of debt to pay for some conservation projects in Ecuador?

Right.

This was debt that Ecuador didn't have to pay and instead the money is used to pay for sustainable development projects in Ecuador.

The way it works is that there is a negotiation between three parties: a foreign donor, a national organization, and the Government of Ecuador. The foreign donors were World Wildlife Fund and The Nature Conservancy. Fundacion Natura was the national organization. So, between the three we set up the conditions and defined the projects, and then finally the donor gives the national organization the money. In our case it was around $1 million. We got the money in bonds from the Government; we can redeem them in 30 years. We finance our projects with the interest from those bonds.

What does the interest on these bonds amount to in Quito?

In Quito it is about 30 percent.

I should invest in Quito, I only get 5 percent in the U.S.

Yes, but once you get it in our money the rate of inflation is 40 percent a year.

How did you decide how to split up this money?

In the negotiation process we decided which projects would get what amount of money.

So those decisions are made in conjunction with the World Wildlife Fund, the Nature Conservancy, and the Ecuadorian Government. Was it difficult to agree with the Government about what these funds should be used for? Did you want to fund some things that the Government did not want to fund because they thought it might embarrass them?

At that time, no, it was not difficult to reach an agreement. Because we accepted this donation does not mean that we have to accept all the Government conditions. We believe that our organization has not only the right but also the obligation to remain independent.

Manuel Baquedano:

Using Symbols to Promote Environmental Action in Chile

 anuel Baquedano M. is President of the Institute of Ecological Politics in Santiago, Chile.

Steve Lerner: *What are your thoughts here at the third Preparatory Committee session of the United Nations Conference on Environment and Development (UNCED)?*

Manuel Baquedano: I like to look at the situation of humanity here on earth as being similar to an airplane flight. Twenty five percent of the passengers are in First Class and Economy and the other 75 percent of the passengers are stuck back in the baggage compartment. At the beginning of this flight everyone is happy. But after a while the people in First Class start noticing that something is not right. The temperature in the cabin is changing, the air smells bad, the food they are served is sometimes hot and sometimes cold, and often not very good. They begin to get a sense that something is not working well. A group of passengers asks the airplane's crew what is wrong? And they are told, yes, there are some problems, but the flight is not endangered.

Nevertheless, there are enough symptoms that something is wrong that a group of passengers demands that the pilot make a survey of the state of the aircraft, similar to the Brundtland Report that was done on the state of the environment after the Stockholm Conference. The pilot agrees to do the study and a report is written that concludes that the flight will not arrive at its destination. It is discovered that there is not enough energy, there are problems with the food supply, the plane is overloaded, there are too many people on board, and there is too much weight. As a result it is determined that the flight cannot arrive at its scheduled destination and an emergency landing is required.

Then the problems begin. The people in first class realize that if the people in the baggage compartment become worried about the emergency landing they may panic and endanger the flight. Some passengers say they want to be consulted about where to land the plane. But others insist that the pilot should make those decisions, since he is the expert.

It also becomes apparent that more is at stake than simply the question of where the emergency landing should take place. There is also the question of what will happen after they have landed. When they reboard the plane after the emergency landing there will still be too many passengers. Some people will have to be left at the airport unless there is a modification of the airplane. And there will not be seats for everybody. So, the airplane will have to be redesigned or a lot of people will be left out.

Tell me about the history of the Institute of Ecological Politics?

The Institute has created a Parliament of students. What is this? In Chile we have not had democracy for about 20 years. So the people don't really know what a parliament is. They also don't know how to discuss ecological problems. The Parliament of students project began with the selection of 25 schools. At each school students took up a theme, such as how the environment of Antarctica should be protected. And each student played a role as a nation, an environmental organization, or an industry. Then they debated the kind of issues that are before UNCED. Now there are 50 schools that are debating the issues raised at UNCED. Each school has a representative in the Parliament and deputies who decide what the international laws should be and what the schemes of compensation should be.

In Chile people have not had the right to vote for 18 years. But now we are beginning to debate ecological issues at a community level. Our organization has created ecological councils in the townships. In Chile the township is the smallest administrative division in the state — there are 340 of them. So we started 20 ecological councils in the townships. They work together with the authorities within the township. These councils were created without the approval of any political body. People just realized that it made common sense to create them. It was important that local citizens be able to participate in looking for solutions to ecological problems. The American environmental organizations concentrate power in the leadership; in our case it is the citizen who becomes concerned with ecology.

What are these ecological councils doing?

They demand to be consulted on matters that concern their environment, to participate in consciousness-raising around these issues, and to be involved in the management of municipal plans having to do with the environment. For example, the Ecological Council of Santiago identified air pollution as a serious problem in its area. The Council lobbied to create a system of using bicycles to reduce the smog. Now it is coordinating its efforts with the City Council, and bicycles have been introduced into the city transportation plan. The plan provides for getting loans to buy bicycles and having places to park the bikes.

We had a competition among the Ecological Township Councils that would provide awards to 20 of them. To win, an Ecological Township

Council had to sign a contract that showed citizen participation in the Council. The mayor had to agree that he would support the program of the Council and take account of its recommendations in the town planning process. We selected 20 townships out of 340. In these townships we helped prepare plans for the construction of waste disposal sites, because many small towns have problems with trash disposal.

These programs are not very expensive. It only requires a symbol of participation to get the township involved. The agreement with the township only lasts for one year because if they do not fulfill the requirements of the agreement, we stop working with them. In this fashion we are creating a new social order using symbols to stimulate change. We are going to publish books about our experience using these symbols; we will give the books to all the countries of Latin America on a reciprocal basis. If a Colombian writes a book, we would trade ours for his. In this fashion the use of symbols can help awake South America.

What other symbolic actions have you found effective to help create environmental awareness among citizens?

We started a hotline telephone number that serves as a kind of "green" telephone line.

What is a green telephone?

This is a telephone number that any Chilean can call if he has a complaint to register about an environmental problem he has noticed in his town. People call us and tell us about problems. We set up a system that allows us to map these complaints on the computer and aggregate these complaints so we see where the problems are most intense. The "green" telephone is a symbol, but it gets people involved. It doesn't take much money to do this.

Can you get a connection going between your "green" telephone line and various radio programs? Can you put some of the complaints on the air?

Yes. We also have a connection with the newspaper. Every week a photo is published concerning one of the calls on the "green" hotline. We also do some television work. If there are a lot of complaints about noise during the week we try to do a program looking for a solution for noise pollution. If there are problems with industry we try to call the companies that are the targets of these complaints. So, we have a kind of telephone inquest into the problem. Anybody can call on the "green" telephone hotline, so it brings environmental problems down to the level of the citizen. This is not ecology for ecologists, but ecology for the citizens.

What does the Government think about these programs?

At first the Government was a bit skeptical; afterwards officials became involved. But the Government is afraid of losing control. This is a process that they do not control. For example, the School Parliament has been sponsored by UNESCO and UNICEF. So we are being supported by international organizations. Ours is a direct form of democracy, but not an official process. Nothing we do is official. We are only an association of citizens. For example, when we started to talk about forming a School Parliament, the Government said all right, but if people start bringing up subjects that are not of an environmental nature, then the censors might become involved. For example, if they start to talk about abortion, then there will be censorship. So, this organization has to be independent of the Government and run by the people and for the people. We are very proud to be able to maintain the independence of these organizations.

What do you do for money?

We sometimes count on the support of foreign environmental groups. We also have another institution called ECO FUNDO which funds little projects for a maximum of $500. For example, we have created a little toy penguin, which was made by a group of women who organized themselves in Santiago. They set up a workshop. The penguin was stuffed with wool obtained locally. This is different from a regular commercial enterprise that obtains synthetic stuffing materials from Taiwan. These toy penguins are sold through a cooperative and a first order has been placed. This kind of symbolic activity is not very expensive. We just have to expend a lot of energy doing the work.

Do you have some ideas about what should happen in Brazil in 1992?

I think we need to find a symbol that is more global than individual. What if we wrote a contract so that the people of the world could buy the earth?

Regina Barba Pirez:

Eco-Tourism in Mexico

 egina Barba Pirez is Coordinator of the Ecological Association of Coyoacan in Mexico.

Steve Lerner: What is the Ecological Association of Coyoacan?

Regina Barba Pirez: In 1982 we started working in a tree nursery in Mexico City. We worked on urban revival through establishing parks and trees. And we tried to reduce air pollution. At that time we were more aware of the problems posed by environmental contamination than with larger social problems. Later we began to see the connection between environmental degradation and social problems.

After six months we closed our urban revival organization and began to study ecology. For one year we had seminars for the people in the group, not only on ecology but also on other social issues that had an impact on the state of nature in our area. During that year we also looked for financial help. We held concerts and put on plays, we sold T-shirts. We also began lobbying the Government on a number of environmental issues. Because of the problem posed by hydrocarbons, we targeted transportation as an issue of special importance to us. We also began to look at the problem of contamination of rivers, not only in Mexico City but also in other parts of the country.

Is Coyoacan part of Mexico City?

Mexico City is divided into 16 districts. One of these districts is called Coyoacan. Coyoacan means the place of the coyotes. It is in the South part of the city.

Is it a wealthy area?

There are rich people, middle class, but also people who live on the margins of society. It is one of the oldest delegations of Mexico City. In the center is the house of Cortez. This is one of the oldest areas of the city dating from when the Spaniards came to Mexico.

How many members do you have in your organization?

In the beginning we had more than 200 members. Now we are working with 25 people. We have five people working on each project area.

What projects have you focused on?

Our group joined the Network of Ecological Groups, which has brought together 53 groups from Mexico City that work on environmental and social issues. One issue we focused on involved the building of agricultural reservoirs in the North of the country. We were against establishing these reservoirs because we did not want to follow the same development scheme in the North that had been used in Mexico City. We didn't want the Government to take all the water from other areas and divert it to the city, causing more people to move to the city. We did an environmental impact statement for the local and federal governments. We have been doing the same kind of work in Guadalajara and in other areas.

Now we are working to protect Mexico's Pacific coast. In Mexico, tourism is one of the main sources of revenue. But if we don't develop an alternative kind of tourism it will be awful for our coasts. So we are trying to develop eco-tourism in this coastal zone.

How do you promote eco-tourism?

First we do an environmental impact study to see where tourist hotels should be located. This looks at the biological and social impact of building these hotels. Also we would want to make sure that the profits from these investments would stay in Mexico, rather than leave the country. Seventy to eighty percent of the investment would have to remain in Mexico. In other words, we would want the people who work at these resorts to come from the local area, rather than from the outside. Local people would have to be trained to do the necessary jobs. These tourist developments would also be required to leave the majority of the local environment as it is.

To supply the tourist hotels, some areas could establish alternative agricultural projects. They could grow food organically and sell it to the hotels. We are looking for people who want to make ethical investments in this new type of tourist development.

Have you had any success?

We have talked with the farmers. At first they did not want to listen to us. But now these people are growing food organically and with eco-technologies. This has taken many years. Similarly, the developers did not want to listen to us in the beginning. But now they are working with us. This is on the Pacific coast in Nayarite, Colima, and Jalisco.

We are also trying to stop developments that we don't think are good for the environment. We are opposed to these mega-projects because they destroy the local culture and ecology rather than improving the way people in the local communities live. Developers were going to put hotels in wetland areas, transforming wetlands into golf courses. We won that battle. We know there are people who like luxury, but we can provide all that they need in a responsible fashion. If these eco-tourism hotels use recycled water and deal with their waste in a sustainable fashion, it will mean that the guests who come for a vacation will learn about nature and a new kind of behavior that will help future generations. So we are cooperating on that with other groups.

Is your group involved in any conservation projects?

Yes. Our group is working on a conservation project with the Mexican wolf. There are only nine Mexican wolves left in all of Mexico. There are only about 34 of them in the U.S. None are in the wild anymore. First, we want to stabilize the population of wolves and then begin to reintroduce them into the wild. The reintroduction will be very difficult in Mexico because it has been transformed into cattle country. Also our population has always been afraid of wolves. So it will be very difficult.

You said you were also involved in some education projects.

Yes. We have put together a "Green Manual" that will tell people about the major environmental problems. It will deal with issues such as water contamination, ozone depletion, air pollution, and public transport. Each of these issues is outlined in two or three pages. Then there is a section that tells citizens what they can do on their own and in concert with others. We are also publishing legal forms that can be used by those who object to what a factory is doing near their house. We have listed organizations that deal with environmental problems by neighborhood, and we are going to publish a directory of environmental groups.

Why are you here at the United Nations Conference on Environment and Development (UNCED)?

When you work on environmental problems and find that most of them are the result of political decisions, then you want to intercede in those political decisions. There are several options for lobbying: first at the community level, second with your city and government, and third in the international arena. From the beginning I have been interested in UNCED not just because of the Rio Summit but also because it is enabling the whole world to look at the impact of human behavior. We are just beginning to address the problems that the next generations will have to deal with.

I don't expect too much from UNCED. Although it will give me an opportunity to network not only with people from Latin America but also with people from the East and the North. If we seek to have more justice and live in harmony with nature there are many different ways we can work together with indigenous people, labor unions, non-government organizations (NGOs), housewives, and other segments of society. UNCED provides a start.

Among the NGO representatives to UNCED from Mexico is a member of a labor union. Are the Mexican labor unions primarily interested in improving the environment in the workplace, or are they interested in broader issues?

In general the unions have been interested in the occupational environment. But now they are aware of the environmental effects we will suffer if we expand trade with the U.S. and Canada. The maquilladores (Mexicans who work in factories owned by transnational corporations in northern Mexico near the U.S. border) play an important role in these issues. It is not only important to take care of conditions that the workers labor under in the factories, but also to deal with the impact the workers will have on the environment outside the factory gates. The North American Free Trade Agreement worries us. In our country the decision to enter into this treaty was not made democratically. It was a unilateral decision. I think the result of this treaty will be that we pull more raw materials out of Mexico and waste more of our energy.

Our fear is that we don't have the legislation in place that exists in the U.S. or Canada to protect the environment. Even if the general legislation on these issues is good in Mexico, we have many states that don't have any environmental legislation. Even those states that do have legislation that regulates the environment don't have any means of enforcing those regulations. So how can we trade on the same level with the U.S.? We also don't have the same infrastructure. We are opposed to the North American Free Trade Agreement. We feel we have to create the conditions that will allow us to trade safely with these countries. We have to harmonize our rules of trade with these countries.

Do you find that northern NGOs agree with you on this issue?

Many northern NGOs are helping us gather information about the North American Free Trade Agreement. I think everyone has to come to understand that our ecological problems don't have frontiers. Problems in Mexico will have repercussions in the U.S. and Canada.

I understand that you and other members of NGOs here at UNCED are trying to form a South American/North American network. What would you like to see come out of that network?

In Canada and the U.S. the population no longer has to fight for food and health care the way we do. You have environmental problems caused by industry and you have been dealing with these problems for many years before us. You have a richer way of life with many comforts. You have taken care of your essential priorities. In our countries we have problems with democracy, with food, with health, and with poverty. We would like NGOs from the U.S. to understand that when they design projects for the South, southerners should be consulted so we can help insure that the projects deal with social problems as well as ecological problems. We can no longer afford the disjunction that has existed between the environment and the economy. We cannot eat dollars.

Uchita de Zoysa:

Combating Environmental Degradation in Sri Lanka

chita de Zoysa is Coordinator of the
Public Campaign on Environment
and Development, Sri Lanka.

*Steve Lerner: When did Sri Lankan environmental groups begin to
focus on the United Nations Conference on Environment and Development (UNCED)?*

Uchita de Zoysa: The Public Campaign on Environment and Development was formed on February 5, 1991. The Sri Lankan Government was preparing a National Report on Environment and Development in Sri Lanka that will be presented at UNCED. Several non-government organizations (NGOs) that knew about UNCED, and were concerned about environment and development issues, felt there was very limited NGO participation in the drafting of the National Report.

It was my sense that the National Report would not reflect the will of the people because they were not being consulted. I proposed to a number of NGOs that we do our own report for UNCED. People laughed at me because they did not think it was possible to bring the NGOs together.

I took the responsibility of creating a coalition to come up with a common process to do something on UNCED. On February 5, 1991, I met with the key figures in eight environment and development NGOs. Among them were the Environmental Congress, an umbrella organization that has more than 150 grassroots groups in Sri Lanka; the Environment Foundation Ltd.; the Sarvodya Movement, a development NGO that has hundreds of centers throughout the island; the Bar Association of Sri Lanka; Environmental Journalists Association; and others. At that meeting we decided to form a coalition and draft a Citizens' Report. We saw that what was lacking in the National Report were the opinions, point of view, and aspirations of the people.

I believe that people living in their own environments have inherited knowledge. When they experience a problem they find indigenous ways of solving it that the present system does not see. We decided to consult the people through a series of public hearings and use these hearings as the basis of our Citizens' Report.

You told me that in gathering information for this Citizens' Report you spent a lot of time in small villages, sleeping in temples, and going to tea stalls in the central marketplaces of small villages where you could talk with the people. When you go to a village, how are you received? What kinds of issues come up?

We decided to make an island-wide tour. I drew up a route that would cover the country. Because of the fighting in the Northeast, we couldn't go there and carry out open and spontaneous dialogue with the people. But we went everywhere else. We hired a van. Other people traveled with me. During one month there were five of us: myself, a priest, a farmer who is a grassroots environmentalist, my technical assistant and a driver. All of us were part of the team. We sat together and ate together; there were no differences among us.

We would stop for a cup of tea in a small village in Anuradapuraya over 100 miles from Colombo in the dry zone. We would sit and talk with the owner of the tea shop. It would take a little time but a conversation would develop.

In Sri Lanka it is customary for people to gather around small coffee shops like that. They would see that something different was going on. They would see that I was seated on the floor chatting with villagers or on a small bench. When we would start talking we'd have no preconceived idea of what the topic should be, but we would start realizing what the topic was and what their problems were. Or, they would tell us about their life-style and what type of problems they had and what they wanted to do.

We didn't introduce ourselves at first. We just talked. But sometimes we'd have to introduce ourselves and explain what we had come to do. Sometimes the people were friendly and sometimes they were suspicious. But when the priest and the farmer were with us we often found ourselves surrounded by 60 or 70 people. We also organized four major hearings in addition to these spontaneous gatherings.

What kind of environment and development issues did you find people concerned about?

We were very much concerned with the construction of huge dams and the diversion of rivers. This has caused a lot of destruction of the environment in our country. We have been campaigning against this. There was a major dam and diversion scheme on the Mahaweli River to divert water to the dry zones. But what happened was that it changed the flow of the water and went against nature. Massive destruction took place. Natural forests were cleared for the diversion. Villages were inundated. Life patterns were changed. Species became extinct. Now there is no water; the river is drying up.

In Sri Lanka we have two agricultural seasons. The first crop is called Yala and the second is called Maha. By diverting the river, the authorities built new colonies in dry zones. People who had homes in the villages that were destroyed by the diversion were moved to these colonies. They had to adapt to a new life-style and it was bloody hard. The first year they were in this new area the water came from the diversion. But after that it began to dry up; no trees were growing or anything. The project was accelerated from an original 35-year plan to seven years, so you can imagine the destruction.

I went into these areas and met the people who were suffering a lot. These are people whose lives have been built around the two-crop system. Yala and Maha are inherited words with an implied life-style. Today the water doesn't just come in those two seasons. There is an in-between season that has been created by the diversion. And now, although the water comes in this in-between season, the farmers cannot raise a crop with it. What is the use of constructing this big dam if they do not plan it well?

Still, the authorities have not learned their lesson. Currently in the South, in the dry zone, there is a project called Lunugamvehera Dam Project. The authorities diverted the Kiridi Oya river that starts in the hill country. But it proved a failure. The authorities moved colonies of displaced people into this area, but now there is no water. The reservoir is going down and there is no water for agriculture. So now the authorities have decided to divert water to the dam from the Uma Oya river that originates in a beautiful hill country area where the soil is very fertile. It is a watershed area. It is one of the best catchment areas in our country and a beautiful place. They are trying to divert it to a dry area. This is a very sensitive issue in my country at the moment. Things are heating up and it is highly political.

Is there an organized movement to stop this diversion?

Not yet. Grassroots groups informed me about the diversion. So this was the major issue at one of our hearings. I was taken to the sites where the dams would be constructed and shown how the river would be diverted. Then I sat down with the farmers and they told me, "Look here, sir. If this river is diverted here, these soils and these mountains will start to break down." They showed me areas where the rocks kept the soil from washing away. They said that if the river is diverted in this fashion, in these areas earth slips will take place. And they showed me an area where an earth slip had already taken place.

Has the diversion already taken place?

No. But they did a small type of water scheme which blocked the water, and suddenly there was an earth slip. About 50 or 60 farmers came to talk with me with their wives and children. The children go to school, but when they come home they go out to the fields. These people are not poor. In their own way they are rich. It is not poverty. We people in the city are poor.

We are talking about conserving those life-styles that are prosperous. Now the Government says that it has plans to damage this life-style. Yet the farmers have been living in this area for generations. This area will provide food for the country: potatoes and beans and everything is planted there. It is a fertile area with streams and trees and it has a good climate. This hill country is a beautiful place.

I asked them how they felt about being moved to another area. And they said: "How can we live there? We are used to this area. We know how to live here. If something goes wrong with the crop, we know how to survive because we have inherited knowledge. If we are planted in another area we will be clueless."

The hill country is a bit cold, yet the authorities are trying to move hill people to a dry zone. For these people it will seem very hot. Their life-style will be corrupted. And already corruption is taking place in those areas where colonies have been planted.

What do you mean by corruption?

Normally, when a farmer gets his crop out he reserves something for his family and his relatives, so that they will have enough rice. The rest he sells. But now it is not that way. Everything has been commercialized. In our country we have lived under the Portuguese, the Dutch, and then the British. These foreigners set up a system to maintain the resource flow from South to North. Sri Lanka is a very good example of this. They came and took control of us because they wanted the spices and other resources from our area. They set up this kind of system, and ever since independence Sri Lanka has remained under colonial influence. The colonial mentality still rules.

It was during the colonial era that the tea plantations were established as an export crop.

Right: tea, rubber and coconut. Those have been the main exports that our economy has depended upon. Now we export our laborers to work in the Persian Gulf and elsewhere. The colonialists created very bad conditions in our country. They sold our gems and natural resources. We have gone from being a self-sufficient country to a dependent country. It is a shame. And still I don't believe that our sustainable life-styles have been smashed to the ground. I believe the roots are still there.

For example, we talk about traditional agriculture. In the past we used no chemicals at all. Our farmers practiced a natural kind of agriculture with cow and buffalo dung and composting. They had their own form of organic farming. Organic farming is now stylish, but organic farming was a way of life for us. Now well dressed people and members of NGOs are talking about organic farming. Our farmers do not know the technical terms for "organic farming" and "alternative development paradigms." But I feel these terms refer to old methods that these farmers have used for centuries. Our farmers say that they and their forefathers have always lived sustainably. Their life-style was balanced with their environment.

That traditional way of life may work in certain rural areas, but Sri

Lanka now has huge cities like Colombo. How can you depend on the old methods for these people who are living in a new situation?

I asked that of an old farmer who was digging the earth in his field surrounded by his buffalos. I asked him if we could farm the land without chemicals using the old system. He said that within the present system that was not possible. Fertilizers and chemicals have weakened the soil. The soil has gotten used to the chemicals, he said. You use the chemicals to get the maximum crop in the shortest period; but year after year the richness of the soil has diminished. I asked him if he could revive the soils and he said that he could but that the authorities would never allow it. It would require treating the soil delicately. You would have to put the nutrients back and rebuild the soil. But he said it is possible to do this under a different system and that if the system were changed they could feed the nation. Other farmers agreed. Even younger farmers recognized that this is a deep truth.

Are some of them still using the old methods?

Very few.

You said the traditional method of farming was working. So why did these farmers adopt chemical methods?

Sri Lanka was an agricultural country. After the colonial powers left, after independence, the country was taken over by an elite group of Sri Lankans who dressed like the British and were educated in the U.K. Their thinking was British and not local. They carried the colonial mentality. And they were very powerful.

Our tradition was to have kings, and people worked for the king. The king assigned tasks to different groups: One village would do agriculture, one village would do pottery, etc. That is the basis of our caste system. I never heard about real poverty under this system in our part of the world. The king had advisors and the advisors were very knowledgeable people. The people who did pottery were fed with the crops of the farmers; and the farmers got the pottery. But now the life-style has changed and the few people who are in power decide everything in the country. So, if the Government says that this is the way we will practice agriculture, that is what happens.

You mean the elites require that the farmers buy chemicals and fertilizers?

What else can they do?

They could refuse to buy fertilizers and use cow manure instead.

The farmers are stuck with this system. They know that if they use chemical fertilizers they will get a crop. They need the crop in order to live. So there is no escape within this system.

The two areas you have spoken about are the building of dams and diversion of rivers and this new system of chemical farming. As you went around to these villages you must have heard a lot about these subjects. How did you use this information?

Everywhere I went I tape recorded what people said and I had a small video camera and an assistant. So everything is recorded from this trip. Every audio tape will be transcribed word for word. No one will edit it. I am trying to keep the emotional factor in this record. We will have great quotations and photographs of people saying things in their own words. That is my vision of the Citizens' Report. It is not for me to sit down and edit and write it the way I want. I am just a facilitator. What I am doing is creating a forum for the common people to be heard.

What were your hearings like and how were you received?

We invited grassroots organizers to set up the hearings. But they set it up with a stage and microphone so that I could make a speech. The first thing I did was take the microphone and introduce our team and the campaign. Then I said to the organizer: "Look here, there is a big divide between the people and me. I cannot communicate this way, because I don't feel welcome. So please excuse me I am getting down from the stage." I did that twice and it was a shock. People had never experienced that. I could have tried to show off like a politician. The other option was to communicate well with the people. If I showed off at the hearings and didn't get the material I wanted, then it would have been a failure.

The way I did it, however, getting down off the stage, meant that I got some really crazy and very direct questions. It felt sometimes as if people were punching me. But I like and respect people like that. If there is going to be trust they should have the right to ask any question they want. People talk about an open process, but usually that is just a figure of speech. What is important is to mix with the people and communicate the vision.

How will the Citizens' Report that you are preparing fit into the UNCED process?

The priority for a man like me is my own country. This Citizens' Report will be presented at UNCED in Rio. World View International, a international media institute, has identified our Public Campaign as something that UNCED and the international community needs. They have offered to come and videotape what we are doing. That video will be shown in Rio.

What is the good of this report?

We are identifying problems and asking what people want. We are identifying and working toward a common vision. I think the Citizens' Report will be a base for that. A lot of people — priests, farmers, fishermen — feel a sense of ownership about this Report and they must implement it.

But the farmers already knew that they didn't want the Government to move them to some other land and divert a river to their new colony. They wanted to stay where they were. How can they do something about that? Do you see this Public Campaign as a group that will empower people to create solutions?

In the independent sector we can suggest and show the way, but when it comes to implementation it must be the Government that does it. We need a mechanism whereby the Government and the NGOs and public have discussions and come to decisions. I am concentrating on that, but it will take time.

Antonio Quizon in the Philippines says that whether or not these reforms are implemented depends upon whether or not you have organized people on the ground. After you have done your Citizens' Report, do you get the sense that this Campaign will become a powerful force? Will it have the "people power" to put pressure on the Government to change its policies?

I believe in conceptual change in our country. What Sri Lankans have been doing every four years since 1948, when we became independent, is appoint people to run our lives. That is not what is needed. There is a sense that we should move from colonial thinking to national thinking. We will not just disseminate our Report. We will organize forums. We will go back to the people with this Citizens' Report. People must be given the freedom to decide how to live their own lives.

Section III:

Defending Biological Diversity

Thomas E. Lovejoy:

Strategies for Preserving Biodiversity

 homas E. Lovejoy is Assistant Secretary for External Affairs, Smithsonian Institution. He is President of the American Institute of Biological Sciences and a member of the President's Council of Science and Technology Advisors, as well as the former Executive Vice President of the World Wildlife Fund. Lovejoy is the originator of public television's *Nature* series and launched the concept of debt-for-nature swaps through a 1984 op-ed article in *The New York Times*.

Steve Lerner: *What do you make of the negotiations on biological diversity. Do you think something useful is likely to come out of them?*

Thomas E. Lovejoy: One thing coming through is the realization that biological resources are not economically inconsequential. This has never been thought about before at a major governmental level. In the past, particularly in tropical developing nations, people have asked why they should care about biological diversity. They have thought of biological diversity as something that those damn environmentalists want us to worry about. Now there is the realization that science is arriving at the point where it can find benefits at the molecular level in biological diversity. And that means biological diversity is perceived as really important.

Second, there is a transition, because people realize that most of the economic benefits that have been derived in the past from tropical biological diversity (i.e. tropical genetic resources) have ended up in the pockets of industrialized nations. That analysis is an oversimplification, but there is a lot of truth in it. If this continues, there is a real disincentive for tropical nations to do anything about preserving biological diversity. Why should they be doing us in the North a favor?

That realization leads into a discussion of intellectual property rights, and that can get extremely complicated. But, in the meantime, there are actual deals being put together that inherently recognize intellectual property rights without going through the angst and philosophical basis of it all. These new deals just say: We in the South have the genetic resources, which are part of the capital that we are putting in; and you in the North have biotechnology resources, which are what you are putting in; and the finances come in addition. On this basis we can make a deal. If something good comes out of it, then benefits accrue to the owners of the genetic resources in tropical nations and to those contributing the biotechnology from the industrialized nations. That is actually happening now in Costa Rica and is being looked at in Indonesia.

So my feeling is that while there may be a lot of dancing around the general principles, in the real world people are making arrangements that are benefiting the people in tropical countries with genetic resources.

Are you suggesting that there will be a lot more of these deals made in the future?

Yes.

And this model in Costa Rica, that I understand is brokered through the Government — do you think it is a promising one? Isn't that a deal between Merck and the Government of Costa Rica?

In Costa Rica the National Institute of Biological Diversity (INBIO) is handling it; but other deals don't have to work exactly that way. However, the real bottom line is that developing countries do not want people just wandering in, finding genetic goodies, and going off with them to make their money elsewhere. I think that is a very reasonable point of view.

There is a more legalistic approach to compensating the South for its genetic resources that would require the people in tropical countries to get a patent or a copyright on their knowledge about the use of biological resources.

That is so overarching and such a fundamental change of the legal system that it may be a long time before that is actually solved. In the meantime, however, these deals are being made.

The Costa Rican deal with Merck is a minuscule amount compared with the value of biological resources and knowledge about the medicinal uses of plants being pirated by northern pharmaceutical companies.

That is true. People say we have to deal with poverty first and clean air and clean water. But I think there is a rapidly growing recognition that these biological resources are economically important. Further, the Merck deal has a royalty when something is found of commercial value.

You have suggested that the deal struck in Costa Rica is evidence of a change that is beginning to happen.

And in Mexico also.

What has been the position of the United States in these negotiations over biological diversity. Is the U.S. position not somewhat resistant to granting tropical countries the right to compensation for these genetic resources?

It is resistant to providing new and additional funding. Yet there is no way that these countries can invest substantially in protection of biological diversity without some help. The U.S. is also resistant to establishing new organizations to deal with this issue. It is resistant to new funds being spent on the preservation of biological diversity. That is probably the greatest fundamental drag on the U.S. position. There may also be some concern about the intellectual property rights side of it. But there have to be ways to work that out. If hybrid corn is going to benefit from wild genetic sources from Mexico, then there has to be a way to make a deal so that the Mexicans are compensated for that. Within some limits the market system will find a way to do that.

But in terms of analyzing our position on the biodiversity convention negotiations and through the Unitred Nations Conference on Environment and Development (UNCED), is it fair to say that the U.S. has been resistant to seeing a significant agreement come out of these negotiations? Or do we have an articulated view of what a biodiversity convention should look like. Do you get a sense from the Administration of what that would look like?

I have the hardest time figuring out what really is going on. I have not been a camp-follower at the negotiations. The impression I get is that we are resistant and reluctant to see an agreement, and some of that is based on real considerations, such as technology transfer. Government entities don't do technology transfer in our system; that is done by individual corporations. But there appears to be resistance to a biological diversity convention for no particularly good reason, in my view. And with biological diversity going down the drain as fast as it is, we have got to do something.

You have just co-edited a book on climate change and biodiversity.

Yes. In many ways the impact of global warming on biological diversity is the most dangerous impact posed by climate change.

And yet, as I understand it, the climate change negotiations have not devoted a lengthy discussion to what the impact of global warming may be on biological diversity.

No, they have not.

In your preface you make the case that if we are interested in preserving biodiversity we have to be interested in climate change; and vice versa.

It is possible, from a technical point of view, to greatly simplify the biology of the world without, at least in the short term, doing something that is going to generate so much greenhouse gas that you get climate change. But the way society and the environment really interact, yes, biological diversity is going up in smoke, in many places in the world, and it, in turn, is contributing to climate change.

Would it be fair to argue that since the United States has refused to set target reductions of carbon dioxide emissions, that the Administration is not very interested in preserving biodiversity?

I don't think members of this Administration have thought very much about it. I think that is far from what they are thinking. When they think about climate change, the focus is on a physical system, not a biological system. That is the real problem. There is very little to worry about unless climate change affects biology. Sure, if temperatures rise we may have to spend more money on air conditioning, and the water supply will be different around the world. But the meaningful impact of climate change on people is at the biological level.

You have written: "I am utterly convinced that the great environmental struggles will be won or lost in the 1990s. And that by the next century it will be too late to act." Here we are in 1992, leaving us eight years to do something about these problems, according to your reckoning. When you go to bed at night, what do you think will be our fate?

It is all so dreamlike. It is impossible to tell whether we are really going to come to grips with these problems or not. There is a Parkinsonian element in the way life works, and I think we are seeing that in relation to UNCED. A lot is being done at the last minute. People are now saying that we had better do something, because there is going to be a conference. Whether that will help us, or whether it will require some kind of other major crisis such as the ozone hole, and whether we will make the changes necessary, I don't know.

Senator Al Gore, when asked whether it will take a further catastrophe before the political will emerges to deal with global environmental problems, enumerated the numerous ecological catastrophes we are undergoing currently.

These ecological catastrophes are all incremental. The growth of the ozone hole was incremental; but the discovery of it was a big leap.

A series of articles was recently published in The Atlantic Monthly *that argued that environmentalists and biologists who warn us about the dire effects of extinction don't appreciate the importance of human evolution that is going on.*

That is a very short-sighted view. I think that a major new source of wealth is going to emerge out of biological diversity. I am working on an article for *The Washington Post* that will show that we are getting at least tens of billions of dollars of our GNP out of biological diversity and biotechnology. No one realizes this.

So there is a financial argument for preserving biodiversity, as well as the argument that if we oversimplify nature, the world will become a less stable place in which our long-term survival is less likely.

Absolutely. It is not as if there are not other important reasons for preserving biological diversity. It is just that so much of this world is driven by economic considerations, that we should not undersell the economic case for preserving biological diversity.

In looking at various strategies to prevent the unprecedented die-off of biological diversity, there are some people who have taken the ap-

proach that we should begin to adapt to these high levels of extinction. This argument suggests that since we can't save all the species on the planet, we will be forced to practice a type of triage. Some argue that we should identify "keystone" species that are very important in the preservation of their ecosystem. Is that practical?

I think the only acceptable approach is to set the target for preservation of biological diversity as high as possible. If we fall short, then we should set the priorities with the best knowledge available at the time. But the fact is that we don't have any very intelligent basis for making choices about which species should be allowed to live.

But we have to do something.

If you look at it in the context of fund-raising, if you are trying to raise $100 million you start by looking for larger sums than if you have set a $5000 goal. You have to set the sights where they should be, and try to get as close as you can. Whatever the gap may be, you take what you do have and spend it as effectively as possible.

But in terms of a strategy for preserving biological diversity, should we be looking to identify species that perform certain very valuable environmental services? Should we be arguing that since biodiversity is dense in certain parts of the world, we should concentrate on protecting those areas?

You do a bunch of things. There are some things that have already emerged from behind the veil of ignorance as being of extraordinary value to us. For example, any wild relative of a crop species is obviously a candidate for protection. The preservation of those species is already being worked on because it is such an obvious thing to do. Beyond that we have to preserve the largest number of species possible. One of the ways to do that is to know more about what there is and where it is.

Do you mean that we have to do a more extensive inventory of species?

Yes, but we should not wait around for the results of the inventory before we take action. We did something called the Workshop 90 Exercise. We got a hundred experts on the flora and fauna of the Amazon together and locked them up (figuratively speaking) for a week, until they pooled their knowledge and created priorities for action to preserve biological diversity in the Amazon now. Then, in our conservation plan, we made efforts to protect obvious centers of biological diversity. That really needs to be done worldwide.

Is a focus on tropical forests sensible because they are the area of greatest concentration of biodiversity? Some argue that those areas where researchers spend the most time are the areas where they find the greatest biological diversity.

However you look at it, from the world-wide picture of biological diversity, tropical forests are very important. We can't be very precise about it, but it is obvious that a good chunk of the world's biological diversity is in seven percent of the dryland surface of the earth. That doesn't mean that marine systems are going to be neglected.

You helped launch the debt-for-nature swaps. Are debt-for-nature swaps going to be an important way in which biodiversity is preserved? Can you give us an idea of what their potential is?

It really bugs me that so much debt conversion is done for ordinary commercial purposes and no one objects to it. But when we suggest using the same mechanism for a socially useful purpose, such as the environment, we meet a lot of resistance. Some people ask why we want to do that. But these are the same people who don't turn a hair when billions are converted for commercial purposes. I am thinking of the case of Mexico and Brazil. There is something about the word debt that, when you couple it with a socially useful purpose, gets people all confused.

The debt-for-nature swap is just a transitory financial mechanism. I will be delighted when the time comes that there is not enough debt around for it to be used this way. It is not a solution to the debt problem; and it is not a solution to the environment problem. It is a financial mechanism.

I have been disappointed that the debt-for-nature swaps have advanced so little. Why are the total debt-for-nature conversions hovering in the hundreds of millions of dollars range when billions of dollars are being converted? It also bugs me when the government-to-government debt is written off without setting aside some of it for these long-term considerations. The Enterprise for the Americas initiative, however, is a conscious effort to do both.

Why is that happening?

Because people sometimes just don't think about it and environmentalists don't get ahead of the game. I talked to the Under Secretary of the Treasury, David Mulford, three months ago. I called him about the debt of the Republics of the former Soviet Union. I told him that these countries have a lot of environmental problems and the Administration should remember debt-for-nature swaps as a possibility. He said I was early in calling about that. I told him that I would rather be too early than too late because much of the opportunity to do these debt-for-nature swaps with Mexico is gone. It is not that I don't want these countries to have their debt reduced. It is just that it would be useful to have some of it set aside in PL-480 fashion for the long-term considerations of those societies even more than ours.

The U.S. is talking about how to get Brazil to protect its biological diversity. How is the United States doing with preserving our own biological diversity?

I don't think there is any "white hat" country anywhere. While it is important to be critical, I think it is also important to get beyond the stage where everyone is running around pointing fingers rather than doing something. I am the first one to admit that we have some serious problems in the U.S. The way we treat our forests in the Northwest is an embarrassment.

You mean the fact that we are still cutting what remains of our old-growth forests?

Yes. We are still doing that with Government incentives and subsidies that you and I pay for, while the Brazilians, at least in the letter of the law, have made changes reducing that kind of incentive and subsidy in the Amazon. In the U.S. we don't have a national biological inventory. We don't have much biological diversity legislation except the Endangered Species Act, which we overuse as a safety net because we don't have the other conservation programs in place.

And as a result there has been a backlash against the Endangered Species Act.

Yes. The real answer is not weakening the Endangered Species Act. Rather we must pass other legislation that will get conservation done so that we can get ahead of the problem. The real answer is more conservation and not less, which is a very hard thing for some people to understand. If we had more conservation, and it was done properly, there would be fewer conflicts.

You have done a lot of work raising consciousness about the threats to the Amazon. What have you been pushing for in this country of a similar nature?

I have been working on creating a National Center for Biological Diversity here at the Smithsonian. I think this is the logical place for it. I have been trying to convince U.S. policy people of the need to preserve biological diversity in this country and what the real issues are about. In two weeks I will have a meeting on the economic opportunities involved with biological diversity. There is money to be made from biological diversity. I am trying to get people to wake up to what global climate change really means. It is mad, utterly mad.

How has this message been received?

The biggest problem is that everybody is treating this as business-as-usual. They want to let the process take its own time.

I will remind you again of your quote that the 1990s is the decisive decade for solving these problems. Do you still feel that way?

Yes. Just look at the numbers.

Which numbers?

First, human population growth. There are a billion more people on the planet since Ronald Reagan took office. There are 100 million more people every year. That is a staggering number to take care of. There is the scale of atmospheric pollution, where we are adding billions of tons of carbon and other stuff to the air every year. The deforestation rate in the tropics is something like 100 acres a minute. These are really big numbers, and the more they build up, the harder it will be to change.

That's what scares me. And these trends are all tied together. So, I try not to lose my sense of humor.

What signs of hope or cause for optimism do you see in terms of our being able to preserve enough biodiversity for the planet to remain reasonably stable?

The fact that there is going to be this United Nations Conference on Environment and Development is a sign of hope. Even if a lot of energy gets expended there, the very fact that it will happen is a hopeful sign. Also promising is the attitude of a lot of young people, as well as the attitudes of some pretty impressive captains of industry. Attitudes are changing. Six years ago no one had heard of biological diversity. I was told to forget it as a phrase. The fact that the concept of biological diversity is now widely used is a hopeful sign. The question is not whether or not positive things are happening; the question is whether or not these positive things are happening fast enough or on a large enough scale. And the answer is: not yet.

People are beginning to talk about creating North/South corridors along which species can migrate as the planet gets warmer. That sounds to me like something people would think up who have given up on doing anything about global warming.

Furthermore, I don't think you can really do very much of that because the landscape is already so modified.

You mean that if animals wanted to move North, they would find Philadelphia in the way? You quoted someone as saying that.

Yes.

Since Philadelphia and other human settlements are in the way, does it make any sense to arrange these North/South corridors?

Absolutely. Wherever you can, do it; it is a sensible thing to do anyway. The ideal way to manage this planet is to create islands of human occupation in a sea of wilderness. That would make it a lot easier for species to survive, adapt, and disperse. And to the extent that we can do that, it is fine. But in a landscape of 100 million more people every year, it is increasingly hard to do that.

It looks as if we are headed for a world where there are islands of wilderness in a sea of humanity.

That's right.

You are doing a study in the Amazon on the Minimal Critical Size of Ecosystems. What have you found out from that experiment? I understand that in areas that are being clear-cut in the Amazon you set aside forest areas to be left standing of different sizes: 1 hectare, 10 hectares, 100 hectares, and 10,000 hectares.

Those are meaningful sizes from a research point of view, not a conservation point of view. We are trying to answer the question: Which is better, a large preserve or a whole bunch of small ones that add up to the same area? The answer to that is that the large area is better.

The answer was intuitively obvious from the beginning, but there were a lot of scientists who would not accept it. That is the simple answer to the question. Then there are all the other kinds of issues such as what is the ideal minimum size and how we manage something that is smaller than the ideal.

Are we moving toward a park concept of preserving biological diversity? Are we going to try to set aside more areas where no one should live? Or are we going to move toward arrangements where people can live in a wilderness area and keep it relatively intact?

You have to do both. But there are a lot of places where we are going to end up with just an isolated preserve.

Jason Clay at Cultural Survival suggests that we must use forests in order to protect them. He calls it a "use it or lose it" strategy.

I am not against that either. If you really want to be rational and scientific about how you manage and enjoy the biology of this planet, you have to have some areas that are essentially (as opposed to virtually) pristine natural systems that are the basis for comparison with the manipulated areas. Otherwise we don't know quite what we are doing.

So we will have to have some areas where there are no people and some areas where we try to help people who are living in the forest make a living out of it without destroying it.

Yes. We have to emphasize these core areas: That is really what the "Man and the Biosphere" program is all about. Biosphere reserves have core areas that are the ecological standard for the natural systems.

Do you think a fair portion of the rain forest can be preserved by helping those who live in it make a living by selling rain forest products, so that they don't have to destroy the forest? You might call this the Rainforest Crunch approach.

I think there are important ways to make money out of the forest without destroying it. The question is: Will we be given a chance to do that before hungry invading hordes destroy it?

One writer on the subject of biological diversity has identified two groups of people. First, the environmentalists, who see humans as a ravenous horde that has descended on the planet and is devouring the world's resources. These environmentalists are said to have a very pessimistic view of the fate of the planet. The second group looks at humans as part of nature and part of the evolutionary process. This group admits that humans are destroying some species, and modifying the environment, but it sees humans as a creative force.

You can be totally fatalistic and just say: Let's do it and see what happens. I think that's really dumb. A lot of people have that attitude about climate change: let's wait and see what happens. But the problem is that there is not much room in Biosphere Two.

Darrell A. Posey:

Protecting Biocultural Diversity

arrell Addison Posey is Coordinator of the Ethnobiological Institute of the Amazon and President of the Global Coalition for Biological and Biocultural Diversity.

Steve Lerner: *How did you become involved in trying to preserve biocultural diversity?*

Darrell A. Posey: I am trained as a biologist and anthropologist. When I went to do my doctoral work in Brazil in 1977, I set out to study how indigenous peoples of the Amazon deal with certain aspects of nature. I was specifically trained as an entomologist, so I began studying how they classify, and use, and deal with insects. I was interested in why traditional agriculture could be successful and productive without using insecticides and pesticides. I was generally concerned about the ecological implications of the use of chemicals on groundwater, pollution of streams, and death of the insects that I used to study when I was a kid.

My father is a farmer, so I not only thought of this as an intellectual process, but when I would go back to visit my family in Kentucky, I noticed that there were no longer any birds because they had eaten the insects that were poisoned. The groundwater was becoming polluted even in rural areas. I thought it was interesting that indigenous people were able to carry out their management of resources rather successfully without these poisons. That is why I went to Brazil in the first place.

I soon began to realize that the categories I had learned at University were simply inadequate. You could not understand entomology unless you understood the relationship between the insect and the plant, the plant and the soil, and all of this together in one ecological system, because the system depended upon using native plants that were adapted to specific soils and microclimatic conditions. Those microclimatic conditions favored certain animals, particularly birds, that would come and be attracted to habitats and be important in destroying the pests.

I had studied ants. That was my specialty as an entomologist: social insects. I was curious about ants and began asking about them, and recording stories about ants, and songs about ants. The old shaman I worked with, a grand old gentleman who is still alive — he must be 75

130

or more — lives in the village of Gorotire in the Kayapo Reserve in the Xingu region of the Southeastern Brazilian Amazon basin. The old man is named Beptopoop. Beptopoop serves as everybody's spiritual grandfather. He is the kind of figure that our society has lost in the U.S. and in many parts of the industrialized world. He is a very wise shaman and respected in his own culture.

Beptopoop was singing for me because in Kayapo culture you don't write knowledge. You don't put it in nice, clear, concise analytical terms and Pythagorean formulas. You communicate it in highly complex visual and verbal images through song and oral transmission. Singing is a very important way of transmitting knowledge. Children learn to sing and they like to sing. It is a very pleasant way to learn. He was singing for me a song about the fields, the gardens, the moon, and the night, and what happens in the gardens when there is a moon in the night. It so happened that one of the things he was singing about was ants. He sang about the ants that come out in the evening and the termites that come out in the evening and protect the fields in the full moon against things that would destroy the crops.

I was involved in an interdisciplinary research project with the Kayapo for seven years working with another entomologist. The team included entomologists, botanists, agronomists, an astronomer, a zoologist, a linguist, an anthropologist, and all sorts of people — twenty of us in all. I told the entomologist that this shaman said that whatever happens to protect the crops seems to happen at night. I asked the entomologist what he knew about what happens in the fields at night. He said entomologists knew nothing, that entomologists don't like to go out at night, they are afraid of the night, and that he had never seen a survey of insects collected in the evening anywhere in the tropics. I suggested that it was time that we did it.

So, we went out to do a collection of insects in the evening. After about a week of this people thought that we were completely nuts, going out with flashlights looking at plants in the middle of the night.

Didn't the light attract insects?

Well no, because there weren't many insects there. In fact we never found pests in these fields during the day or the night. They just don't exist. The system is balanced so that you don't have the problem of insect pests. You may get an infestation that results in 20 to 25 percent leaf damage. But now we know, scientifically, that leaf damage is minimal compared with production, and in fact can stimulate production, because what you are doing is forcing the energy of the plant from the leaf into the fruit, or whatever is being produced.

To make a long story short, this entomologist and I were in the field with the moon out. I was on one side of the field, he was on the other, and I heard this scream. I thought the guy had been bitten by a snake. I went running over to see what was wrong. He said it was his toe. We looked at his toe and there was this huge termite with a great mandibles that had attacked his toe. We looked around and there were hundreds of these things. And they were out after these leaf cutting ants, Sauva (*Atta* SPP.) which come out at night and destroy the fields.

The termites are attracted by the straw. In a modern agricultural plot they burn the straw or bale it and take it away. But the Indians don't. They leave it and that attracts termites that use it to make nests down in the ground. The termites are only active in the evening. If ants get in their way, the termites just chop off their heads.

There is another type of ant, called the Azteca. The Indians call it the smelly ant because its pheromone system gives off really strong odors. The leaf cutting ants won't come near the smelly ants. These Azteca ants work in the daytime, and the termites work at night. There is a nice balance between the guys who work in the daytime protecting the field crops and the guys who work at night. These were just two of the little secrets that we were learning.

So we began to realize that Beptopoop wasn't making this stuff up. These weren't just funny little stories that you put into your songs to make the kids laugh. In fact, these songs were full of very important and very powerful ecological information. If we were to take seriously the oral traditions of indigenous peoples, and begin to analyze what they were passing on orally, we would discover very complex ecological relationships that might take forever to discover on our own, were already encoded. It took looking very seriously at the knowledge and analyzing it in a sophisticated way. It takes a long time to learn a language; it takes a long time to know how to get to these things.

It must also have taken a long time to meet Beptopoop and have him sing you his song.

That part was not too hard. Beptopoop loves to sing. And most indigenous people are very willing to share their knowledge. The problem is for us to have enough knowledge to be able to interpret it, and to not just see it as pure folklore that it is really quaint and cute.

So, I became more and more fascinated with this work. I also did a study of indigenous knowledge of bees. Not the European bee, which we all know about, but the native bee, which became completely extinct in North America and is under great threat in some parts of South America because of deforestation and the introduction of the European bee — the hybridized European bee, which is the so-called African killer bee.

With another shaman named Kwyrà-kà, I was able to collect 54 species of bees. We collected them by name, by how they fly, what they eat, where they collect pollen, where they get their water, how they differ morphologically one from the other, which type of habitat they live in, when their honey is good and when it isn't, and how the honey is used. There was just an amazing amount of scientific knowledge available.

I took this knowledge to the best specialist in Brazil, João Camargo, who is also one of the best in the world, and who works at the University of São Paolo. We published a number of articles that were among the first studies that compared the incredibly complex and rich folk knowledge to scientific knowledge. We discovered nine new species of bees. Nine. Some of them haven't been named or described to date.

One can learn from these people and make quantum leaps in knowledge about classification of animals, and about ecological relationships between the soil and animal and plant behavior.

And the knowledge about these bees came from indigenous sources?

That is how we found them. I went to the bee shaman, Kwyrà-kà, and he told me everything I ever wanted to know about bees and more. I knew nothing about bees. He would take me around and he would say, "Look, there is this big black bee that lives in the trees and builds its nest on the outside of the tree in the bark, and has an entrance tube. Then there is another big black bee that looks almost the same that also has an entrance tube, but his nest is not on trees but is on the side of the rocks. Then there is another bee, a little bit smaller, that builds its nest inside the tree and has an entrance tube that is very thin and looks like the penis of an Armadillo." Seriously, that was one of his examples. Then there is that other black bee, he explained, that he didn't like very much because it builds its home in the ground and it tends to mess around with animal excrement, so we don't mess with that one; however, the wax of that bee is pretty good when you want to use it for your arrows, but we wouldn't use it for medicine. Then, if you want to know about the other little black bee that lives in the cane, it is very small, but it produces this marvelous resin that can be burnt, which we use to purify our houses. This goes on and on, and you write all these things down. Then you discover, like Columbus "discovered" America, that what you have just collected is a complete taxonomy of bees, which is more sophisticated than the taxonomy that the scientists use.

You can do this with ecosystems also. Some scientific texts will describe 20 basic classification systems for all of the Amazon. That is ridiculous. The Amazon is extremely diverse. We have never adequately recognized the diversity of it, and we have never been able to describe it. But if you go to the indigenous people who live there, they can tell you the names, the characteristics, the soil-plant-animal relationships and seasonal changes within these environments, the migration between ecosystems. These people know these ecosystems; it is just a question of learning from them. But Western science is reinventing the wheel all the time. Scientists have been too arrogant to learn from indigenous people. They don't think traditional knowledge is scientific.

At UNCED a debate is going on about intellectual property. Some of the delegates from the South argue that traditional knowledge is worth something in monetary terms.

It is worth a hell of a lot.

Yet, the reward it has historically received has been minimal. How does your work fit in with the debate over intellectual property at UNCED?

I have just given you some examples of how sophisticated and how important and how complex the knowledge systems of these indigenous people are. Yet, no one seems to want to talk about the relationship of human beings to the environment. As soon as we start dealing with that we have to start dealing with some of those nasty problems that most countries don't want to solve such as land tenure, or empowering local communities instead of maintaining all the wealth and power in the hands of the urban ruling elite.

People have not been nice to each other throughout the ages. There have been inequalities since the beginning of recorded history. There have been unequal trading relationships, military occupations, enslavement, and other nasty things that people do to each other. Now, when we begin to face this global environment/development crisis, people talk about having to fix everything: the global economy, the exploitative relationship between the North and the South. I sometimes feel overwhelmed and powerless when people suggest that we have to solve all the problems of inequality in the world in order to stop accelerating environmental degradation. If we have to change human nature at such a fundamental level, then our chances for survival seem slight. Yet when I talk with people from the developing world about what will be necessary to make a deal between the North and the South, they genuinely feel that we have to deal with these equity issues before tackling the symptoms of environmental degradation. What do you think?

I don't think we have time to do one before the other. The excuses that man has always been that way, that man has always been unjust to man, that there has always been unequal trade, that we must have all the scientific evidence before we can do anything, these sound like the kinds of excuses made by George Bush. True, there has always been inequity. But in the past, inequity threatened local or regional or even national resources and human beings. It has never before threatened the entire planet.

Human evolution works in the following manner. You can survive by maintaining your old standards of behavior, but when conditions change abruptly, some organisms are able to survive and some are not. We have now reached the point where the systems that we have created require enormous amounts of natural resources, wastefully utilized. At the same time we are expanding this same system into Eastern Europe, Asia, Africa, South America, and everywhere else. If we are already facing an environmental crisis, why do we continue to use the same model?

If we have deforested 50 percent of the planet over the last 50 years, then we are going to deforest the next 50 percent in the next 10 years, because the demands are so great. Not only is the population growing, but this model of wasting resources is being rapidly expanded. So, I don't think we can learn from the past, because we will just give the excuse that "we have always gotten by".

I think we can learn from indigenous people. We can learn from them not just because of their knowledge about the environment, and their knowledge of ecological systems. It is also important to listen to indigenous people because they depend upon the earth, and they have never lost the belief in sacred place. If you believe in the concept of sacred place, it means that you believe that the physical surroundings in which you live have a sacred nature to them.

We in the industrialized world have no sacred place. To us, all the earth is the same, and it is just simply a question of economics. We ask whether or not it is economically feasible to develop an area. If it is, we ask how best to do it: is there enough money; are the returns adequate? There is no concept of sacredness. We can turn an environmentally, bioculturally rich area like the Amazon into a desert by planting a single species, for example Eucalyptus. The result may be green, it may produce something, but in terms of biodiversity it is still a desert. I don't want to pick just on poor Eucalyptus. You could use, for example, soya beans, or sugar cane, or other monocultures. Even the forests in Europe are impoverished. The Swiss think they have a very sophisticated and advanced forest management system, but all they know how to manage are eight species at the maximum. In the Amazon we are talking about a forest that has 6,000 species in it. Do we want to give it over to foresters who have never been able to successfully convince anybody that they can manage more than eight species? To turn over to them the management of tropical forests would be absurd — frighteningly absurd.

My personal feeling is that we have to change. It is an intuitive feeling. Human beings are above all intuitive. We have convinced ourselves that the solutions to the world's future problems will come from technology, logic, and science. I am afraid that does not satisfy the spiritual necessity that human beings feel. We now see in societies that are the most technologically advanced, the sincere desire to return to a sense of the sacred. The church is not offering that because it has been co-opted into thinking in terms of the number of people it attracts, how to manage all these people, and how to get church business attended to in Congress.

Suddenly the concept of sacred place is becoming fascinating to people who live in the technological world. I think that is why we have a new interest in traditional knowledge. This opening is for spiritual reasons as well as for some very hard and crass economic reasons. The economic reasons are that — parallel to this new spiritual desire, this seeking of an alternative life-style — people are looking for alternative markets and products. So they want to have natural foods, natural hair products, natural insecticides, natural colorings, and natural medicines. And the only people who really have these are indigenous peoples.

A discussion is going on at UNCED about arranging a fair trade relationship between indigenous people and the pharmaceutical companies of the West. It involves the intellectual property rights of indigenous people who have specialized knowledge about specific uses for botanicals that they have used over the ages. Can you tell me how that debate is moving and how you see your role in that debate?

There is a threefold reason that indigenous people must be a central part of the UNCED negotiation. First, there is a spiritual desire of the human species to once again recognize the earth as a sacred place. Second, there is a need to understand the scientific complexities of ecological systems so that we can better preserve them. And third, we need to look at economic incentives for maintaining environmental and cultural diversity. The people who run the planet are not interested in the science or spiritual part. They are interested in the economics. The planet is run on an economic model that states that if something does not have economic value we should tear it down. So we have to build value into these economic systems.

For example, how can we calculate the economic value of a tree, given the ecological services it supplies?

Or how much is indigenous knowledge worth? Or how much are 6,000 species of medicinal plants in one indigenous village worth? What is the worth of the world pharmaceutical industry? Answer: $54 billion per year. What is the worth of the seed industry that is built on biogenetic resources mostly from the Third World? The answer to that is that it is worth more than the pharmaceutical industry. What is the economic interest in natural hair and body products? We don't know what the world market is, but we know that just one company, the Body Shop, has an annual income of around $60 million, with a 50 percent growth rate in the last three years. So, one of the great growth profiles is in this area of natural products. Look at all the clones that have come after the Body Shop. It is big business. People are realizing its potential, but they also know that they have to learn about these natural products from indigenous people. So, the knowledge is as important as the resource.

If you take indigenous people and remove them from their land and if you take biological diversity and export it, you have lost most of the information. You have lost the information about the ecological interrelationships of that plant with all the other animals and soils; and you have lost the knowledge about that plant that the native people know, because you have pushed them off their land.

The history of Western industrial civilization is that we use up a resource and then move on to the next.

Yes, that is what we used to do, but there are no more frontiers.

The Amazon appears to be a frontier.

The Amazon is hardly a frontier. There is hardly anywhere you can go in the Amazon where you cannot find roads and gold miners. Anyone who thinks that the Amazon is the last frontier doesn't know the Amazon. The last frontiers are over. There are no more last frontiers.

Look at what is happening to the Yanomami Indians. The Yanomami were one of the largest indigenous groups in South America. Unfortunately, they happened to occupy the border area of Brazil with Venezuela, and they happened to be on top of significant deposits of uranium and gold. As a result, the Government divided up their lands and let the gold miners clear it out so the Government could get to the uranium. The Government never said that this was its intention, but we know the real interest there is uranium and cassiterite. The Indians are seen as barriers to progress and getting rid of them is seen as worthwhile. So, the Government lets the gold miners in and they wipe the Indians out. We have lost at least 50 percent of the Yanomami population in the last five years. This is clear cultural genocide. They die from malaria, flu, and tuberculosis.

The area has also been opened up because the military wants it for geopolitical reasons. The military says it needs the region to defend Brazilian territory, yet nobody knows against whom; the military is another of those beasts that has to learn that world strategy has to be built on ecological security, not geopolitical security.

We have to recognize that the Indian people who are linked to the earth have the answers we need. They have the spiritual answers, they have the scientific answers, and they have the technological answers, because they know the alternative products we need, and ways of preserving them. They have been doing this for a long time.

How do you get people to realize this? One way is to point out to those who make economic decisions that the Indians know a hell of a lot, that their knowledge is worth a lot of money, and that the forest is full of new products which the industrialized world knows nothing about. If money were invested in developing these forest products, it would become clear that the living forest is worth a lot more than the uranium and cassiterite, the use of which may not be permissible in the future.

So, we have to explain to the economic decision-makers what the potential source of wealth is in the forest. And we have to make them understand that they will have to share this wealth. But there is a problem here. If you want to talk with the people at the World Intellectual Property Organization (WIPO) or the Union for the Protection of New Plant Varieties or even the General Agreement on Tariffs and Trade (GATT), one of the things you have to make clear from the beginning is the following: Indigenous people now know the financial value of their wealth. They know its financial value because over the last 10 years ethnobiologists have held a real dialogue with these people and have helped them to understand that their knowledge is worth a hell of a lot. We have helped them to understand that their knowledge is important to science, it is important to the earth, and it is important to business. As a result the Indians are no longer willing to give that knowledge away freely. They will restrict it. It is very easy to restrict it. You can't make me tell you anything.

How about bribing? The flesh is weak. If I came to Brazil and was shopping for that knowledge, could I not buy it?

Some of it, maybe. But not the best of it. You wouldn't have the tools to buy it. You would have to know the culture and the language very well.

Can't I pay some hungry anthropologist to go in and get the information I need for my pharmaceutical company, or natural hair products company, and then retire to the Riviera?

The pharmaceutical industry has, over the years, managed to rip off an enormous amount of information. But basically it is a very small amount of the total. Their success rate is incredibly low. They even say that they are not interested in studying traditional knowledge because it is too hard and they never get anything out of it, which is not true. But it is true that they are very inefficient. Why is that? Because they ask these shamans in a foreign language, "How do you treat this disease or that disease?" They have their concept of disease. They don't accept the basic anthropological truth that there are no givens on this planet. Culture classifies reality for everything from smells to colors to diseases. There are symptoms that you clump together and give the name of a disease. We give a name and assume, because our medical system is so arrogant, that that is the way the entire world must operate. But that is not the way the world operates.

People from the pharmaceutical industry use these scientific categories and ask the indigenous shaman to give a response. To the shaman it sounds like a really foolish question, but they give an answer. And the people from the pharmaceutical company go back and test it in their laboratory and discover that a very small percentage of what they found is interesting.

So it does not translate.

It doesn't translate because they didn't try to make it translate. They didn't get to know the person, they didn't get to know the language. They didn't get to know their concepts of disease and curing. They didn't get to know even how they prepare their medicines. These so-called ethnopharmacologists go in and they don't even study how the shaman prepares the medicines, let alone how he classifies concepts of disease. If you are willing to learn about indigenous knowledge, put in the time to learn the language and the customs, in the process the Indians end up knowing who you are and what you are up to. You come out of it, as I have, dedicated to the indigenous peoples' cause. You are not going to do something unethical that will show disrespect to those people.

But the pursuit of knowledge, and the interest in disseminating knowledge, is a powerful force in the world. There will always be people, such as yourself, who are fascinated by traditional knowledge, who study it, and publish articles about it. This is our way. We want to know the secrets. And once we learn the secrets we want to tell others. In the past, the local people who gave of their knowledge were not well rewarded. Now we are talking about rewarding them.

Yes, now we are talking about rewarding them because it is in our interest to do so, because if we don't reward them they will not tell us what we need to know. Or because they are not going to be here to tell us. Or because the resources that they could tell us about will no longer be around. Or because they not only know how to use this stuff but also how to manage and control it.

The new research we have been doing in ethnobiology over the last two decades shows that indigenous people don't just live in these areas, they manage them. And in many cases the diversity of the region is a direct result of human input in the region. The same thing goes for soil fertility. The richest soils in the Amazon, called "the black soils of the Indians", are human produced. They cover an enormous area in the Amazon. The Indians know how to improve soil fertility, something which no modern agricultural system can do without using very costly and ecologically dangerous chemicals. Yet the indigenous people do it naturally and organically. So if we want this information we are going to have to give them the ability to survive.

I am not convinced that our side is sophisticated enough to do this. Not at all. But I am convinced that there are a number of instruments and tools that allow us to force this question into some of the major world debates including UNCED. That is why I insist on two things. First, if UNCED is serious it is going to have to deal with the question of local control over resources. Second, it is going to have to recognize existing sustainable models of natural resource management practiced by indigenous peoples.

Yet, this has been largely absent from the UNCED debate.

It has been largely absent because none of the countries want to deal with it. The delegates represent the elite who are not in the least bit interested in empowering people and sharing the wealth. I think the elite of Brazil are scared. I think they know they cannot hold on forever.

What have you been doing in preparation for the Earth Summit?

We have an interesting strategy. We get key artists from films, music, and theatre and take them into the forest — where our friend Sting went. We know they will not come out the same. If you take them into the forest with indigenous people, in three days you achieve more than you could in 30 years of talking. It is a question of feeling it. People have been alienated from their feelings. So, we take them into the forest to understand what is going on there, and then let them speak to the world through their music.

How do you see intellectual property rights evolving?

The debate over intellectual properties is interesting because the right to one's knowledge is a basic universal right. It is being declared by the U.N. in the Universal Declaration of Human Rights for Indigenous Populations. It is also clear in International Labor Organization (ILO) Declaration 169.

So, there has already been an effort to establish that knowledge is property and property is a right. I have the right to say to you that I told you a great secret about medicine, but you don't have the right to commercialize it without my consent. Everyone has these rights. If we can get these rights for indigenous people who have been considered to be savage, primitive, and backward for all these years — if we can get these rights respected, then for all the peoples of the world it becomes easy.

They should have the right to say no, that we don't want to commercialize our knowledge. It is sacred, special, and secret. They don't have that right now. If they do want to commercialize it, they should have the right to be compensated for it, and the right to be able to say that that knowledge will not be abused. All we are doing is asking that they be recognized as equals in this system. Intellectual property rights are a tool for making that happen. They state that I have the right to say no, or yes, under specified conditions, and if you commercialize my knowledge I have the right to compensation. Those are the basic rights. That is the link between intellectual property and human rights.

The link between intellectual property, and biological diversity, and the questions being discussed at UNCED is that if we want to be able to control and maintain the biodiversity of the planet, there are not enough police in the world to do it. There are not enough military people in the world to do it. And besides it is not just maintaining the diversity. Don't we also want to maintain the knowledge of how to use it and knowledge of how this diversity was produced? We have scientific evidence that the biological diversity of the Amazon was produced by human presence in an interplay between human beings and the forest, human beings and the savannah, human beings and the rivers. We should want to preserve all of that. That is why we started the Global Coalition for Bio-cultural Diversity. We want to preserve the knowledge about biodiversity, the knowledge about how to preserve it, in addition to the plants and animals themselves. Human beings have to play a central role in this.

Many agree that traditional knowledge should be rewarded, but they ask how, in practical terms, it would work. Our system rewards people who gather knowledge from disparate sources and then apply that knowledge within a market framework. That is where the patents and copyrights are generated. How can we now take traditional knowledge, which is often diffuse, and create mechanisms by which it can be protected and rewarded?

The mechanisms by which it can be rewarded already exist. They are called royalties, contracts, trademarks, appellation of origins, and trade secrets. All these mechanisms exist. The reason they have never been applied to indigenous peoples is because no one has ever asked, and because there is a concept that we can only protect private property, and not collective property.

Consider a community. A community consists of a number of individuals; those individuals share bits and pieces of common knowledge. Some individuals have specialized knowledge. Some take common knowledge and invent something new. Or, someone expresses a traditional, historical concept that no one else has. It is their unique inheritance. It is one of those cases in which one might say: My grandfather told me, and his grandfather told him, and his grandfather told him. Suppose I have that knowledge. How do you know if what I represent to you is my unique inventive act or something I learned from my great grandfather? It is impossible to know. The burden of it is on the other. If I say that I came up with this and present it in the patent office, they have to prove otherwise.

Someone can take out a patent on an invention not in his own name, but in the name of the community. Is that different from a corporation, which is a group of individuals, and in which one individual makes a unique inventive act which is then patented not in his name but in the name of the corporation? I think not. I see no difference whatsoever, especially given that many indigenous communities are already corporate entities. So, we already have a lot of legal instruments in place that can be used to protect traditional knowledge.

These legal instruments available to protect indigenous knowledge must be implemented. If they are not implemented, what must I say to indigenous people? In the Global Coalition for Biocultural Diversity we have indigenous groups, environmentalists, and scientists in 85 countries. The only thing I could tell this coalition would be to stop transmitting knowledge. As an anthropologist and an ethnobiologist, I can write scientific articles without ever revealing the scientific name of the plant I am talking about. I can write about a plant, describe it, and give its indigenous name. But in order for someone to learn the scientific name they would have to go to that community and get it. And the indigenous people are going to have to say, OK, you can have it.

If the indigenous people are informed about the implications of what they are doing, information can become restricted. Obviously there are always groups that are going to be fooled. There are individuals who are going to be corrupted and bought. No doubt about it. But since we now have less than .0001 percent of the profits from indigenous knowledge going back to the communities, the worst that could happen is that we would get at least one percent; that is already a thousand percent improvement.

Why do you think all these people from all these organizations at UNCED are interested in this issue? First, because they are afraid of bilateral agreements that would put them out of business. Second, because they know, even though they claim otherwise, that they need biodiversity. They say that they do not need biodiversity. "We have biotechnology," they say. "We can invent everything." So it is time to say, "OK, you are right, you can invent everything. And since you don't need any of this stuff sign on the dotted line a contract that says I agree to recognize and compensate indigenous peoples for their knowledge from this time forward."

You are talking about organizing indigenous peoples' communities around the world to strike.

They don't have to be organized. Many of them are already doing this. Western scientists are saying no. In the last meeting of the Society for Applied Anthropology, a number of leading scientists said they had to take on their shoulders the ethical responsibility for this. They have to educate their members about the ethical responsibility they must take for what they are writing.

Once I describe a plant and its use in a scientific publication, it is then in the public domain. Thereafter, indigenous people can never protect it. Scientists have never understood the implications of what they are doing by writing and putting this knowledge in the public domain. Many, if they did know it, would not do it. Including me.

Have you held back writing a series of articles because you do not want that knowledge abused?

Exactly. There are other ways you can hide it. Anthropologists, over the years, have invented names for communities and people in order to protect their sources of information and the communities they are describing. It is perfectly possible to record in enormous detail what it is that indigenous people are talking about, then give a plant a fictitious name. If some company is interested in the information, it can contact the community and negotiate. That is what I think many of us will be doing.

What if you have researchers from, say, the Smithsonian who are doing an inventory of the plant species in areas of the forest where indigenous people dwell. This is not applied research, but rather an inventory. Is the conflict over compensating traditional knowledge going to interfere with the inventory of species?

It depends where the inventory is made. It could be if the inventory is made in an indigenous area. Here we should talk about partnerships. These partnerships cannot just take place on paper at UNCED. They have to take place at all levels of society, and they have to take place in my life, your life, and everyone else's lives, whether they are scientists, politicians or environmentalists. If we are going to have environmental inventories in indigenous areas, we are going to have to explain to indigenous people why doing the inventory is important to us, and why it is important to them. If we can do that, they will be happy to help us, and we can then set out the contractual arrangements. You don't write a book for a publisher without a contract. I don't work for an institution unless I have a contractual arrangement. Why should indigenous people work with Western people without a contractual arrangement, when everyone else demands one?

What progress, if any, has been made on intellectual property rights at the U.N.?

There has been an enormous amount of movement. The first time I felt movement on this issue was last year when I came here for the working group on indigenous people. Annually, here in Geneva, in July or August, there is the U.N. Working Group on Indigenous Populations. Last year, in July, we were able to introduce into the formal U.N. system a proposal to include protection of intellectual property rights for indigenous people, as part of the Universal Declaration of Human Rights for Indigenous Populations. That was accepted and included. There was a background paper done on this, which brought the entire concept officially into the U.N. system. That set a precedent.

At the third Preparatory Committee session at UNCED, what we have been able to do is to discuss the issue in a very broad way on four or five occasions. Now we are asking that this Universal Declaration of Human Rights for Indigenous People be introduced into the UNCED plenary and that it become a central request for action by the U.N. secretariat to use this as a tool for change.

If we were fortunate enough to be sitting with the shamans Beptopoop and Kwyrà-kà, and they had been listening in on this discussion, how would they feel about the fact that we are talking about the placing of a material value on this sacred knowledge?

I think it is important to remember that we are not trying to place a material value on all of their knowledge. We are just saying that a small percentage of their knowledge, which for us would be large, has commercial value. This would be of great interest to them because they need economic alternatives.

The whole reason that I got into this is because I have lived and worked with the Indians on a daily basis for 15 years. I've gone through this entire process with them. I have seen them opt to sell lumber, mine (and pollute their waters with mercury in the process), and cut the forest to raise cattle. Why? Because there are no other options. They cannot live the way they lived 10 years ago. The children need to read and write to survive, or at least some do. They need lawyers to defend them in

Brasilia. They want to have radios, because it helps them to communicate between villages. They like to have video cameras, because they can record the images of their relatives, and send it to other villages since they do not have the ability to travel that we have. These are wonderful things for them that tend to strengthen their culture, not destroy it. But they need money for that, and if it is necessary to destroy the resources around them to do it, I am afraid that is what they will do, just as anyone else would. My concern is to help them find options.

I think the shamans will be very pleased to know that in the United Nations, in the highest world forum, we are discussing the relevance of indigenous knowledge and its importance in the world market. We could call a meeting on intellectual property rights and indigenous people and have representatives from ILO, GATT, WIPO, the Center for Human Rights, UNCTAD, UNCED and others. They would think this was really incredible; maybe our knowledge really is worth something. And I think that would give them the strength that many of them need to convince the younger generation that traditional knowledge, which was lost in the West due to the generation gap crisis, need not be lost.

What do you think about the forestry principles that are being discussed? Do we need an international legal instrument on forestry to stop deforestation? Is community control of forests a better approach? Need these two approaches be in conflict?

In the principles of the Forest Convention no one is willing to talk about local control, or land tenure, or who is going to implement whatever it is that they do about forests. Whatever is done I think we should do outside the existing technical expertise we currently have about forests. The existing technical expertise is inadequate, and in the case of foresters, negative. If I had to rank the most destructive forces in the Brazilian Amazon I would have to put foresters and agronomists above missionaries. These guys are terrible. What we are currently talking about at UNCED, in the forest convention, is empowering foresters. That is the last thing in the world we want to do. That is like handing over the chickens to the fox. Even the most enlightened forest convention I have read still treats the forest as some kind of special interest. But the forest does not exist in isolation. There are no such things as isolated forests, they exist as part of a larger environmental system. So I don't believe that even the concept of forests is valid.

One of the problems is that the we in the West tend to make a distinction between forests and agricultural areas. Indigenous people don't separate the two. Agriculture is a phase of forestry. You clear down a limited amount of forest, you cut it, you burn it, you use the ash. You plant domesticated plants in it because they grow fast and cover the earth and protect it from the sun and the rain. Then you begin to introduce, or allow to grow up, the natural reforestation sequence, some of which you cut as weeds, and some of which you favor by putting ash and fertilizer around it; or you plant seeds to develop into trees. The whole point is to plan the forest. Agriculture is the first phase because you put domesticated plants in; you do that because they grow quickly and cover and protect the soil. You start molding the resource system. Then you have a system that can go from 8, 10, 12, 30, to 40 years, depending on the soil and forest of a reforestation sequence. The concept of fallow, which we in the West still use, allows us to think that the first phase, agriculture, is important, and the last phase, tropical timber, is important, but that everything that happens in-between is unimportant. But for indigenous peoples this in-between state, which we in the West see as useless, represents 98 percent of their natural resource base. That is where they find the resources, and that is why they manage their forests. They are managing them for biodiversity. The areas where they have managed for 10 to 12 years are of higher diversity than the mature forests or the agricultural plots. They are increasing biodiversity and using 80 to 90 percent of all of the resources.

Do you mean that if the Indians had left the forest undisturbed there would be less biodiversity than after they cut it down, burned it, and planted it?

That is right. We have scientific proof of this. What is more amazing is that you can take a forest that has been managed under this system and it will have a higher soil fertility profile after this 40-year management cycle than before. That is even more revolutionary. There are no other systems that do that in the world. So why are we dividing up the structure of the world into forests and agriculture? Timber and crop products are only 2 percent of the species that are available to us.

Anil Agarwal suggests that an international forestry agreement is not a good idea because in fact the forests should be managed by the local people. Forests are different in different parts of the world, so there is no single, centralized global authority that should set out how they should be handled. Is that congruent with what you are saying?

That is exactly what I am saying.

Do you believe it would be better not to have an international forestry agreement?

If a forestry agreement took into account all the related environmental systems that feed into a forest, OK. If the forest agreement took into account that local communities could decide what they wanted to do with whatever they called forests, and those related ecological systems, then that would be an interesting prospect. Without those two elements it would not be interesting at all, because then it would only be a plan to empower foresters, who have proven in the past that they are incapable of helping to manage biodiversity. They are capable of destroying biodiversity and managing monocultures. They are not a positive force.

There are large portions of the world where people are not organized to protect their forests. If there were a global agreement, however im-

perfect, it might help.

I would not be against a global forestry agreement if there was some kind of local override. We could have environmental statutes that would determine what local communities could and could not do. We could set minimal standards. Local autonomy does not mean you can do anything. It is not permissible to cut down all the trees in your front yard just because you want to. It doesn't matter if you are an indigenous person or the mayor of the city.

What you seem to be suggesting is that an international agreement and community control are not mutually exclusive. We could have minimal international standards and local standards that are stricter.

Of course. As long as those standards had meaning. Then you get into the problem of what in the world "sustainable management" means.

You would also get into the problem that in many areas they would cut up to the minimal standards.

Right. That is why we are in a stalemate situation at UNCED. But, would people want to do that if all of a sudden those forests were valuable? We go back to the central question: Are we not talking about how to give value to local communities in the forest? Would the indigenous people want to cut the forest if they didn't have to? Why would Malaysia want to cut up to the minimum standard if the forests were worth more standing than cut? That is the key. Until we find the economic mechanism that gives value to the forest, all this other stuff is going to be logjammed.

In this respect the world has gone into the consumer mode even in China. The old chief Raoni, who travels with Sting, was asked 15 years ago by a colonel what he thought of Communism and Socialism. Raoni answered in halting Portuguese (but brilliantly put): "Well, I don't know much about these 'isms.' I have heard about Communism, Socialism, Capitalism and Consumerism. To the Indians the isms are all the same. All the isms want our land and our resources."

It appears you are at least as interested in preserving cultural diversity as biodiversity.

Biodiversity is an interesting concept if it can be merged with cultural diversity. What we should have is a convention for biocultural diversity. That would be an interesting convention. Then we could talk about how we could preserve the local communities and the biodiversity. Biodiversity as it is currently being discussed has very little to do with local communities. It has to do with the selection of areas that have the most species. It has to do with defining these areas with the goal of protecting them. Since we can imagine that these are going to be dominated by First World countries, we are talking about park models, which usually don't include people. We are not talking about how we make it interesting for the people near these areas to want to preserve them. We are not talking about how these areas can be used to serve the people who are around them; it is a very inadequate concept.

The "Man and the Biosphere" model is that you have a central area that is highly protected and then you have a buffer around it, and then you have a zone where extraction takes place and people are allowed to do what they want within certain limits, and then you have a zone for industry. You could have the opposite model where in the middle you have indigenous people, then a buffer to protect them and their resources.

Jason W. Clay:

Use Forests Sustainably or Lose Them

ason W. Clay is Director of Research for Cultural Survival. He is also Director of Cultural Survival Enterprises, the trading arm of Cultural Survival, and a Research Associate at Harvard University.

Steve Lerner: *Many people from the environment and development community are skeptical about the whole United Nations Conference on Environment and Development (UNCED) process. Some of them see it as a "black hole" for energy and resources that could be better directed at projects that are closer to the ground and have a more immediate payoff. What connection is there between the UNCED negotiations and your work helping indigenous people find a way to make a living without destroying their environment?*

Jason W. Clay: I participated in two of the U.S. roundtable discussions on UNCED put on by the Council on Environmental Quality (CEQ). One roundtable dealt with consumers, trade, marketing and the environment; the other had to do with indigenous people. I don't think that the UNCED roundtable discussions in the U.S. were done in such a way that citizens in this country had any input at all. The few not-for-profits that did have input were the ones with connections and the ones that knew about the process. But my sense is that a lot of the people who are doing the on-the-ground work in the U.S., and certainly in other parts of the world, never heard about these roundtables.

In Brazil UNCED has diverted the attention of some of the most qualified people away from the necessary tasks at hand so that Brazil can put on as good a face as possible for the UNCED summit. That bothers me. Brazil is in a crisis situation. The fires in the Amazon are picking up again this year and even if not all of them are in primary forests, too many of them are.

The groups in Brazil have a political opening now because of the new democracy there that has not really jelled yet. There isn't yet a national elite that dominates politics. The past 25 years of dictatorship pretty much destroyed previous political machines and coalitions, and they haven't been replaced yet. But in the next two or three years they will be replaced. Diverting all of the non-government organization (NGO) people's attention toward UNCED, and away from forming their own political lobbying group at a very critical time in Brazilian history is going to have real implications for policies that affect the Amazon.

Yet the formation of the Brazilian non-government organization (NGO) Forum — some 600 environment and development groups that have joined together to focus on the UNCED negotiations — is not a bad thing. In a sense this is a new network or lobby of environment and development groups.

But how many of those groups are actually affecting the lives of people on the ground? How many are run out of one person's office? How many of those are "ego NGOs": a single individual and maybe a cluster of followers? How many of them have a meaningful budget? How many of them are approaching issues that are substantial? There are not that many of them in Brazil that are doing substantial work. Another related issue that is causing problems is that international organizations are establishing offices in Brazil, often to facilitate communication. We at Cultural Survival are considering doing that ourselves. You want good people to run these offices so what do you do? The tendency in the past has been to raid Brazilian groups of the best people. That is not an appropriate thing to do. So in our efforts to establish an office, what we are looking for is Brazilians who have never been traditionally involved in these issues. We are looking for business, trade, financial management and accounting skills. One of the biggest problems with conservation in the Amazon is that the groups can't manage budgets, cash flow, and revolving credit funds. They can't do fund balances and fund accounting. Those things are very important. Without those skills they can't run a factory. Even if you can get the money to build a factory it is not going to be run well without these skills. We think we can bring that kind of person into the environmental movement in Brazil rather than stealing activists from other groups.

I think that UNCED is going to play out in such a way that it pits states against states. The best-case scenario is that southern states, probably led by Brazil, are going to say: "If you want us to save our rain forests, save the genetic diversity, save the areas that may have crop genes or medicinal plants, then pay us. You must pay a carbon tax or some type of remittance to us for saving these areas. That will provide us a way for our citizens to make a living."

The Group of Seven (G-7) industrialized states will say, "No, we don't want to do that. The per-capita production of carbon in the Amazon is 12 times higher than our per-capita production of carbon in the U.S. So forget it." It will be a battle fought in an us-against-them fashion, rather than states sitting around a table recognizing that we all have a common resource, the planet, and we have to figure out how to manage it, because all our lives depend on it. The representatives of the various states will thus be fighting among themselves, rather than following the admonition to "Be concerned about the future because you are going to be living in it."

Would you nevertheless agree that we do need the kind of negotiations going on under the auspices of UNCED? At UNCED, after all, the "world brain" is finally beginning to grapple with the need to halt environmental degradation by promoting sustainable development.

I question that. Who is the "we"? States do not represent people anywhere in the world, including in the U.S. — although it is much worse in many other countries. Until we build democracies from the bottom-up, rather than the top-down, any international structure that we build is going to end up with a top-down hierarchy. That is what UNCED is all about: It is a top-down series of negotiations by what you call the "brains of the world." But they are not the brains. They are the powerful. And they have specific ideas that often reflect self-interest.

I have heard this perspective from Anil Agarwal. He suggests, for example, that we should not have an international forestry convention. Rather, forests should be managed at the community level. People in positions of power in some distant place should not try to tell communities in diverse parts of the world how to manage their forests. However, we do currently face a global environment/development crisis. So does it not make a certain amount of sense that we should approach this problem through a negotiation among nation states? After all, nation states are a reality in terms of the power that they wield.

I think the power of states is being questioned everywhere in the world. The break-up of the Soviet Union is an assault on our notion of what a state is. Now there is an assertion of substate identities — national identities, cultural identities — that many thought had vanished 70 years ago. In fact, ideology turns out to be less important than culture in the world today. The emperor has no clothes. People are beginning to see that states have little legitimacy.

All the Soviet Republics want control over their resources because they know that that is where their future lies. I think increasingly the control of resources by the groups whose future depends on them is essential. I don't think we can have people on the other side of the world making decisions the consequences of which they are not around to see. We have seen too much of that kind of decision-making. That being said, I also don't believe that you just turn it all over to the local communities because they can make mistakes, too. But it is a question of relative emphasis.

The relative emphasis of UNCED has been to try to create a suprastate. The problem with that is that you are building it on a superstructure of 170 states that are not legitimate, that do not reflect the values, interests, concerns or votes in most cases, of the people they claim to represent. So how does the suprastate ever claim to represent the common person or the village?

You make a distinction between the larger "states" or countries that we are familiar with on the map and "nations," which are comprised of smaller groups that have a strong cultural identity. But it does not seem to me necessarily the case that international treaties by definition must run counter to the interest of these nations or groups of indigenous people. The treaties that come out of these international negotiations could have the effect of empowering communities in states that are less than democratic or less than representative. These international treaties, if they are properly shaped, could be used by local communities as a way to gain control over the sustainable use of their own resources.

Treaties, by and large, do not protect nations and never have. In fact the United Nations is about destroying nations. Under the League of Nations, following World War I, nations were protected under international law. Under the U.N., individuals and states are protected, nations are not. There is a working group within the U.N. on indigenous populations, but it is dealing with the smallest, most isolated remote peoples of the Amazon, the Kalahari Desert, etc. It does not include some of the largest nations, such as the Kurds of the Middle East or the Oromo of Ethiopia, which pose a threat to states.

States are run by a few elites who are going to define the peoples who are to be protected in such a way that it won't threaten the state. States are out for themselves and for their own livelihood. They are not interested in representing people. That is the distinction. States throughout the world have been created by other states to facilitate trade. And the buy-off, the way you keep these state systems going, is to pay the elites who rule them enough money that they keep them going. That is why nearly all the shooting wars in the world are in the Third World states. The U.S. model of a melting pot state is simply not going to be a reality in the Third World. We are not likely to get the people of Kenya to think of themselves as Kenyan and not ethnic Masai or ethnic Luao or whatever. Kenyans are just people who live in Nairobi.

We have had more treaties and conventions in this century than we have ever had regarding things like the environment and human rights. Despite all the treaties on human rights, we have had more genocide in this century than in any previous century. Have the treaties helped? I think it is arguable that they have not. I know that because of the treaties people are more aware of genocide, so maybe genocide is being reported more often. But I think we are in the final throes of trying to eliminate indigenous societies. The numbers are quite high in terms of how many we are eliminating. These people are not killed by lining them up and shooting them. It is much more subtle. It is denying the language, taking the kids away, and relocation that is eliminating indigenous people. Some 150 million people have been relocated as a result of "development" programs. These moves destroy people/land relationships that have evolved in a sustainable fashion for centuries.

Let's look at the Law of the Sea and how that might be a model for empowering communities. This is a law that gave states 200 mile off-shore territorial limits. The Law of the Sea brought fishing under state control. It has had disastrous consequences for every fishing village in the world because the 200-mile limit provides states with the impetus to sell the fishing rights to large state- or elite-dominated companies. Local villages are shut out. So, the traditional systems of managing these marine resources that are 200, 300, 500, or 1,000 years old are being destroyed overnight. Instead of traditional fishing methods, people are now coming in huge boats with huge nets and collecting all the fish. If you look at Indonesia, Malaysia, and the Philippines the impact of the Law of the Sea has been to destroy the marine resource base or degrade it severely.

That is why I am afraid of these international treaties. That is the kind of top-down treaty that does not work because it is created by the elites of these states and plays into their hands. And it is used by them. Now there may be other more benign treaties, such as the Montreal Protocol on protecting the ozone layer, but I am not convinced that they will be helpful. If we cannot even get acid rain legislation in the U.S. — where we can see the consequences and the causes of acid rain — if we can't correct this kind of problem in our own backyard, why are we going halfway around the world and trying to legislate solutions?

The recently passed Clean Air Act did something to mitigate acid rain. It is not entirely a fraud. But I take your point. Still, if you are not impressed with these large international treaties designed to slow environmental degradation and promote sustainable development, then what do you favor? Do you think that organizing at the community level will solve the global environment and development problems that we face?

My position on this is probably complicated and contradictory. There is no single solution. I think people have to work on all fronts. My concern about UNCED is that too much time and attention and too many resources are being focused on UNCED, and that other things are being excluded.

Environment and development problems took centuries to build up and the solutions will take at least decades to unfold. So I am personally going to focus my attention on working with indigenous peoples and with nations to help them retain the economic base that they require to survive. I think the people who have the most to gain or lose through the protection or destruction of a resource base are the ones who need to be given the most play in defending it.

Around the world there are people who are pushed onto smaller and smaller pieces of land, which means the land must be used in ways it was never used before. There are some problems, such as the problem posed by logging, that will probably require knowledge beyond the capacity of local groups. To find solutions on such issues there is a need for outside input. What we are talking about will require that some of the most traditional resource management systems interact with some of the most sophisticated modern systems.

Are the strategies of solving these problems through international treaties or by organizing local communities mutually exclusive?

Not at all.

Is it necessarily a bad thing to enter into an international treaty that would require nations to do something to halt global warming?

Is global warming itself the problem, or is it a symptom of a deeper problem? Global warming in its own right is a problem; there is no doubt about that. But it is not the underlying problem. What causes global warming? Specifically, in the U.S., it is the use of gas-guzzling cars that is causing global warming. Now, we are not going to do away with cars overnight, but let's get 40 miles to the gallon. Let's improve the system. We are not going to stop deforestation in the Amazon, but let's try to stop some of the burning and let's come up with alternatives, let's come up with income-generating schemes, let's spend our money on alleviating the kind of poverty that pushes people into the Amazon.

Isn't the global warming negotiation putting pressure on the U.S. to do something about its gas guzzling fleet of cars? I think it is. It has not been effective pressure yet. But the fact that the states of the world are grappling with this problem helps. We now read regularly in The Washington Post *and* The New York Times *that the U.S. has refused to set targets for the reduction of carbon dioxide emissions and that it is out of step with many other industrialized nations, which have come to the conclusion that we all must take concrete steps to minimize CO_2 emissions. That strikes me as useful.*

That's fine. But if you want to look at who is doing what, look at China and the Soviet Union in terms of CO_2 production from using high-sulfur soft coal. They may sign documents, but they will never live up to them. So what is the point of these international agreements? If you want to change the U.S. position on this, why don't we educate Americans? Why don't we start at home and work from the bottom-up? We don't need an international convention to force the U.S. to do something. Why don't we educate Americans to get the U.S. position to the point where it is leading the world towards an agreement, rather than being dragged into it?

I think this process works from both sides. I think it is useful to have the U.S. embarrassed on the international stage about its 23 percent contribution to the global carbon dioxide load that is contributing to global warming.

But why stop there? Why not talk about consumption in general?

I agree. The UNCED process should concentrate more on the fact that excessive consumption levels in the North are causing the environment/development crisis. International pressure should be brought to bear to make people in the North less wasteful of resources. But what I hear from you is that these international negotiations are a distraction, and that they are draining resources from the work that we really should be doing.

I guess it depends on what kind of world you want to live in. Do you want to live in a world that is governed by laws from the top down? Or do you want to live in a world that works more from a consensus built from the bottom up? It strikes me that much of what is wrong in the world, from soil erosion in the Midwest to overuse of pesticides, could be dealt with very effectively if consumers in the U.S. cared. So why don't we work on that side of the equation also? Consumers in this country are not just fouling our own waters. We are also fouling the waters of the world. And our consumption patterns are not just driven by IBM, AT&T, and Madison Avenue admen. Damn it, people want to buy things. The problem starts here at home. That is where we have to turn it around. Eventually, that means cutting consumption. But in the short term that is not going to happen. So we have to figure out what our vision is, and each of the steps to get there, because it is going to take a while. So in the short term let's offer some alternative products. Let's at least allow consumers to make connections between their consumption patterns and some of the problems they create halfway around the world. Then, as they see that connection, they will begin to see the effects in their own backyard.

A lot of the approach to the consumer movement in the U.S. — the Ralph Naders, etc. — has been focused on safety and health issues affecting Americans. I think that has been a typical, egocentric American approach. The consumer movement has failed to educate Americans about their role in the world. It has allowed Americans to be more isolationist. That type of approach has helped us to clean up our own backyard, no doubt, but has pushed the pollution into someone else's. We don't care that the asbestos is manufactured in South Africa, then sold to Korea where it is used to make brake linings for our cars, as long as the asbestos does not affect our workers.

A book published in the 1970s, *The Circle of Poison,* talked about contaminated meat and fruit coming to the U.S. with high levels of pesticides and other substances that we in the U.S. had banned. The book didn't really point out that when we reject this stuff at the border it goes back and is eaten by Third World citizens. We have to begin to look at that. And if the fruit is contaminated, imagine the environment in which it was grown. Imagine the quality of the water supplies that people are drinking in the country where this fruit was grown. It must be really polluted. We Americans have to get out of this egocentric view of the world.

That brings us to a fundamental issue that should inform all of this debate. Americans at best will be environmentalists. I am using the term "environmentalist" as someone who doesn't know anything about the environment and has to learn about it objectively. These are people who do not really see themselves as part of the environment. That is a real problem here. When you grow up on the tenth floor looking down on the world, it is a very different situation than if you grow up on a farm, much less in a rain forest, and know the relationship between rain and erosion, pesticides for crops and fish kills in the stream. If you are close to the environment you understand these relationships because you see them. If you flush paint down the toilet it is going to kill stuff somewhere else. I really don't think most Americans know that. So what the world is facing as we become more and more urbanized is how to teach people environmentalism when they don't see themselves as part of a living environment.

Negotiations are proceeding on biodiversity. Have you been following them, and how would you describe the progress of these negotiations?

I don't feel qualified to discuss that because I don't follow it very closely. But let me tell you a little bit about biodiversity. My sense is that we don't know what biodiversity is because we don't care. If we care about something as a society we find out about it pretty damn fast. We know how many shares are traded each day on the New York Stock Exchange and we know the price of gold in cultures throughout the world. But we have lived for hundreds of years on this planet with science and still not figured out how many plants and animals there are, much less how many we are losing every day. So, clearly, we don't care about it. If suddenly people start caring about biodiversity, that triggers a few alarm bells for me because it means that somebody has decided that there is money to be made or lost on it.

What we do know about biodiversity, which is driving certain of the funding sources, such as the MacArthur Foundation, is based on a few incomplete forays into the forest. Our assumption is that the hotspots of the world (where there is the greatest density of biodiversity) are in certain areas. But that may just be because that is where all the research has been done; in fact there is good evidence to suggest that this is the case. A study that just came out of Brazil concluded that the more days scientists spend in the forest, the more diverse it is found to be. That stands to reason. Yet a lot of funding has been focused on hotspots that may not be particularly hot when compared with other areas that have not been studied. That is not to say that these areas are not fairly dense. But it is clear that we have not got a clue about the extent of biodiversity.

We are losing between one and a hundred species a day as we sit here and have this conversation. We can't save the world's biodiversity. This is where some of this top-down thinking needs to take place. What areas are we going to save? What are the most important regions? If the only criteria for choosing those regions to be saved is that they have the most genetic diversity based on this questionable evidence, then I think we are really up a creek. We need to choose the areas we protect. We need to choose areas that have traditionally proved to be the source of the most medicines, the most plant genetic resources, the most food crops. The Americas are the source of 60 percent of the world's food crops, so we damn well better be concerned about Brazil, and Colombia, and Central America. Most of the grains as well as a lot of fruits come from inner Asia. We had better be concerned about those areas just from the perspective of our current economy and food system. If we start having blights or diseases or pests, we will need to be able to go back to the genetic stock. So these are the areas we have to be concerned about.

We also need to ask: What is attacking the genetic diversity of the world? I think it is poverty. By poverty I mean a lot of things. I don't just mean that the problem is poor people cutting down a lot of trees. I mean that the problem is a system that creates poverty. Indigenous people are not poor when they come in contact with the West. They become impoverished. It is having resources stolen from them that causes the problem. It is being discriminated against in the marketplace. So issues of environmental degradation cannot be divorced from issues of social equity. The two are locked together in a dance to the death.

Intellectual property rights (IPR) could be used to bring some resources back to indigenous people so that they would not be forced to destroy the environment that supports them. You mentioned that Cultural Survival, while it has played middleman in an effort to help indigenous people find a market for non-timber products, has not traded in medicinal plants. The reason you gave was that a system was not in place to compensate indigenous people for their medicines. Is it the debate over intellectual property rights that must be concluded before you feel you will be able to help indigenous people get a fair return for their plants, and the knowledge about the medicinal use of those plants?

A lot of the debate over IPR has focused on securing for the state the money that would come from the sale of these plants and knowledge. Brazil would get the rebates for Amazonian genetic materials and medicinals. To me that is not right. Brazil has done everything it can to destroy the Amazon and get rid of the people there who have often identified, used, and in fact created compounds that have medicinal values. Anywhere else in the world a scientist who did that would have rights — maybe exclusive rights, and certainly co-patents, royalties, licensing agreements, or profit-sharing.

I think the precedent that Merck pharmaceutical company has established in Costa Rica is extremely dangerous. Merck has set up a system where it pays an exploration fee to an NGO and the Costa Rican government for access to a national park. This park area is not inhabited. Yet this system establishes the precedent of the state receiving the right to compensation for genetic materials exported to the North.

Under English law, and American law also, I believe, a community can own a resource base and claim rights to it even if it hasn't exploited it, as long as it has protected it. This case first came up in the U.S. over some clam beds in New England where a community hadn't harvested them but had not polluted the waters and had not destroyed this resource. So when a fishing fleet came in and took it, the community could charge them to do so. I don't know if this works in Latin America under Napoleonic law, but there might be a similar mechanism. At the very least, if an Indian group has medicinal knowledge that is taken out of the forest and patented in St. Louis by Monsanto, we can make a class action suit against Monsanto in the U.S., on behalf of that indigenous group, to negotiate the rights to some of the profits.

The strategy is not to put the pharmaceutical companies out of business, but rather to work out a system that protects the pharmaceutical company investment in the development of a drug — which is often quite expensive —as well as protecting the rights of the people who originally discovered it, or who are providing the raw material. It is our assessment that what we need is an industry-wide standard that assumes these rights of nation-peoples as a cost of doing business, and simply adds it to the price of the drug. It is not a difficult thing to do. They do it already with scientists and many other people.

Give me an example of how this would work.

Let's look at the example of a compound that a group in western Brazil discovered and developed as an anticoagulant. It was a substance they put on their blow-gun darts that caused an animal to bleed to death. That compound is being developed as a drug for open heart surgery and has tremendous medical and market potential. It is a compound that this group discovered after much trial and error. Under most legal systems the group's interest would be protected, because theirs was clearly an act of invention. But, currently, the drug has no protection.

There are other situations that are not as clear cut. Let's say a traditional group has identified a single plant that has a certain property. And they have, over centuries, cultivated that plant or selected from that plant the properties they like best and adapted that single plant from its wild brothers and sisters. That would be protected under another type of right, not as clear cut as the first case.

What the smart ethnobotanists and pharmaceutical companies are doing now is finding the parts of the world where native peoples are using plants from the same family for the same kinds of diseases. In this case you can bet you have a medicine. Those indigenous groups should get something, but not as much as in the more clear-cut cases.

Then you have the situation where people have used a plant for one thing and a pharmaceutical company comes along and uses it for something else. In this case the indigenous peoples would have even fewer rights. Finally, you have the case where it is just a plant in the forest, but

the forest was protected by the people. They didn't destroy it or eliminate that plant, so they have some rights to it, at least under English law
— but much less right. That is the spectrum as I see it.

How has case law been evolving in this area?

The first case that we wanted to bring to court we decided we could
not ethically support. It would have to be a class action suit on behalf of
the group in the western Amazon that has used a compound they discovered as an anti-coagulant. There are less than 50 of these people left.
None of them speaks Portuguese, although they live in Brazil. One of
the members of this tribe would have to be present in a U.S. courtroom
for a class action suit to proceed. And it would not be right to bring one
of them out of their environment. They have never been in an airplane.
The court will not accept any other Indian from Brazil, or a videotape.
That would have been an ideal test case because it was clearly a compound. But our concern is that if we brought a member of this group out,
he would never be the same. The trial could take years. It would be such
a crass thing to do. But, the press would be interested, and the pressure
brought to bear on that company to make an out-of-court settlement
would be enormous.

In the final analysis what is really in question here is not just the
intellectual property rights of the people in the forest, but the ability of a
pharmaceutical company to patent something that has already been
used. If you can demonstrate that something has been used in another
place, then the company has no right to patent it in the U.S. Pharmaceutical companies are scared that this could jeopardize their 20 years of
development of the drug, which is why we would want an out of court
settlement.

*Can we expect that there will be a whole series of class action suits of
this nature?*

Yes, this issue is going to come up; but this particular example may
never be tried.

*At that point will Cultural Survival become interested in finding mar-
kets for some of these medicinal compounds and botanicals used by indigenous people?*

Yes. That is where the real value of the forest is — that and genetics.
We are already involved with the genetic material of foods. For example, we at Cultural Survival have begun to talk to spice companies
and chocolate companies about the fact that the genetic base or origin of
almost all spices (not herbs) such as chocolate, vanilla and coffee comes
from tropical forests. We have trademarked "Forest Flavors." Any company that puts that label on their package has to pay us a percentage (say
1 to 5 percent) on all the raw materials they use, as well as a percentage
of the profit. That money would go back to the South to make sure that
the genetic base of that particular spice or flavor is protected in its
natural setting. So for chocolate, for example, that would be to the

western Amazon and Colombia because that is where chocolate came from. For coffee, it is Ethiopia. And for nutmeg, cloves, mace, cinnamon and vanilla, it is the rain forests of the Philippines, Malaysia, Indonesia, Madagascar, and even Brazil.

But I think we can do this without international legislation. I think we can do this by getting one company to sign on. It's similar to the effort to protect dolphins when catching tuna. When one company announced it would use nets that would not trap dolphins, within six hours two other major companies signed on. They could not afford to be the ones who were killing dolphins. It is the same with this. My sense is if we get one spice company to sign on, they are all going to sign on. It can be an industry-wide standard. You get one chocolate company to sign on and the others will follow: Hersheys, M&M's, Cadbury's and Nestlé. When one of those signs the others will follow. Someone will convince them it is in their interest. It is a public relations thing. They will make money on this. The first company that sets this industry standard is going to get a lot of press. The other companies will be just covering their assets.

In your Smithsonian sponsored lecture you suggested that to protect rain forests we have to find ways to make them productive. You used the phrase: "Use it or lose it." That runs counter to a lot of myths those of us in the North have about rain forests as pristine jungle areas that are largely uninhabited, except for a few small tribes of traditional people.

Most people think that Indians are just not in the market. They are not buying and selling commodities. That is also a myth. Every indigenous group that I have worked with, and the vast majority of the rest of them, sells or trades something because they all need to buy things.

But suggesting that the way to preserve rain forests and preserve biological diversity is to make the rain forests productive, in terms of marketable goods for the people who inhabit these areas, is a relatively new concept, is it not?

It gets back to the point that we are going to lose some of the rain forest. You have to accept that. There is not a single habitat that people have lived in without losing some of it. Botanists say that there are not 10 square kilometers of rain forest anywhere in the world that have not been altered by people. That blows most people's idea of a rain forest. For hundreds of thousands of years people who live in the rain forest have been chopping down trees that don't provide them with food and allowing something else that is more useful to them to grow in their place.

Darrell Posey argues that the indigenous people in the Amazon have, for centuries, been practicing a kind of resource management that improves the fertility of the soils. He goes so far as to say that they manage for greater biodiversity. Do you agree?

No. I'm not an expert on this but I keep my ears open. In the Cambrian and Pre-Cambrian period there was a flourishing of biodiversity.

The geologists and paleontologists say now that there was more diversity then, and that it has been diminishing since. I think that for at least the last 1.5 million years, or perhaps always, the dominant species has tended to eliminate biodiversity. That can mean plants as well as people — trees for ferns, etc. So I think I would disagree with Posey. I think indigenous people manage for diversity, but for greater diversity? No. Because I think they are managing for the diversity that they want. And what they want is what they know about.

For instance, tomatoes in the wild, the genetic base for cultivated tomatoes, have all 20 of the amino acids. Beans are similar. But the one tomato that was selected by Indians in the Americas, in the pre-conquest period, had only one of those 20 amino acids. So what they selected was a deficient food source that then had to be eaten in combination with other sorts of starches to get the type of protein that you need. People don't always manage resources for the best, because they don't have the knowledge, or the desire because it doesn't taste as good, or it takes too much labor.

That is why I would argue that we don't just need local control of these resources. We need the most up-to-date science in conjunction with local control. We need both systems. Yet I am concerned about the state system setting up a suprastate umbrella. I would rather see NGOs do that. I would rather see a lot more power in the non-governmental sector. That being said, I would be the first to point out that there is not a single NGO officer who is elected. We members of NGOs are not a representative group of anybody. All of us are self appointed. So let us not kid ourselves. This is not a democratic system we are talking about.

Tell me about the role of Cultural Survival in helping indigenous people find markets for their non-timber products in order to help preserve both the rain forest and a diversity of cultures within it.

Our strategy is that we need to change trading relations. We need to ensure that the producers of the raw materials get more back from the manufacturers. If they do get more of a return, that will slow or maybe even halt the destruction of a lot of this resource base. It will also help preserve the cultural diversity if these indigenous people have an economic base.

How effective could this effort be to provide northern markets for rain forest products? If we all start eating Rainforest Crunch and we all start using these products, will it protect the rain forest?

This is a short-term strategy, not a long-term process. For one thing, there probably will not be enough of these products for everyone to eat. But in the short term I think we can identify those areas being destroyed that are biologically and culturally diverse. And we can support their preservation through consumption patterns that use sustainably produced rain forest products. That is why we are talking about Brazil, parts of Indonesia, and parts of Malaysia and the Philippines where there is a lot of biological diversity that is going down the tubes very fast. That is why we want to work in certain parts of Africa where the same kind of thing is happening. In all these places you have cultural diversity pitted against biological diversity. But it is not an either-or situation; it can be both.

Are you referring to the park approach to preservation of biological diversity, where people are kept out of certain areas?

That is the Nature Conservancy view. They want to get rid of the people in these areas and build fences around them. That is how they justify buying land.

How did Cultural Survival get started?

Cultural Survival was founded in 1972 by anthropologists who were outraged that the societies they were working with, somehow, in the name of progress, had to be destroyed. These cultures were being steamrolled into the 20th century and eliminated. The anthropologists did not think this was inevitable. They thought it would be possible to have Indians living as Indians in the modern world, and yet be part of the modern world on their own terms. So the vision of Cultural Survival from the outset has been that there could be a world of difference. The original focus of Cultural Survival was on small societies of a few thousand people.

We have since begun to work on why these groups disappear. And that is why our programs have focused on land rights and resource rights, and helping groups reorganize after having been de-organized by states. We work at figuring out how these groups can make a living in the modern world. We focus on how they can trade, sell, or barter products to get what they need to have better health, better education, or whatever. We are interested in what skills they need in the modern world that will not destroy or degrade their resource base. This requires working with them and providing them with technical assistance,

Give me an example of an intervention you have made to help one of these groups.

There is a group called the Kayapo Indians in Brazil. Right now the two main ways for them to earn income are selling mahogany logs and selling gold mining rights. One of the things we have worked on with the Body Shop — which funded the program — is a system that uses a press so the Kayapo can harvest Brazil nuts, press them into oil, and sell the oil to the Body Shop. They make a lot of money doing this because the Body Shop pays them a fair price. The Body Shop also pays a Kayapo women's cooperative to make bracelets that they sell in their stores. This is just a small thing with one culture. But it allows them to use traditional skills and interests to make a living in the modern world without degrading their resource base.

Another example is our work with the Huichol Indians of Mexico who make benches and earn 300 times more per log because they use carpentry to turn the lumber into products instead of selling the raw log. They have better lives, retain their own culture, and cut fewer trees so that reforestation can occur naturally.

Do you help groups lobby the Brazilian Government for better enforcement of their rights?

Some groups are becoming quite sophisticated in terms of land rights. But the Yanomami in Brazil, who are very isolated, aren't really prepared to lobby on their own behalf in the capital, Brasilia. Cultural Survival was able to support a law group in Brasilia with profits from trading Brazil nuts. This law group took a case to court that was one of the landmark civil rights cases. The finding in the case basically said that Brazil has a new Constitution, the Executive Branch is in charge of protecting indigenous areas, and those areas have been invaded by gold miners. The judge found that it was the Government's responsibility to get them out, and in three months 45,000 gold miners were gone. The case was won. To get the gold miners out required that one branch of the Government forced another branch to carry out this program. But it was the Brazilian Supreme Court that made the decision.

Cultural Survival also bought a computer for the largest human rights movement in Brazil with money we generated through publicity surrounding our trade in forest products. This is a very sophisticated $100,000 computer. It allows this human rights group to take all the maps of Indian areas in Brazil — about 11 percent of Brazil's surface area — and feed them into the computer where they are digitalized. Then they can take satellite photos and scan them to see where the areas have been invaded by settlers. They also plot out who owns the land adjacent to the Indian reserves so that when the invasion occurs they know the person who is responsible and they can take that person to court. As a result, years do not pass during which a house is built, pastures are established, and claims are made that the settlers have been there for years. It will take a couple of years before the entire system is in place, but this is the kind of use of modern, sophisticated technology in the defense of indigenous rights that is possible.

Some groups are extremely isolated and cannot speak for themselves. Other groups are getting to the point where they don't want others speaking for them. So our role is to open the door, but not walk through it. Let the indigenous people walk through it themselves.

Many of the schemes that you are talking about are essentially export oriented.

That is how they appear from the perspective of what I am doing. Our position on this is that Brazilians are not going to consume many products from the Amazon unless people in New York, Paris, and London consume them. There is a cultural dependency that exists. That is one of the rationales for exporting these products. The other is that we do not think it is our role to create markets in Brazil for these products. We think it is the role of the Brazilians.

What we are trying to do is get a processing plant up and going that produces quality products for international exporting. Then it can be sold wherever. It can be sold locally or internationally. Within months of when the first product, Rainforest Crunch, began to be distributed, I was talking to a Brazilian who has founded an environmental group. She said that there should be a Brazilian company doing this. I told her to go for it, and that Cultural Survival would give her whatever help we could. A Brazilian company is going to make two million candy bars similar to Rainforest Crunch. They are going to donate the profits to rubber tappers and the environmental lobby. These things can take place. But outsiders can't set it all up because if people don't own the process, they don't own the result. And if they don't own it, it won't work. It will just be a subsidy of one type or another.

There is an issue that remains, however, about whether traditional societies should be encouraged to plant crops that they sell or crops that they can use themselves. Would it not be better for these groups to become even more self-sufficient than they already are, and grow what they need, rather than depend on producing a crop either for sale to other parts of Brazil or other parts of the world?

I would agree in principle with the promotion of bio-regional self-sufficiency, but not with a rigid definition of what that is. We have to have a vision, but we also have to figure out how to get there. The vision may be more self-sufficiency. But that is not going to happen overnight. Besides, you never have complete self-sufficiency because the world is interdependent. In some ways it is good to have indigenous people selling a product. We create jobs both in Brazil and in the U.S. out of this export of Brazil nuts. That is not bad. What we have to look at now is how much energy we use to transport commodities and whether or not there is a net protein drain. These are the kinds of issues that we need to begin to address.

There may even be ways to deal with that issue. For example, one of my goals with Brazil nuts is to turn most of them into oil to be used in the cosmetic industry — oil that is of very high value. Oil is easier for shipment than the nuts themselves and the profit margin on cosmetics is much higher than on food items. What you are left when you press Brazil nuts into oil is a flour by-product that has more protein than meat. We can add that flour to pasta and bread and use it in school lunch programs for kids in Brazil.

Why is it that the development groups have not been performing the function that you have taken on as a conduit for rainforest products?

Many people, and this includes U.S. Agency for International Development (USAID) and the World Bank, see development projects as an end in themselves. In some ways it is like reforestation schemes where you pay a person to plant a tree. From my point of view it is better to guarantee a price for a product from the tree, focusing on value rather than production volume. That way you make sure that the tree not only is planted but that it survives to produce. It is a question of emphasis. Do you want to say, "we planted 20,000 trees," or do you want to say "we bought 40,000 pounds of, say, apples?" It is a different approach. The traditional development approach is to ask how many hectares have been planted; the question is not usually: How productive are those hectares? Taking that one step further, it is not enough just to produce. One must ask, what is the value of what has been produced? What are these development groups doing to ensure that producers get good prices for their product? You only need to use half as much of the resource base, if you get twice the price for it, to have the same level of income.

One of the reasons USAID and the World Bank and those kind of entities have not really looked at price is that very quickly it would have an impact on where the money is coming from. If you pay producers twice as much, then it is going to be passed on to consumers who are mostly in the points of origin of AID or the World Bank money in western Europe, the U.S., Japan, and Canada. Ultimately, we are talking about the transfer of resources through this kind of marketing approach. This is not just true at the international level. Raw material producers around the world are getting a "raw deal". Midwestern farmers in the U.S. only get 7 percent of the value that is being added to their product. Brazil nut collectors get 2 to 4 percent. And that is what has to change. If those producers, those people who are the most connected to the environment, are being impoverished or kept at a very low level of income, then they are going to degrade the resource base. And they are the first line of defense for the resource base. It is like paying the users of a product to conserve it, in a way. You are supporting that conservation by increasing the price you are paying to the producer. You are not supporting preservation, and that is a very important distinction. The saying should not be "use it or lose it"; but rather "use it without abusing it."

Oren R. Lyons:

Sustainable Life-Styles of Indigenous People

ren R. Lyons is a chief of the Onondaga Nation. He is also a member of the Executive Committee of the Global Forum of Spiritual and Parliamentary Leaders on Human Survival, and of the International Indigenous Commission.

Steve Lerner: *You mentioned that when you were young you were put in jail for not going to school.*

Oren R. Lyons: Well, they caught me for not being in school because I was fishing every day. I didn't like several teachers who were making life painful for me. They were doing it deliberately and I knew it. I said to myself: "Why should I have to go through all this?" I will just go fishing. So I spent some great instructional time in the woods, you know, by the creek, by myself. I got very good at writing excuses for myself and handing them to my mother and the school. Nobody knew where I was half the time.

But they finally caught me and I was really captured. I must have been 14 years old or so. They dragged me in front of this guy who sat there. I remember he was chewing a cigar and looking down at the desk. He was a white man, you know, and I was aware of that. He said: "Well, boy, why are you running away from school?" And I would not answer because how do you explain all that to teachers and everything. "Ah," he said. "That's why. You dumb Indians. You can't talk. You don't want to go to school. You don't want to learn nothin'. You're just stupid."

I was really angry. And I was measuring the distance between him and me, figuring, well, at least I will get one good punch at him before they nail me. I was literally measuring the distance, I was so angry. Then he started laughing, you know. And, reading my mind, he said: "You think you can do it?" And I didn't care because I knew I would get one punch in. But he said: "Well, you dumb people. You dumb people. You are just a problem. And we are going to put you where you will learn how to understand things. We will make you understand things. And maybe then we will talk."

And I made up my mind right then. I said: "We'll talk then. I'll learn your language. I'll learn your language and I will talk. But when I talk you might not like what I've got to say."

So he really got to you, didn't he?

He sure did.

What is your primary work now?

My primary work and concern lies with the Onondaga Nations and the Haudenosaunee, the Grand Council. I am one of the chiefs of the Onondaga Nation, Turtle Clan, Faith Keeper. And, of course, our nation has all of the problems that any community has, so the chiefs are called upon to do a lot. We have our Grand Council, our National Council, which is a division of powers and is an early form of bicameral government. It provides a forum for political exchange and decisionmaking. We reach agreement by consensus, by discussion, and by accommodation. Fundamentally that is our government structure. We have to do all of that in the process of running a community. We also have to deal with the national issues that surface concerning the Onondaga nation. And we have to gather ourselves when subjects such as federal taxes, environmental concerns, or national issues involve the Haudenosaunee itself. We also have to move in the broadest arena, the international field. So those are the arenas that we work in.

Within the nation itself, we all belong to various medicine societies, so we are called upon for that kind of involvement. There is a constant pressure on the individual to give. You spend all your time with and for the people. We are not paid. The Council does not receive any money. All this is done of our own free will. We receive traveling funds, if they are available.

I have also been a teacher at the University of Buffalo for the past 21 years. I am an American History teacher with a decided slant, which I announce to everybody. I enjoy it. It is an opportunity to catch a lot of our Indian kids before they get completely brainwashed by another society. We catch them there and we have produced some wonderful individuals with our program at the University of Buffalo. It is a Native American program that looks after all of the Indians that come through the area. We have different classes we teach within the University community. We have a lot of influence there. The University of Buffalo is one of the largest universities in the country because of its outreach. It is a great huge plant. I've been there a long time. At first I didn't think I was going to be a teacher, but I am. And I do not mind it. I keep a close hand on the pulse of the young people and what they are thinking and how they feel. That is very important. I commute from the Onondaga nation, which is about 150 miles from Buffalo. I prefer living on our own territory. All my family is there.

What is the International Indigenous Commission ?

That is an organizing, information gathering, facilitating commission that is a non-governmental organization (NGO) based in Geneva to help indigenous people prepare for the international meeting in Brazil in 1992.

So this is a group that came together specifically as a result of the United Nations Conference on Environment and Development (UNCED) process?

Pretty much. Where it will go from there we are not sure. Whether it is permanent or not we don't know. It is vital to our organizing because we don't see our South American brothers very often. And when we do we have to coordinate our activities.

Is this the first time there has been an international indigenous network?

No, we have been coming to the U.N. in Geneva since 1977. But it is the first time we have tried to organize really specifically around these issues. And we need it because UNCED is a huge operation. Next time, at the fourth Preparatory Committee meeting in New York in March, 1992, UNCED will be coming to Indian Country. And we will try to see if the Indians get served at all. As you have observed here, it is very difficult to even get to speak. You just heard us battling for a few opportunities to speak and it is tough. Countries don't want this voice of indigenous people to be heard. The intrigue here at U.N. headquarters in Geneva is stupendous. The intrigue is a fact of life here and everybody knows it and works with it. But it makes life difficult for people like us who don't have the infrastructure to absorb time and money and mistakes. A mistake for us here really costs us.

The issues of UNCED, the environmental issues, the political issues, the economic issues that are surfacing, the power plays that are going on among countries, the differences in perspective between the so-called Third World and the Western industrial states, the power structure, are different from the discussions that we have with indigenous people.

We are operating at a lower level. We are involved with all of this, sometimes directly, but most of the time indirectly. The way states perceive it, it is not in their interest to have to deal with the indigenous perspectives at all — whether they are developing nations or the U.S. or Canada. We indigenous people are a difficult subject matter for states. Indigenous means original, it means you come from the land, you have priorities, you have rights, you have the aboriginal rights to territory. That it is very difficult for nation states to recognize.

Watching the events that occurred in Iraq permitted one to see very clearly the attitude toward the Kurds, who are an indigenous people. You could see clearly the attitude of Turkey and Iran toward the Kurds. The Kurds were stacked up on the border dying in the rain and snow with no one caring and everybody very careful about what they said. The U.S., in particular, was careful. Seeing this the Indians were saying: "If that is your position with the Kurds, then what is your position with us?"

So we are not a commodity here at the U.N. that nation states like to deal with because we are in a sort of a no-win situation.

In an official sense you are among the unrepresented groups, along with the Tibetans and others.

Yes indeed. That is a major issue here. UNCED accredits organizations and NGOs. But we certainly will not subject our nations to a non-government organization status. That disenfranchises us from the discussion because there is not a specific place for us. We are requesting special accreditation for indigenous nations and peoples. That is a major step and if they take that step it will help us and clarify things. Relations are not altogether hostile. We have some friendly people in nations who really support this initiative. Because if one thing is clear it is that the voice that knows what is going on about environment comes from the indigenous people.

In the course of the UNCED deliberations one hears talk about creating an alternative system that is more in harmony with nature than mainstream society. But indigenous peoples' traditional life-styles have always been in harmony with nature; this characteristic almost defines indigenous culture. Indigenous people argue that instead of reinventing a system that is in harmony with nature, we should focus on protecting indigenous groups, giving them clear rights to the territories in which they live. Is this message being heard at UNCED?

I think your description is very good. Essentially what you say is true. The missing parts of it are that it does not fit in the economic loop of nation states. The attention that the major corporations give to sustainable development is nothing but lip service. The forces that drive modern society are the market forces and the forces of profit. That is, I guess, where we differ.

Frankly I don't see any solution to the global environmental crisis. I don't see the nation states suddenly waking up tomorrow, after being touched on the head by the good fairy, and saying: "Well now. We have been doing all these bad things all our life here and we really have got to be concerned about the coming generations. It is about time we just revised our whole structure." That is not going to happen. No. I mean, obviously, it is not going to happen. To really, literally expect that to happen is living in that fairyland I just talked about.

So, what is the reality then? I perceive the structure, the process of, well, I guess you'd call it capitalism or industrialism or whatever. To me it looks like a horse race. You might imagine that this particular horse race involves all of the Sneaker People. So we have a race going on between Adidas and Reebok. In this race the jockeys are the CEOs — the ones who run these corporation horses. Now, what is the race? Well, it is a competitive race to be Number One; everybody is striving to be Number One. The jockeys who are up, these CEOs, they are not monsters. They are human beings. They have families. The are quite friendly, quite nice people, at times, if you get a chance to meet with them once in awhile. Often they are churchgoing people who recycle their newspapers. They do all that. I even talked with a vice president who ran a Boy Scout troop in the evening.

So, then, what is the problem here? Is it that they don't understand? No, they understand precisely. But they are jockeys up on horses; they cannot for a moment or a second be reined in. If that horse is reined in, they are going to be overrun. Number Two becomes Number One. Number Three becomes Number Two. And maybe they stumble, they go down, and they become like Keds, way back somewhere trying to catch up, but still in the race. Or else what? If they are not in the race they are out.

As a matter of fact, this race is out of control at the moment. All over the world, in all of the areas, this race is out of control. Now, these jockeys who are up watch a horse go down. They know all the damage that happens to the jockey who goes down. But the most they can give that event is a glance. There is no intention on their part to stop, pull over, get off, and help him up. Why? Because they would lose. They have a responsibility to a certain group of people: the stockholders who are sitting there, who are demanding this profit.

And who are the stockholders? They are just people. A lot of them are just very ordinary people. And sometimes they are people, you would be surprised, whom you would term poor. But, you come to find out that they are holding stocks and they are all somehow trying to secure a piece of reality, or security in this life. And that is what it is all about.

Fear.

It is fear. Yes, it is driven by fear. Now, is that a good system? Well, I don't think it is a good system, because it doesn't allow for any practical impulses such as looking about and seeing what condition the track is in. You know? Let's look at it this way. In the distance you can see a big wall. Do you think they are going to slow up for that wall? No. They are going to run full force into that wall. Even seeing it. Even looking at it. And if at the last moment...I mean, what is the alternative? Are they going to sit and say, "Look here. Let's negotiate a situation here, all you jockeys now, wait a minute. Shall we all negotiate to stay in the same place and go over and help this person get back on and start our race again?" There is no discussion in that direction. But there is some concern at the moment because the track is getting pretty rough now. There are a lot of holes in the turf. They are having to run very much more carefully.

So do you think we are looking more now to indigenous people because their model has proved more sustainable?

I think people will look at it in a very cursory way. I don't think most people are looking at the indigenous model as an alternative system. I think they only look at it as maybe a way to patch up a few holes and allow us to stay mounted. No, I don't think so. But let's say that the fences that are holding the spectators from the racing field are receiving a lot of pressure at the moment. Now what can happen is that those fences can break down and the spectators will all come onto the track and disrupt the race.

The horse race that you are describing is the dominant culture now.
Absolutely. Everybody bought into it.

If you go to India, Argentina, Canada, places where there used to be indigenous people with very strong cultures, they are no longer the dominant culture. What do you feel the indigenous people have to teach us that will help us toward a true form of sustainable development that is practical and applicable in the world today?

(Laughter) Well, what is practical and applicable is the indigenous system. That is the only practicality there is. We have made some tremendous interventions here. We have challenged Christianity.

I heard you call on the delegates to bring the fish, the birds, and the trees into the room where the UNCED negotiations were going on and let them be represented also.

Beyond that, what I said was that the Judeo-Christian religion is responsible to a great extent for the problems we are having today, because they have covenants that exempt them. They also have a process of redemption. They can go and be redeemed, once a week or even three times, as many times as they want. But what is this redemption for? Well, let's say a particular person is the president of a chemical corporation that has been pouring toxic wastes into Niagara River. Now, he feels very bad about this. He knows that this is water that people drink, and that he is responsible. He feels so bad about it that on Sunday he goes to church and he says: "Please forgive me." And they say: "OK, I'm glad you came here." They pat him on the head and he goes out and he now feels a little better. Nothing has changed in the river. So, here is something that has occurred in a person's mind, but in reality nothing has changed. What I am saying is that this covenant of exclusion and forgiveness builds into the human mind the idea of a limitless frontier.

Maximo Kalaw, Jr. from the Haribon Foundation in the Philippines says something along the same lines. He quotes a tribe from the southern Philippines that dates big environmental problems to the time when the Christians came and placed God too high up in the sky. God was so high up in the sky, they said, that people could no longer recognize the sacred in trees, people, or other aspects of nature.

That is a very common-sense observation. Indigenous people all over have a very strong belief in the Creation, in the Creation process, and in the power of an Ultimate Authority beyond human beings. Everywhere I have gone indigenous people believe this; they also understand the process and the cycles of life. So, any kind of development is going to have to follow a cyclical process. It cannot follow the linear process that is currently driving the forces of this world and the market. Development is going to have to fit into a cyclical process; it is going to have to correspond to the powerful cycles of life. If the forces of development do not understand that, if they don't have enough of a belief in it, then the last source of salvation for humanity and future generations is that the people themselves will have to rise up and change it.

You have been to New York City. You have been to Geneva. You have been to mega-cities all over the world. We are not going to return to the small village, the sweatlodges....

I don't think you have to. Technology is an extension of the human mind. The human mind is a gift from the Creator. So obviously technology is what you make it. You have been given the properties to do something. It is a question of what are the motivations. Now, almost all older societies, proven societies that have sustained themselves for long periods of time, have always controlled certain emotions. They have built societies to control greed, to control jealousy, avarice, and anger. Society is built to be able to function, but also to control these emotions.

But we saw something different when the Pilgrims came to what they called the "New World." It started right out with Columbus. The first words out of Columbus's mouth to the indigenous people when he landed were: "Do you have any gold?" The first words. There was no "Hi, how are you? Are you feeling good?" or anything. He said: "Do you have any gold?" And then it was only a very short time before he was cutting off people's arms and hands and so forth when they couldn't produce gold. So, you know, obviously, their purpose was to enhance and enrich an empire.

To what do you attribute the growing interest in the traditional knowledge of indigenous people?

Why are you interviewing me? Why aren't you interviewing some of these powerful people? You are not interviewing them because you know what they are thinking. But over here, what is it that Indians are thinking about? That is why you are interviewing me. Because it is different. And that is what we are trying to do. We are trying to safeguard our homelands, our people, our way of life by illustrating to people that ours is probably the last wellspring of authority and knowledge that you are going to have in this battle for survival.

The laws are very real. There is this law of life that we are under, you know. This sun — that everybody celebrates and has ceremonies for — is going to become a killer. The sun itself will kill you. Daylight is going to kill you. The air that you breathe, you know, will kill you. People get up in the morning, open the window and take a deep breath and say: "That air is good." That is going to kill you also. And the water, which is the first law of life, even now the water is killing people. That is on its way. These are the laws that have been violated and as a result of that you are going to suffer.

I read a quote by some movie star who said that we have created a pinball society, and people are knocking themselves crazy at these machines. In the inner city of New York, and in Newark, you have people killing for sneakers. What is that? How did that happen? It is because no one is paying any attention to those people. They don't have any teachers. Everything is on a survival basis. How am I going to get something to eat today? Drugs have just taken over. What you see in the inner city now is what you are going to see in the world at large. It is just happening in the inner city faster. It is like a cancer. But eventually it is going to cover everything. So, I don't see a solution. I see this horse race heading toward a wall at full tilt and just piling up there.

In the interventions you have made here, and in your efforts to protect indigenous cultures around the world, what specifically have you tried to accomplish? And how is it going?

Well, not badly considering everything. We have picked up allies. Life is a wonderful thing and everybody loves life. Everybody is afraid of death. And everybody denies death. Indigenous people have great processes to deal with death. Everything is in twos: the sun and the moon, day and night, man and woman, life and death. Everything is in twos. So death is as common as life. But in Western society people do not talk about it at all. It doesn't occur to people, except when it happens. Then they discuss it.

So people in modern society don't live in reality. In our indigenous societies the realities are there. I am not saying that the Onondaga Nation is any kind of panacea for the ills of the world, because it is not. We have all the problems with our young people and everything else that anybody else has. Maybe we've got an edge. Our leaders are true leaders. They are for the people. They are not paid. We have a little edge. But it doesn't last. All you need is a generation that doesn't listen and then here come the pipes of Pan, the pipes of materialism.

I watched my grandson play the Nintendo game and he is an expert. I can't play it because I am in a different cycle. He just laughs at me when I try to compete with him. Yet, on the other hand, he sits there and listens to what I have to say. So I think we have to find this communion between the young people and that force. If anything is going to change it is going to have to come through the young people. And through the other part of humanity, which is the women. I think the women and the young people have within them, along with the indigenous people, the only opportunity to turn this around. Because this is a male-oriented problem.

As I said, male and female can't exist without one another. So the two make the whole. Each is a half. When they come together they make the circle, the complete circle, and life goes on. That is the way it works all over this circle of life. Women cannot deny the male half of the world, although some would like to. Some women would like to get rid of all the men. But of course that is not right. We tell them, we understand why you are mad, but it is not a good thing to try to kill off all the men or do without them because the children need both.

Western society has been able to disenfranchise the family. This is a very controlling society. The industrial society much prefers two people without children or a single person without a child because the child interferes with the work hours of the adult. This is not high-tech thinking, but it is fundamental. Modern society produces working hours but it destroys the family. This is not a problem until the society itself becomes chaotic, which is happening. Then it becomes a problem for everyone.

You pointed out that there is considerable interest in traditional knowledge and indigenous people among the children of the industrialized nations. What do you feel the chief lessons are from the indigenous people that would promote a new version of a sustainable culture?

It is not a new version. It is an adjusted version. We have to go with what we've got. Obviously what is out of balance, out of kilter, is the dominance of humanity over the rest of the natural world. We have scrunched up the elephants into a little area, a string of woods where they almost have no place to go. The tigers in India are scrunched into smaller and smaller areas so they are losing ground.

And the wolf in North America has lost his territory.

Well, the wolf is a mystery. He is special in this creation. He is in every continent. All the special creatures are in every continent. The deer, for example, is in every continent. But the wolf is a good family man. And he is a good survivor. I think he is like the Indian. He is mystical. Others fear him. He is supposed to be very courageous. You don't want to deal with him on a one-to-one level because he will tear you apart.

You may end up inside the big bad wolf.

Yes. There are all kinds of myths. But, actually, he is very friendly, and tolerant to a great extent. He has to kill to eat just like we kill to eat. No one eats live meat anymore. Except here and there. I was in Nebraska in this little town on the border of Iowa where they have to shut down the slaughtering plant 8 of the 24 hours it runs just to get rid of the 6 inches of blood on the floor every day. Every day. Eight hours are spent to get rid of the blood. This is not a well-known fact, but it goes on. I just point this out because if you ever happen to be down wind from that plant, you will know something is going on in there that is not too good for something that is alive. You can smell it. Nothing smells worse than rotting blood.

So anyway, what I am saying is that this goes on. And the wolf is part of that chain. And we're part of that chain. But he is a mysterious being. And he is always singled out in our cosmology as a powerful individual. I think he is. One of the songs of our most sacred ceremonies talks about the good road, you might call it heaven or whatever, but it is the road that leads up. And in the preamble of the song, as they sit there speaking in song, they talk about this beautiful path that we are on. And what we are doing in this ceremony is that we are enhancing that path. They talk about the flowers and the strawberries that line the path, and how beautiful it is to be on this road that we are on. And then they say that on the path alongside us is the wolf.

Now, what does that mean? See. He may be the spiritual leader of the four-footed creatures, you know. It is hard to say because the bear carries that as well. And if you go to different parts of the earth, different animals are noted for their power of spirituality. But that is a singular note. There is no instruction at all. It simply says that on that path, side by side with us, is the wolf. So, that says something very, very clearly. Now this is old, old wisdom. And you hear it so often that you don't think about it. But when you stop and think about it, it certainly has some qualities of mystery to it.

I think that the wolf is like the Indian, like the indigenous people. He is a barometer of the natural world. And how it is going with him is how it is going with the world. And if you say there are only eight wolves left in some part of Mexico, well then things down there are bad for the world. Bad for you. So it may be that there are only eight of them left, but that means that it is too bad for you because you are not looking out for him. If there were more of him it would be better for you. But this kind of thinking doesn't occur here in the courtrooms and conference rooms in Geneva. The African peoples would know immediately what we are talking about. They would respond.

There is no ritual here at the UNCED negotiations. There is no initiation. There is no connection with the earth. There was even a bureaucratic hassle finding a place to plant a ceremonial tree.

Yes. That involved a big discussion with the gardener. But, if you note, the ceremony had a major impact on the people who were there. That story, which was a very abbreviated story, the one he told about the Peacemaker had an impact on the people who were there. I don't care who they were. Whether they were wearing pink tags or white tags. Nobody left and they waited for him to finish. And he talked about a different time, but a very important time.

What do you think will happen? Will the environmental crisis engulf us?

We chiefs, we know all this stuff and we know it is going to happen inevitably. But as Handsome Lake said to the Four Protectors, whom the Creator has given to look after the world, he said to them: "Well, as long as this is coming, then what is the use? Why try to do anything?" And they said: "Well, because the generation that lets it happen, the generation that is going to be responsible for the destruction of the world, that generation is going to suffer beyond any understanding that they have. So we instruct you to tell your people: don't let it be your generation."

174

Section IV

The Bargaining Table: North vs. South

Martin Khor:

Searching for a New Model of Development in Malaysia

artin Khor Kok Peng is Coordinator of the Third World Network in Penang, Malaysia.

Steve Lerner: In a statement you made at the third Preparatory Committee session of the United Nations Conference on Environment and Development (UNCED) you suggested that if Third World countries are to keep their forests standing for the benefit of all the people of the world, they should be compensated in a number of different ways. First, this compensation should be provided to retrain loggers who lose their jobs because the forests are left intact. Second, there should be compensation to make up for the lost revenues from trees that are not cut and sold. And, third, there should be compensation for the revenues that would have been generated from the agricultural crops, industrial plants, or other developments that would have been grown or built on the cleared land.

If you use this formula of compensation for not destroying some part of nature, it could be applied not only to the Third World but also in Canada or the U.S. or in the Soviet Union. Are we all going to end up compensating each other for every benefit provided to the earth's ecosystem?

Martin Khor: There are three things to keep in mind here. One is the principle of it, the second is the implementation, and the third is the ability to pay. What is the principle? Do we accept that there is an opportunity cost if we leave the forest alone? There are benefits to the country that leaves its forest standing, as well as to the world. But the country that leaves its forests standing also suffers an opportunity cost. From an environmental point of view, we would say that the long-term benefit of leaving the forest alone is greater than the short-term benefit of chopping it down. But economists can demonstrate that by not cutting the forest down in the first year, the nation will lose income from the timber it would have sold; in subsequent years the nation will lose income it could have gotten from palm oil, for example, or rubber, or cattle.

On the other hand, it is very hard to demonstrate the economic benefits from leaving the forest standing. It is harder to place a value on the benefits that would accrue to that country as compared with the benefits to the rest of the world. In principle we must accept that there are some costs and there are some benefits. Yet, the benefits go to everybody in the world, while the costs are born by the country that leaves its forest standing. Those who benefit from the country that leaves its forest standing should help that country bear its costs for performing that service.

Who should be able to apply for compensation for bearing this opportunity cost? The South argues that if you are in a country that only has 5 percent of its forests left, you have already benefited from chopping your forest down. You now already have all your plantations. In my country, Malaysia, the authorities claim that 60 percent of the forests are left. This is debatable because there is not much primary, unlogged forest left. But, for argument's sake, take a hypothetical country with 80 percent of its forests left. Do you agree that if I have 80 percent of forests and you want me to preserve it, I am making a sacrifice? Everybody agrees with that. Should you pay me something? Yes. Then let's work out a mechanism.

Should we pay the country that has 5 percent of its forests left for the 5 percent it leaves standing? Maybe. We will pay him for his 5 percent if he pays us for our 80 percent. In the end he ends up paying us 75 percent. So, in net terms it would still be equitable. Or we could say that all countries should maintain at least 30 percent of their forests, and those countries who have cut beyond that are more culpable, and therefore should pay a penalty. And if some country has more than 30 percent of its forest cover left, say 80 percent, then that country should be paid for its 50 percent surplus. If the principle is adopted then technicians can go into the mechanics of it. There is no point in going into the mechanics of compensation if the principle is not adopted.

Is this a principle that you would apply to areas other than forestry? For example, we could apply it to the ratio of people to automobiles in a country. Or we could take a carbon tax approach. The principle of compensation is slightly different than the old principle that he who creates the pollution pays for the damage he does.

Yes, this new principle suggests that he who conserves gets paid for it. You get a conservation fee instead of a pollution tax. We have two environmental crises. One is the depletion of resources. The other is contamination and pollution. In one the person who pollutes should pay, while in the other the one who conserves should get the benefit.

Let me play the devil's advocate. If we looked at the amount of sewage flowing into the oceans of the world, we could argue that some nations are spending enormous sums to process their wastes and to not let everything go into the ocean. Other countries have not made as much progress in this area. Should we penalize those countries that have not made substantial investments in waste processing equipment? My point is that many countries do not have the money to invest in the equipment to process their sewage. It is good for the entire world that the U.S. has invested billions of dollars in pollution prevention equipment. We can talk about all the bad things the U.S. is doing, nevertheless, billions of dollars go into waste purification plants and other pollution control technologies. Should the U.S. be compensated for that?

We should put the two principles together. First, we must all agree that pollution is bad, and that all countries should take the responsibility for their own pollution. Second, while we recognize that all countries should deal with the pollution they generate, we must also recognize the relative abilities of countries to accomplish this. If a country has the financial resources to build pollution control devices, then there is no excuse for *not* using pollution control technologies. If a country can meet the basic needs of its people, then we need not compensate it for taking responsibility for its pollution. But if a country does not have the means to meet basic needs, and it has developed a proper program to stop pollution, and it is doing its best by readjusting its expenditures, then we must look further back in history.

Part of the problem in the Third World is that because of colonialism many southern countries are now in a dependent state, their nature has been stripped bare, they were paid miserably for the destruction of their natural resources. Therefore there is an historical economic and ecological debt owed by the people who did the destruction to the people who are suffering from it. Maybe at the time the colonists destroyed the economies of these Third World nations they did not know that what they did was destructive, because who knew about nature then? But now that we know and we say, "Oh my God it is true, we decimated those poor Indians in Amazonia, we cut down all the trees in Malaysia," now the former colonists owe a kind of debt. And we are going to pay back that debt through the process of aid and setting the prices of commodities higher. If that principle is accepted then the mechanics can be worked out.

After Iraq invaded Kuwait and was ousted, it was forced to pay compensation to Kuwait for the damage caused to its oil etc. Indeed, Iraq is being forced to pay a very heavy price. The compensation principle was recognized and applied severely. What Iraq did to Kuwait is the same thing that Britain did to Malaysia, or to India, or that Spain did to Latin America not so long ago, but, of course, on a much larger scale and with immeasurably more damage. They invaded, they conquered, they took away all the natural resources. They took the oil, trees, and everything. No one ever called on the colonial powers to compensate the colonized nations, because when the colonies won independence, we did not ask for compensation. We did not have the enforcement capacity. We didn't have the force.

But we are now, supposedly, all people of good will, sitting around the table at UNCED. We come to the realization that to save humanity and all our children, we need to address this historical problem. We are not saying that the U.S. has to pay $50 trillion to the Third World or whatever. But the rationale exists that aid to help Third World nations engage in proper sustainable development programs should not be seen as charity, but rather compensation. People in countries that caused these problems must understand that their ancestors did something wrong in the past.They may not have known quite what they were doing. But now there is a need to compensate the victims of colonialism. This is the principle of compensation.

Ensuring that the country that receives this aid or compensation will really do something sustainable with it is the subject for a global agreement. We must build a consensus that aid will be given for sustainable projects rather than unsustainable projects. And that must be negotiated.

Do you think that because there is this growing awareness that we all must cooperate to survive, the Third World now has a kind of leverage and power that it did not previously enjoy? Does the Third World now have the power to say to the First World: "We won't go along with these international agreements to protect the environment unless you compensate us for the trade imbalance that has impoverished us?"

The Third World means so many things. There are the Third World governments. There are the Third World people and non-government organizations (NGOs). So I don't think there is a consolidated thing called the Third World view, just as there is not a unified northern view. There are many northern governments willing to agree to the principle of compensation because of colonialism. Others will say: "Go to hell and I will kick your backside."

But I hope Third World leverage will not be characterized as a bargaining chip in which the Third World says: "If you don't compensate me then let's all die together." All of us have to realize that it is one world. And each of us has to retain our humanity.

If there is one world and there is a crisis, there are two ways of solving it. In the first approach one could argue as follows: "There is one world. There is a crisis. I am strong and you are weak. I'm going to get your resources. If you die in the process I do not care." That is one way of dealing with the problem. In other words, we would go back to the colonial approach where one country dominates another. This is what colonialism was all about: fighting over prices and supply of raw materials. That could happen. That, on balance, is what is probably going to happen. It looks like a 60 or 70 percent likelihood now. That's what I think.

But it would be a horrible way of solving the problem, because the person with the power who does this would lose his humanity in the process. As Jesus Christ said: "What does it profit you if you gain the whole world and lose your soul?" Is it worthwhile to remain rich and powerful and continue with "our way of life" if you lose your humanity in the process?

The other way of solving the crisis in this one world is for me to retain my humanity even if I am rich and powerful. In this scenario, I cannot sleep at night, knowing that my richness is causing nature to suffer so that future generations will not survive. Moreover, I am troubled that someone is starving to death at the same time that I am overconsuming. Since I cannot sleep at night because of my humanity troubling me, and my conscience, I want to solve these equity issues in the spirit of one world where all human beings should be guaranteed access to a decent standard of living. And if it can be proven to me as a rich person that I cannot continue my life-style and my production system, then I will be willing to change. I will be willing to voluntarily give up part of my wealth and power in order to get the real wealth and power of humanity. I will trade my material wealth and power in order to regain my spiritual humanity or whatever you call it. Each one has his own name for it. Some are religious and some are not. But it is that part of you that makes you fulfilled as a human being. That is the internal conflict that people in the North face.

The argument that we should help the Third World out of altruism is perhaps less powerful in a materialist world than is the argument that unless we cooperate with the people in developing nations we will all die.

But you need not die. You can take over the South. You don't need to cooperate with the South. Just take over the southern countries. You can do it. You can say: "If you don't stop chopping your trees we will drop a nuclear bomb on you." You can use that kind of horrific response based on sheer power and terror.

But, realistically, how can you stop deforestation with armed forces? It would be impossible.

You don't have to do it with armed forces. You just have to drop a bomb and demonstrate in one or two cases what you are willing to do. There is that extreme possibility as well.

I am more interested in a statement made by a member of the U.S. delegation, who says that the political reality in the U.S. is that if you ask the voter in the U.S. for more money for aid to the Third World, the voter will say: "No. We won't do it. We have a crisis in our own country. We have poor people in our country." If you try to sell a massive aid program to the U.S. voter in this election year, you will lose. The delegate goes on to say that if UNCED rises or falls on additional financing from the First World, it is going to fail for political reasons. He suggests that instead of doing this we should, for instance, correct the way the Third World uses its money on the generation of electric power. They do it inefficiently. Let's teach them to do it more efficiently. Let's take the Third World state-run energy generating systems and privatize them the way we do in the U.S. They will become more efficient. That money will be freed up.

That is a pragmatic way of looking at things. It is how to retain the system and satisfy public opinion. He is making sense in that short-term context. But if you were looking in the long term, 20 to 50 years ahead, at the lives of your children and grandchildren, then you would say something different. You would say: "How can we survive unless we look at the North/South economic relations, because that is a precondition to solving our own environmental problems."

Secondly, we must look at the internal economic model in the North at the same time as we examine the flawed development model in South. As I said, the development model is just a subsidiary of the flawed economic model in America. The fact that you have so many poor people in the U.S. means something is wrong somewhere. So the solution lies in reforming that flawed social and economic model in America.

You must have a more just distribution of resources in America so that everybody has a security blanket, so that no one is homeless, so that everybody has a job. Supposing you develop that kind of system and then you tell the people: "We have to adjust our economic model in order to make it more environmentally sustainable." People will accept it because they will see that the burden for this adjustment will fall fairly on all. But if you have a socially unjust system in which people are starving and homeless even in the richest country in the world, and then you tell people to tighten their belts further, they will refuse.

That is why economic adjustment has to be accompanied by socially just policies. Social, economic, and ecological problems have to be addressed simultaneously for a long-term solution. We are not just talking about what kind of policy will be promoted by President Bush or whoever is going to challenge him. That is the short term. Maybe we even need to change our political arrangements so that a politician can bring up real issues. Maybe candidates can have a kind of all-party arrangement whereby they all agree that they will bring up the real issues and not just look at the short term.

What has happened to the traditional type of stewardship of the land in Malaysia? Does it still continue?

In the past, Third World communities did not have multilateral agencies like the World Bank imposing policies or technologies on them. If you were a farmer from a Third World community who owned 10 acres of land, you were bound by a traditional system of social arrangements in which farmers decided among themselves who could make use of what kind of land. They had their own dispute settlement system. These were the traditional systems that existed in the Third World for thousands of years. People had been able to survive. Life may have been physically hard but there existed these helpful community relationships. There may have been some elements of feudalism as well, of course. But a kind of patron-client relationship existed in which the feudal chief performed certain services in exchange for which you had to surrender some of your crop. In this system some resources were shared, and you also had your own individual resources that belonged to your family.

Today, this would not even be considered part of the formal economy. It would be considered part of the informal economy. If you are a small firm selling food in an urban area, or a small farm producing food in a rural area, today that is called the informal sector. It is a local system within which local communities are able to take control of their own resources. In the Third World our traditional system has been that land is not owned by anyone privately. Neither is it owned by the state. It is owned by the local community. That land belongs to the community as a whole.

This is still true in large parts of Sarawak in Malaysia, for example. A family has the right to make use of the land that belongs to the community, as long as they are making productive use of it. The moment they stop making use of that land productively, it reverts back to the community, which then has a social arrangement by which the next family will be assigned to use it. That is really the whole concept of stewardship: communal ownership, but individual stewardship with local sanctions requiring that the land be used in the proper way.

This kind of community control over local resources and local technology has been progressively taken away by the centralized state. The centralized state takes away the resources that used to belong to ordinary people, in the name of development projects. By development projects they mean projects that are commercially profitable to the people who control the projects.

What is your view of the way the UNCED negotiation is shaping up? Has Maurice Strong, Secretary General of UNCED, made a credible attempt to see that the development and equity issues important to the Third World are attended to?

If we look at the global environmental crisis we have to analyze the global economic model that is now dominant. We must examine the model in the North. We have to look at the production, consumption, patent system and so on. And we have to understand that the development models in the South are a subset of the northern economic model.

From this perspective we should not just be looking at the global environmental crisis, the development crisis of the South, and the environmental problems that the South has with the forests and population growth. The dominant economic model in the North, which is responsible for 80 percent of the use of resources today, is really the model that has to be scrutinized.

Do you think that the economic model prevalent in the North is the cause of the environmental and development problems this UNCED conference is meant to address?

Of course it is. People focus on the development model in the South, but they don't look at the parent body in the North. The interconnection between the parent body and the development model in the South is what we call North/South economic relations. I think we have to ask ourselves: "What is the interrelationship of this whole set of problems to the global environmental crisis, both in the North and the South?"

This is an enormous task. Can we solve all these problems at the same time? Is UNCED the right place to take on reforming the global economic system? Or should we try to get concrete results by attempting to solve some specific environmental and development problems?

There are two different approaches to tackling the subject matter of UNCED. One approach would be that we want very concrete results. But that leaves the larger issue unsolved.

Are you suggesting that just trying to solve s_i ·cific problems would leave us dealing with the symptoms instead of the causes?

That's right. Through the UNCED process we are all educating ourselves. The UNCED process has restarted the North/ South dialogue. At least it has brought the North/South actors together. This time NGOs are playing quite a catalytic role in pushing their own delegations on a variety of issues.

It would be helpful if UNCED could actually create a framework of understanding by the time of the summit in Rio that says in essence: "We realize there is an environmental crisis that affects all of us on this earth and our children, but this environmental crisis is linked to the equity problem of an unjust world economic system." Let's use the example of forests. Once you see that deforestation is a social problem, then you have to solve the environmental and social issues simultaneously. Otherwise it won't work.

If UNCED became a process by which international cooperation is put back on the agenda, it would be a much greater achievement than simply arriving at a few concrete results.

Our national systems in the Third World have been significantly influenced by the international system, including the process of exporting the dominant northern economic model to the South. As a result, even if you look at the national problems in the Third World today — in terms of poverty, environment, social institutions — many of them were put in place in the Third World through international processes.

It is not possible to tackle environmental problems only at the national level. You have to look at international processes as well. And I think the UNCED negotiations will make this clear. The summit in Rio is only a milestone. It is only important in that it allows us to make politicians more conscious of these problems. The Preparatory Committee sessions are also milestones, and after Rio there will be more milestones. If we look at it in this way, then UNCED could play a unique role in restarting genuine international cooperation.

The danger in this approach is that we could have an endless process without serious actions being taken and treaties signed with enforcement powers that allow the international community to make real progress toward a sustainable world economy. Unless there are some conventions signed that are meaningful, I fear that UNCED will be seen as just a lot of talk. What do you say to that?

Because heads of state will be involved in UNCED, more priority is given at the national level to this conference than to most U.N. conventions. If heads of state are going to go to Rio they are going to be jolly well sure that they know something about what is at stake. That means government machinery in the capitals of the world is involved in the UNCED negotiations.

Malaysia, for instance, places a lot of importance on this negotiation because our head of state is going to Rio. Moreover, I think many countries are realizing that this is not just an environmental affair that the environment ministries should attend. They realize that the heart of this negotiation is an economic matter. The environmental issues are in front, but the economic issues are just behind them; indeed they are the larger issues. Governments are realizing that UNCED could lead to changes in the economic systems and structures of their respective countries, especially in the Third World. Heads of state realize that if they sign some kind of global agreement, it may mean economic adjustment. So they place a high priority on UNCED.

Many activists from Third World NGOs seem less than enthusiastic about the legally binding international instruments coming out of these negotiations. This is also the position of many Group of 77 (G-77) developing nations as well. Do you think that the equity deals have to be made before there will be international, legally binding agreements? Or do you think we are witnessing two essentially different approaches in which the developed nations are more interested in top-down, international treaties, while those from developing nations are more comfortable with community-based control of resources? Are the G-77 and Third World NGOs opposed to these international conventions and would they prefer to see the local communities left with the final responsibility?

Both. If the environmental crisis requires that we change economic models, then those who will be required to change are very frightened; they want to see how others will be required to change. Developing nations will ask if they will receive help in changing their economic system, or if they are just being dumped in the deep blue sea to change by themselves. If that is the case, delegates from the Third World will see UNCED as an effort of the rich to get richer while making the poor poorer. They will not see why they should go along with these treaties. That is basically the G-77 argument, which I think has some merit to it. That is why we say that the equity or the economic and social issues have to be looked at simultaneously with the environmental ones.

It appears that the Third World Network has quite a sophisticated and multi-layered strategy. What is it that you are really trying to achieve?

In the Third World there is a conflict over the control and use of natural resources between local communities, the larger nation states, and the international agencies that are forcing their economic model onto the Third World countries and the local communities. Members of Third World grassroots NGOs who are able to analyze the whole situation are trying to fight at two levels. On the North/South level, we want more justice for the South. We want less control by northern institutions whether they be northern-owned institutions or northern-controlled multilateral institutions. We want more accountability, more democracy, more say in the decision-making process for the South.

At the national level, we want more power, control and say for local communities *vis a vis* the state. We also want more of a voice for local communities within the international agencies. When we argue for democratizing the World Bank, for instance, we mean democratize it so that the southern governments have more say, but also so that local communities have more say.

Some Third World NGOs, including the Third World Network, are very critical of international agencies such as the World Bank. They believe that these agencies have been exporting unsustainable models of development to the South and destroying sustainable technologies and systems in our countries. International agencies, such as the World Bank, impose this on us, but they use the nation states to do it.

Listening to this perspective, some Northerners will say: "People from the Third World are blaming all of the problems on the North. They take no responsibility for the damage that they are doing to the environment in their own countries; nor do they take responsibility for the economic and social systems that they permit to exist." Can you answer this charge?

I think that criticism is not fair. Perhaps it could be launched against Third World governments. NGOs are different. While we are very critical of the international system for all the reasons I put forward, we are equally critical of our own governments, and of our own national systems of development and economy. Third World governments are not so critical of themselves — or they are not able to be so openly critical of themselves. But, within the Third World there are vibrant NGOs, that are very critical of the development and management models in their own countries. Of course it varies from country to country

186

and group to group. In Malaysia, for instance, we have been pointing out to our government why we think certain development policies may be damaging to the environment, or to communities. We point out why there should be more balance in our development policies and all the different ways in which these policies should be amended or changed, including the Malaysian forest policies, pollution policies, corporate policies, food safety policies, and public accountability in the use of financial resources. If you distinguish between governments and NGOs you will find that the NGOs are critical and are fighting for democratization. We have quite a sophisticated view of what democracy is. From our perspective democracy includes economic democracy: the right to food, the right to shelter, the right to jobs, the right to public housing. Democracy also means international democracy.

When you come to UNCED you must find yourself in a dual role. You have been critical of the Malaysian Government at home. But here quite often you find yourself arguing the same position as the Malaysian Government relative to the First World. For example, you agree with the Malaysian Government position that the South is getting a raw deal from the North. That makes you, at least temporarily, an ally of your Malaysian delegate at UNCED, whereas at home you are more critical of your country's policies.

I don't think we are just the allies of our delegates. We are allied on certain things and we disagree on others. We make our differences with our government clear even here. Take our position on the forests. I think our position is quite different from the Malaysian position and the G-77 position. If you look at the G-77 position and our position, we both agree that the North/South issue has to be taken into account and that there has to be some kind of financial mechanism to help the Third World countries protect their forests. But if you look at the conservation aspect of our position, we are very radical there. We talk about the drastic phasing out of logging, and all commercialization of forests, and an eventual moratorium on logging. Western countries have not dared to breathe a word about that. We have looked at the North/South consolidated document on forests and we are very critical of it because it does not say a word about having to tackle the root causes of deforestation. There is not one single word about it.

Similarly, if you look at our position on giving rights to forest peoples and local communities, we are far stronger on insisting on those rights than is our government. The western point of view is also very weak on this. So in some areas we would say that our government's position is deficient, and in other areas we agree with them. We insist that there must be an ecological aspect that is very strong. We talk about phasing out logging and all development in primary forests, including mining, cattle ranching, agriculture, and hydroelectric dams. But we are also saying: "Take care of the forest people and their rights." Finally, we insist that we must find the economic mechanism that will make this possible.

What do you think of the role NGOs such as yours are playing at UNCED?

I am not accustomed to attending United Nations meetings, but I think a serious attempt was made to bring the NGOs into the process. I imagine that this is quite an innovation in the sense that NGOs are directly involved and not just running a parallel event, which is what normally happens. When the World Bank has its annual meeting, NGOs often participate in parallel events.

Here at UNCED, in addition to their parallel activities, NGOs have also been able to participate in the plenaries and working groups, and have been given the opportunity to speak and to mingle with the delegates quite freely. In a sense the delegates now accept that the NGOs are partners (or junior partners) of governments in the process. I think that this is a positive development and something that should be encouraged further in other U.N. and international fora.

This is a kind of democratization of the process. Of course we have many criticisms of the process and there are many shortcomings. But there has been some democratization. NGOs are present and they are witnessing the process. They may not be granted space equal to that of the governments, but they can witness what is happening and talk to delegates and hold their own events. A lot of space has been given to NGOs for meeting rooms and xerox facilities. So, I think that while we do come from critical and independent NGOs, this is something very positive that has to be said for the process.

Robert J. Ryan, Jr.:

The U.S. Position at UNCED

 mbassador Robert J. Ryan, Jr. is Director of the United States Coordination Center for the United Nations Conference on Environment and Development (UNCED).

Steve Lerner: The U.S. negotiating posture at UNCED has been characterized by some as a damage limitation exercise. Critics point out that the U.S. stance at UNCED is largely negative on three major issues. First, the U.S. insists that there be no new and additional resources made available to developing countries for the promotion of sustainable development. Second, the U.S. wants no new institutions created within the U.N. system for the coordination of international efforts on environment and development issues. And third, the U.S. refuses to set targets for the reduction of carbon dioxide emissions, a key point in the climate change negotiations. How do you respond to these criticisms of U.S. policy at UNCED?

Robert J. Ryan, Jr.: To deal with the third one first, climate change, that is not my bag. I have enough to do worrying about the rest of the UNCED process. It is quite true that we have been criticized for the position we have taken on the climate change negotiations. I wouldn't want to say too much about it because the negotiations are ongoing. But I think the climate change negotiations have a political momentum to them that will make them succeed. I am optimistic about that, but I wouldn't want to get into the details.

On the issue of new and additional resources for developing nations, I think the discussions about financing are evolving in the UNCED negotiations. You should wait and see what happens at this negotiating session before you judge the U.S. position on finances.

On the institutional reform issue, I was just with a group of very high-ranking people in the UNCED process and one of the representatives of the Group of 77 (G-77) developing nations described their two bottom lines. First they want more money. And second they want no new institutions. So I don't think the U.S. is out of the mainstream on this institutions issue.

I have heard a number of non-government organizations (NGOs) say that the U.S. position is just no, no, no. They see our position on no new institutions is part of that. But I think the U.S. has provided a lot of leadership in moving forward on the institutions question. We do not think we need brand new institutions. We do think we have to restructure existing ones and reorient them toward sustainable development. I think that the U.S. is far ahead of any other nation in making concrete, detailed proposals on how to do that. Our proposals have been well received, so I don't think the countries involved in the UNCED process, as opposed to the NGO community, perceive the United States as lagging on the institutions issue.

In fact, I think what you would get if you talked with delegates is that what the United States is doing on institutions is very constructive, and that we are trying to move the process along. We haven't tabled a formal proposal on institutions, we are not trying to set our ideas in concrete, but we have tried to put some suggestions on the table and get some exact language out there. So, I think the criticism of the U.S. on our position on no new institutions is a bad rap. As a matter of fact, the other two criticisms are also bad raps.

Beyond that there has been far too much attention to greenhouse gas targets and timetables and the financing issues and not enough attention paid to what the rest of the UNCED conference is about. In any one of a number of areas there are things that people would disagree with us on, but I think you could find many other areas where the U.S. has been leading the pack, not following it.

Right now there is a discussion going on about oceans. If you look at the history of the oceans discussion at UNCED, I think you will see that the really innovative and constructive ideas come from the papers the United States tabled in the second and third negotiating sessions. Those papers have really structured the debate. I think in that area, environmentally, we have been way ahead. We have been pushing for conservation of marine mammal resources. The U.S. has been the strongest voice against drift net fishing. We have tried to set a agenda on land-based sources of marine pollution and focus some attention on that for the first time.

Similarly, on forests, there probably would not be the movement toward a forest convention that you see now without the United States insisting on it. In the area of technology, if you look at our proposals, people have now rallied around them and forgotten that they are U.S. proposals. That is fine, but the fact is that a lot of them have really been well received.

So I think this perception that somehow the United States is not providing leadership is really pretty far off. Partly it is determined by the fact that a lot of the media, and to a lesser extent the less-informed NGOs, think of this as the United Nations Conference on Climate Change. They don't like the U.S. position on greenhouse gas emission controls, and so they assume that the rest of what we are doing is not to their liking either. I think if they looked at the rest of what we are doing in any detail they would find a very different story.

The U.S. position at UNCED has been criticized as being hypocritical. The U.S. suggests to Third World nations that they cease burning and cutting down their forests, when here in the U.S. we continue to cut our remaining old-growth forests. It also appears as if the U.S. wants southern nations to keep their forests standing as a sink for the greenhouse gases that we generate, yet our energy policy and our position on the climate change negotiation suggest that we are not willing to do much to reduce our emissions of greenhouse gases. Do you think the charge that the U.S. is hypocritical on these issues is supported by the facts?

No. On the forestry issue, I think some of the early statements probably left the wrong impression. But by now it has become clear that we should make commitments on all kinds of forests, not just on tropical forests. So, in that sense, I don't think we are hypocritical. I personally think that the issue of primary forests, more generally, is one that has got to be strengthened in the Forests Principles text partly for this reason. I certainly think it would be wrong of us to be pushing developing countries toward a sustainable development agenda that we were not willing to embrace ourselves.

Yet it remains a stubborn perception that the U.S. has not moved quickly toward a sustainable energy policy. The Third World is understandably reluctant to enter into agreements on forestry before we do that.

You are getting into an area beyond my real expertise. If you look at the proposals we made at the end of the last round of climate change negotiations, we laid out a program of various new elements that might go into an energy strategy. Of course, some people will always be unhappy with whatever we do, but I think if you look at those new initiatives carefully you will find a lot of very constructive elements.

Are you referring to the new energy efficiency initiatives?

Yes. I have not had the time to look at them in detail, but they seem to have been very well received along with the new contribution the U.S. announced to the Global Environment Facility (GEF).

The position of the G-77 developing nations, as I understand it, is that they are willing to do a deal with the industrialized nations under the following conditions: (1) we give them new and additional resources for the promotion of sustainable development, (2) we provide them with debt relief, (3) we improve terms of trade, and (4) we cut our carbon emissions substantially.

The World Resources Institute in Washington has made a similar suggestion in its "Compact for a New World." It found, at least among experts in the Western Hemisphere, that if the North took the initiative and made clear that it was willing to provide the South with debt relief, new and additional resources, and cut carbon emissions, it would help break the North/South logjam we are experiencing here at UNCED. If the northern countries make clear that they are willing to help the South and change northern consumption patterns, there will be a willingness among southern nations to do more to halt deforestation and to make further efforts to control population growth. Why is it that the United States seems unwilling to enter into a real partnership with the South to promote sustainable development?

I am not sure that there is a logjam between North and South at UNCED. Certainly this idea of partnership has gained a lot of credence. I don't know if you have looked at what came out of the United Nations Conference on Trade and Development (UNCTAD) a couple of weeks ago. The spirit at UNCTAD was very constructive and tried to take UNCTAD from being an organization that was essentially a G-77 lobby group to being an organization that could really build a partnership between the North and the South. I think that is the kind of spirit we are trying to create here at UNCED as well. And I think we are succeeding. The atmosphere in the meetings the last eight days has been excellent. People are trying to work together to get the text as good as it can be. That is extremely welcome.

I also want to say something about debt relief. We just dealt with all these international economic issues at UNCTAD so I don't think anyone is looking to break new ground on them here at UNCED. I think there is a recognition that you need a supportive international economic environment, and that on certain topics there is a clear sustainable development angle that needs to be dealt with at UNCED. So I am not saying that we should not deal with these subjects at all.

But look at the record on debt relief. In the mid 1970s I was the U.S. representative to the Paris Club on international debt rescheduling. At that time I would not have believed that we could be where we are today on debt relief. We have essentially forgiven the official debt of the low income countries. We have started, particularly in the Western Hemisphere, a process of forgiving a lot of the official debt of the middle-income countries such as Bolivia and Jamaica among others. And in return for this debt relief we have asked for environmental conditionality. In other words, we have signed agreements with these countries that we will reduce their debt service if they will do something positive on the environment and sustainable development side. So, there is a lot of movement there.

Furthermore, some of the countries that we used to worry about most on the debt issue are turning into great success stories and are coming to good arrangements with the banks. Who would have believed what Mexico is like today, if you had thought about it 10 years ago? So, I think there is more movement that is constructive on all of these issues than people realize.

Nevertheless, when the South looks North they want to know what sacrifices people in developed countries are willing to make in order to protect the global life support system. If the southern nations are told not to cut their forests, they will be unable to expand their croplands and industries, and as a result we will forgo opportunities to develop. What sacrifices is the North willing to make in return for the sacrifices it is asking of the southern nations?

Let me say something about the sacrifices in the South, first. Environmental groups in the United States may be saying to southern nations: don't cut down the trees, but the U.S. is saying to the South that it should manage its forests sustainably. Those are not the same thing. Sustainable management leaves room for logging that would help economic development and it leaves room for other uses of the forests that can be sustainable. That is the idea of the Forest Principles. So, I would not put it quite as starkly as you have.

On the other side of it, if you look at forests as sinks for greenhouse gases, if we are going to get a credible climate change convention, there will have to be clear commitments from the United States and other developed countries as well. And I don't think it is unreasonable for the southern countries to expect that.

Clear commitments on what?

On greenhouse gas emissions, on energy policy. As I say, I don't know the details very well. In terms of financing, I think the Global Environment Facility (GEF) negotiations are proceeding rather well. Everybody recognizes that the pilot project has got to be changed quite a bit.

Do you mean the governance of the GEF?

The governance and aspects of the way the GEF relates to the conventions under negotiation. That all needs to be sorted out. The U.S. has been playing a constructive role on that issue. We are not saying that the GEF has to stay exactly the way it is. We have been discussing proposals for changing it. We think the GEF should be the main vehicle for dealing with the fact that developing countries don't always have the wherewithal to undertake the projects that they and we would like them to be able to undertake to deal with some of these global issues. The GEF should help them do that. The fact that we made a new contribution to the core fund of the GEF is, I think, quite significant.

Are you referring to the $50 million contribution made by the U.S. to the GEF?

Yes.

In listening to the discussions on financial resources at UNCED I am beginning to hear the G-77 nations talk about the "compensatory" nature of aid from North to South. There is also beginning to be some talk about the concept of an "ecological debt" owed by developed nations to developing nations. Do you think the U.S. will be willing to recognize

*that it owes money to developing nations for the damage we have done
to the biosphere?*

No. I don't think that is the right way to think about it at all. We talked
earlier about partnership and people working together to solve problems. I think, clearly, some nations have more to contribute than others.
But I don't at all like the approach of finger pointing that talks about
compensation and says: "You owe us something for your past sins." I
don't think that is going to get us very far. In fact, I see developing
countries backing away from that. Every time we come to that para-
graph in the G-77 paper they really would prefer that we forget that they
ever said it.

*But is this description of the North owing the South an ecological
debt not accurate?*

There is no question that the more developed a country has been in
recent years the more strain it has put on the world environment. The
U.S. has recognized that, and that gives us a different kind of responsibility than a much smaller country that is less developed. But I don't
think that we should be pilloried for having given our people a higher
standard of living over the years, a standard of living that other countries would have been absolutely delighted to achieve. And I don't think
you should forget that a lot of the countries — not all of them — have
sectors of their economy that are acting pretty much the same way we
have, when they get the chance.

*Nevertheless, there is a limit to how much pollution the oceans and
atmosphere can absorb, and it is undeniable that the U.S. has taken up
more than its share of the absorptive capacity of the global commons.
That is what the debate about ecological debt and the compensatory
nature of financial aid from developed to developing countries centers
on. The U.S. has taken up more than its share of the global commons
both in the amount we consume in energy and raw materials and in the
amount of pollution we generate.*

I don't like this zero-sum game approach. What we should do together is figure out how we can reduce the strains we all place on the
environment to a level we can live with. This question of "environmental space" really troubles me a lot.

More generally, it seems to me that this whole question of consumption and life-styles is not framed in quite the right way. For example, one
of the main reasons that the United States consumes proportionately
more energy than other countries is that we provide more living space
per person to our population than even the average developed country. It
seems to me what we should be saying to the American people is not
that we all have to live in smaller apartments or smaller houses and
somehow approach a lower standard of living. That is not the way to
frame the debate. What we have got to say, and what I think most people
would accept, is that we have got to be more efficient in heating, light-

ing, air conditioning the space that we have. If we frame the debate in that fashion we can get a lot of agreement. And I think we already have a lot of agreement on the need for energy conservation, and more recycling, and things like that. But if you frame it strictly in terms of consumption patterns, as such, that is not a very good way to go about it. Politically, you are going to have a hard time convincing the American people to live in smaller spaces. We have to look for ways of providing the essential services at the same level, while using our resources more wisely in the process. If we redefine the debate that way, we could get a lot more convergence on the ideas.

I don't like the proposals in Agenda 21 that say that we should look at consumption, and that propose that we have a new U.N. unit to look at consumption. That doesn't seem to me to get anywhere. We should be looking at how we can more efficiently use the resources, how we can minimize waste, how we can invent new processes in our industries that will be much more efficient.

Many NGO activists would say that it is not surprising that the United States does not want to look at consumption patterns, and instead is more interested in talking about efficiency, because the U.S. is at the top of the list when it comes to consuming most of the world's resources.

And that is not all bad. You and I have benefited from that.

Yes we have.

There are rumors that the Japanese and perhaps the Germans may announce that they are willing to put billions of dollars into a fund to promote sustainable development in developing countries. The United States has come up with only $75 million. Is there some chance that if the Japanese or Germans announce that they will contribute billions for sustainable development in the developing world, that the U.S. position will shift? Is it likely, given our economic reality and the timing of our election, that we might signal to the developing nations that the U.S. recognizes that there will be a need for more financial resources for sustainable development projects in the Third World in the future?

You will have to ask the Japanese what they are doing. I am told that they have their own problems with their Parliament on this. I don't think the U.S. will develop its own strategy on financing in response to the Japanese or Germans. This is something we will have to decide in terms of our own system: what we can really do ourselves. The U.S. has always been for adding resources for sustainable development. Look at the London Summit communique on sustainable development, for example, which we joined enthusiastically.

Is the U.S. heading in the direction of conditioning aid to developing nations on national plans that show promise in terms of sustainable development?

I don't like the word "condition" there. I would say that there has to be a country-driven process. I expect that we will come out of UNCED with a very meaty Agenda 21 that lays out an approach for possible activities in the 20 program areas. Then each developing country will have to look at Agenda 21 and say to itself: What are the most important things here for us, what parts of Agenda 21 do we want to start with right now?

I think developing nations will need some help in terms of their analysis and planning. But that should not be construed as interference in any sense. Developing countries should put together good sustainable development plans based on Agenda 21 and the commitments they have taken in Agenda 21. Then they can come to the donors (multilateral, bilateral agencies in these country consortiums and roundtables) with projects that are based on very sound sustainable development planning. At that point I think financing will go to the countries that do a good job of that.

But I would not think of this as extra conditionality, because instead of making these conditions part of the lending process, we would be putting it up front where countries accept Agenda 21 as a compact mutually entered into. Obviously, there would still have to be some of the more traditional conditions on loans. But, more generally, in terms of the policies, if countries have accepted Agenda 21 and the approaches in Agenda 21, and they do the sustainable development planning, that is the element of partnership that substitutes for conditionality in the more traditional sense. You might want to call it a different kind of conditionality, but conditionality is a loaded term and I would like to get away from it and just say that we have a new approach here. UNCED is putting into motion a new way for countries to relate to each other.

Could this not lead to a situation where the U.S. has funded a number of developing countries' sustainable development plans, but no one has the leverage to force the United States to adopt a sustainable development plan?

Developed countries will make commitments in Agenda 21, the Forest Principles and in the conventions. But since the U.S. does not need money for that, there is no international process at the financial level.

In other words there is no financial leverage on the U.S. to adopt a sustainable development plan as there is on developing nations.

But UNCED is a high-level conference that is getting international attention and will get a lot more in the coming months; the commitments we make here will be very serious. Anything the U.S. signs we are going to do.

Is the U.S. going to attempt to divide Agenda 21 into two parts: that which we are willing and that which we are unwilling to sign?

No. Within Agenda 21 there will have to be different levels of commitment for different kinds of actions, not just for the United States but for everyone. Some things we will commit to do; other things we will commit to look at further. I would hope the latter category would be rather small. The U.S. has been among the nations insisting on negotiating the whole text of Agenda 21. Some delegates have been talking about prioritizing Agenda 21 and taking just four or five things to work on. The U.S. has been strong on saying that we should negotiate the whole thing. That is not to say that we don't have our own priorities. There are some issues that are more important to us than others: forests, technology cooperation, biodiversity, conservation, and some of the oceans issues. But we recognize that our priorities are not everyone else's and that it is not appropriate, or even feasible in a body such as this, to single out one section and say it is the most important. What is most important to one country is not necessarily going to be the same for another.

Do you think that the U.S. will join with other nations at the Earth Summit in Rio in signing a climate change convention, a biological diversity convention, an Agenda 21, and an Earth Charter?

I am optimistic on all those.

Do you think President Bush will go to the Earth Summit in Rio?

That will depend, among other things, on how well we do our work here.

What do you mean by that? If you come up with a result that he is comfortable with, then he will go to the Summit?

I would not say that. There are a lot of other things going on for him. It is his decision and I have not discussed it with him personally. Certainly, I would say a necessary but not sufficient condition for his going would be that these negotiations go well and it looks as if there will be a good product coming out of the conference.

Senator Al Gore said recently that 20 years ago, in 1972, the U.S. took a very clear leadership position at the Stockholm Conference on the Human Environment, while at UNCED the Administration has failed to take a leadership role. You have already said that this is an inaccurate analysis and on a number of different subjects we have taken a progressive stance.

Right.

If we have taken a leadership role at UNCED, what would you say the United States wants to get out of these negotiations?

At the most general level the U.S. wants to get a commitment to integrating environment and development considerations at all levels of policy-making in all the operations of different international agencies and the policies of governments.

Do you think we will get that?

Yes. Particularly in the last few days I am very heartened by the kind of convergence we are seeing, that we didn't have at the last negotiating session, on the integration of environment and development. I hear both from developing and developed countries that we have to integrate environment and development issues, and that is very heartening.

How is policy made on the U.S. delegation to UNCED? What is the chain of command? Does President Bush tell Secretary of State Baker, who tells Ambassador Bohlen, who tells you what our position should be on various different issues? What is the framework for making policy at UNCED?

It depends on the issue. We have a very elaborate structure that deals with at least 30 categories of issues. We have people who are designated to be the coordinator for an issue. These people have an obligation to consult with their colleagues all over the Federal Government who might be interested in that issue, with the Congress, and with NGOs, in order to formulate a position on the texts we are working on at UNCED. Some issues are either controversial among the agencies or are so important that they need to get higher-level guidance. So we get as high a level of guidance as we think we need. We have access to the highest policy levels on any of the issues where we need guidance.

Does that mean the President?

In cases where we need it, sure.

Have you consulted with him?

Personally, no.

How about Ambassador Bohlen. Has he consulted with the President about issues being negotiated at UNCED?

I don't think he has discussed this with the President either. The President is certainly well aware, through his people at the White House who are close to him, of what is going on at UNCED.

I read today in the Earth Summit Times *a headline that says that the "White House is Bullish on the Earth Summit." Have you gotten that impression? Is that accurate?*

I saw the article. I was not there at the meetings. I don't know what happened when Maurice Strong saw people there. But the message that I am getting very clearly is that the United States is very positive about this conference, we want it to succeed, and we are going to work very hard to make sure that it does.

Section V:

Reforming International Organizations

David Runnalls:

Reforming the U.N. to Coordinate Sustainable Development Activities

 avid Runnalls is Director of the Environment and Sustainable Development Program at the Institute for Research on Public Policy in Ottawa, Canada.

Steve Lerner: In your assessment of progress at the United Nations Conference on Environment and Development (UNCED) you write that there has been "little progress," and that "the omens are not good." You describe the biodiversity convention negotiations as "stalled." You describe the central deadlock between North and South as being a result of the industrialized countries' unwillingness to come up with new and additional resources, which in turn causes southern countries to be unwilling to sign on to global climate change, biodiversity, or forestry conventions. Is there any hint of where a breakthrough may come in this deadlock?

David Runnalls: I think the forestry convention is a dead duck as far as UNCED is concerned. The best that anyone is hoping to get on forestry is an agreement on some set of principles. On the central issue I don't see any movement at all. My hope is that we may get a coalition of the European nations on this issue, led by the Germans. I have just returned from Berlin, and the Germans are quite scared about climate change and are determined to take quite radical action. They have committed themselves to a 25 percent reduction of carbon dioxide emissions by 2005.

Why are the Germans more concerned about climate change than anyone else? Are their voters better educated on this subject than ours?

I think it is a combination of things. The Germans have taken a terrible beating from acid rain. Go into the Black Forest. Whereas we just talk about acid rain in Canada, you can physically see it in Germany. Secondly, they have been horrified by what they have seen in East Germany. The level of environmental deterioration in the old industrial areas of East Germany has changed public attitudes on the environment. They have discovered such a series of eco-catastrophes in East Germany that environmental consciousness in Germany, which was quite high to begin with, is now even greater.

The Germans and the Japanese are doing what they usually do. They have recognized that environmental deterioration is a serious problem facing the world. They have recognized, in addition, that not only do we have to do something about it, but that whoever does something first is going to have an enormous competitive advantage. German industry or Japanese industry, after doing a lot of grumbling, will invent the energy efficient technology of the 21st century. Later, when all the rest of these countries wake up to the fact that they have to do something, guess whose equipment they will have to buy? The Germans are doing this. They are also pushing the European Community quite hard to have a community-wide carbon tax and a community-wide policy on carbon dioxide emission reductions. I don't know whether that will work. The Germans have also said on several occasions, both on their own and via the E.C. in the climate change negotiations, that they are prepared to talk seriously about a fund that would help developing countries in the transition away from fossil fuels. The Europeans have taken that position for at least a year.

I am also finding that there are rumors coming out of Japan that the Japanese are readying a major initiative on the whole question of financing. Sums of $5 and $10 billion dollars are being bandied around with some frequency.

For what?

It is not clear. I think it will be in the realm of a global environmental fund — not the Global Environment Facility (GEF) at the World Bank. Some, if not most, of it will be devoted to providing cleaner technologies in developing countries.

If the Japanese created a $5 to $10 billion dollar fund, would it lead to other countries purchasing more energy efficient technology from the Japanese?

Exactly. A Japanese friend of mine said, "Look, we know we are going to have to do this sooner or later; we also know we are the only country in the world that can mobilize large amounts of capital in this day and age. We know as a society that in the next 10 to 15 years we are going to have to move towards far more efficient means of production, both in terms of energy and material use. So, why not combine that together into a positive political initiative by Japan? In this fashion we don't get caught on this the way we got caught on the Gulf war, where we were publicly beaten by Baker into putting up money to support the allied effort because we simply had no policy response."

If the Japanese and Germans do get the technological jump on creating a new generation of energy and resource efficient technology, does it mean that the U.S. and Canada will once again become colonies for cheap labor and abundant resources? We are countries with a large land mass, while Japan and Germany are relatively small, and depen-

dent on import of raw materials.

When the Global 2000 Report was published in the early 1980s, I remember everyone in Washington being amazed when it became a huge best seller in Germany and Japan. But I don't know two countries that are historically more concerned about running out of resources than Germany and Japan. These two countries became involved in wars at least partly because they were worried about security of access to natural resources. Neither one has any basic stock of energy resources of its own with the exception of some coal in Germany.

For Japan to take up international environmental problems, however, is a double-edged sword. While Japan is more energy efficient than the U.S., Japan is also well known for buying up raw materials all over the world with little regard to the environmental damage it causes. So, if it enters into the North/South dialogue, it can be faulted for a resource-rapacious foreign policy.

That's true. I think the Japanese are worried about the kind of image they are getting internationally. It is not yet clear that Japan will make the financing available for an international environmental fund; those are just rumors. But one of the factors driving them in this direction is a real worry that Japan has a dreadful reputation, particularly in Southeast Asia, for its forestry activities. One of the ways to counteract that would be to disburse substantial aid money — which Japan has already agreed to spend anyway — in favor of the environment, and particularly in favor of reforestation and preservation of biological diversity. The Japanese are all too aware of the fact that their ability to trade depends at least partly on how people perceive them.

Are you suggesting that new Japanese funds for improving energy efficiency in developing countries would not go through the World Bank GEF fund?

What I meant was that this new money might go to a global environmental fund. I did not want to suggest that this necessarily implied the GEF. I don't have the impression that these decisions are very far advanced, yet. My guess is that the Japanese will disburse most of this money through bilateral channels. But Japan was instrumental in the creation of the GEF and in the creation of a major technical assistance fund in the World Bank for dealing with the environment. I am sure they will not turn their backs on the international system. If such a fund or funds were created, I'm sure that chunks of it would go through the GEF and chunks through United Nations Development Program (UNDP) and United Nations Environment Program (UNEP).

Do you believe that there is the basis for a breakthrough on providing new and additional funds for sustainable development?

Perhaps. I am trying to be hopeful. Fundamentally, I am still very pessimistic about UNCED's prospects. But I think if it is going to succeed, it will require some type of alliance between Europe and Japan that the United States might be persuaded to join. I don't see leadership in this area coming from the United States at all, despite the U.S. having traditionally provided important leadership on international negotiations. These are now sufficiently serious problems that the usual collection of so-called like-minded countries — the Scandinavians, Dutch, and Canadians — are not going to be able to do it on their own. One or two of the major financial powers will have to say to the developing countries: "OK. We get the point. We are going to have to put up some real money here. Now, let's hear what you have to say on population questions, on the question of biological diversity, on forestry, etc."

If suddenly there were new and additional resources made available by industrialized countries, would it lead to a breakthrough? Perhaps the developing world would simply up the ante and ask what the North was going to do about overconsumption of resources. Could the South not press an infinite number of demands upon the North before agreeing to conventions on global warming, biodiversity, and forestry?

In a sense that is what any international negotiation is about. My perception is that there is so little movement on either side that there is really no negotiating taking place. This promise of money, either ephemeral or real, could well unblock the logjam to the point where countries started bargaining on some of the other issues. It is not going to solve the whole problem. But at the moment I get a real sense that there is no bargaining going on at all; instead, there is just maneuvering for position, with everyone saying: "You have to do this and you have to do that." The negotiating parties are frozen in place; someone has to break that deadlock.

The most convincing argument to India, and Malaysia, and some of the other hard-liners in the South would be a major concession by the North on money. I don't know how much money would have to be involved. It certainly has to be many billions of dollars. It can't just be a few hundred million. If the Europeans put up $5 billion and the Japanese $10 billion, is $15 billion sufficient? It is certainly sufficient to get discussion going on the other issues.

That would put the U.S. in an awkward position, would it not? We are in an election year, and the public is concerned that Bush is spending too much time and money on foreign issues, and not enough on domestic problems. It will be hard for the U.S. to ante up the same kind of money that the Germans and Japanese might be willing to spend.

I think the U.S. has got itself into a very rigid position from which it is going to be hard to back down and still save face. At the same time, I am not sure, if I were President Bush, that I would want to be deserted by my major allies. If there were an agreement or common initiative from Japan and Western Europe, it would not be very long before the Canadians, Scandinavians, Australians, New Zealanders, and other "like-minded" countries threw their lot in too. That would leave the U.S.

as the only developed country not prepared to seriously talk about some of these financing issues.

President Bush is in a very difficult position because he faces domestic criticism that he is spending too much money overseas and too little on the poor at home. Yet I suspect that he does not want to be put in the position in which the U.S. becomes not only isolated from everybody else, but also less able to influence the course of some of these negotiations. For the U.S. to change its position on financing there will have to be a certain amount of effort expended by everybody to allow the U.S. Government to save face and go along with the initiative in some way.

Another obstacle to a breakthrough in the deadlock between North and South could be over the institutional arrangements that come out of the UNCED negotiations. Institutional reform has been the last question to be taken up by UNCED. The U.S. is not alone among developed nations in saying that it wants to talk about the substance of a sustainable development program before it discusses the institutional reform necessary to make it possible. But unless institutional reform is adequately addressed at the last Preparatory Committee session of UNCED in New York, there will be no institutional focal point following the Earth Summit in Rio to support the carrying out of Agenda 21.

I agree. I also think that this next Preparatory Committee session in March, 1992 is almost too late to do a lot of these things. Some things are going to have to happen before then if Rio is not to be a failure. One of them will have to be an initiative in one or more of these areas, like the Japanese/ European initiative. I think those have to surface pretty quickly, because the next Preparatory Committee session is only a little more than two months before the Rio conference. If the UNCED delegates are going to make decisions of major importance, they are going to need more than two months to cook them. So I would expect that some major initiatives have got to surface, if not before Christmas then certainly shortly after. They would be in one or more of the three nasty areas: the institutional question, the technology transfer question, or the financial question — or maybe all three. I think it is unlikely that they will all be resolved.

In the institutional area, you have written about a number of options for reform, some more ambitious than others. You begin with a discussion of possible reform of the U.N. Security Council, in which you suggest that Japan will have to be allowed a seat if the Security Council is going to work. What would have to happen to the Security Council in order for it to take environmental security seriously?

Let me go back a little bit and say that the Brundtland Report was right. For the next five to ten years the whole question of the relationship between environment and economics may be the major international political issue. If that is true, the existing international institutions are totally ill equipped to deal with it. We do not, for instance, have anywhere in the system a regular meeting place for top senior political figures to discuss these issues. The message of the Brundtland Commission and its follow-up is that economic decision-makers actually have to sit down and discuss these issues for there to be any progress. That is why one naturally turns to institutions like the Security Council.

As the Cold War continues to peter out it is perfectly obvious that the U.N., an institution that was set up to reflect the political and military realities of 1945, is simply not adequate to deal with the realities of 1995. That means that despite the fact that no one wants to talk about it, we are going to have to swallow hard and fix the U.N. system. That is going to require modifying the U.N. Charter, which everyone is terrified of touching. If fundamental reform of the U.N. does not take place, ancillary institutions will spring up all over the place on an ad hoc basis to try to institutionalize discussion of some of these issues. I have a tidy mind so I prefer to say it is about time that we try to reform the U.N. system so that it is ready for the 21st century. The time for coping with the middle of the 20th century is long gone.

Is that type of U.N. reform not scheduled for after UNCED, leading up to the 50th anniversary of the U.N. in 1995?

I think UNCED can do two things about U.N. reform: one good and one bad. It can either propose a whole series of changes that will facilitate broader international reform — or at least won't complicate it; or it can rush off and create a whole bunch of free-standing institutions that have a will of their own and get in the way of any attempt to reform the international system. I tend to prefer a solution for UNCED that relies either on existing institutions or creates what I call a "non-institution" such as the Group of Seven (G-7) industrialized nations.

The G-7 is a non-institution. It has no legal base, no legislative base whatever. If a non-institution such as the G-7 were established by UNCED to deal with its agenda, that would allow the reform of the U.N. to proceed, while at the same time creating some responsibility for following up UNCED. In that fashion, UNCED and UNCED's follow-up do not become the victims of protracted discussions on reform of the U.N. system, because reform of the U.N. system is the biggest international bag of snakes you could imagine.

You have written about a non-institution similar to the Group of Seven (G-7), but you suggested that to be effective it would have to expand its membership to include not only the G-7 nations but also the Russians and a number of developing countries. What would that look like?

There is a precedent for this. Right after the Report of the Brandt Commission in the early 1980s (a commission on international development chaired by the former German chancellor) there was a summit conference organized in Cancun in Mexico, which was comprised of the

G-7, plus a representative number of developing countries. It was a much broader grouping than the G-7. It was not 150 countries, but it was not 7, either. About 20 countries were invited. India and China were there, as was Venezuela. There was some method of sounding out the G-77 bloc to make sure they had a representative selection of developing countries. As a result no country could say that it was not represented, that it had just been a conference for the rich.

Cancun came very close to a major breakthrough, but subsequently fell apart. In fact, it was then viewed as a failure and was never tried again. But it had all the characteristics of the G-7 in that it had no legal or legislative basis. It was brought together at the invitation of former German Prime Minister Willi Brandt who at that point was not an official anything.

What was the focus?

The focus was on the Brandt Report and on what was needed to get the developing countries going again economically. It took up all the financial issues, trade and technology etc. It had a very full agenda which is one of the reasons that it didn't work.

But you can bring something like this kind of non-institution together just by having three or four influential world leaders who say they wish it to happen. That is how the G-7 Summit was created. It means that for three to four days a year the heads of state or heads of Government, those people who make decisions at the highest levels, have to focus on the relationship between environment and development. Otherwise they won't do it. Were we to create such a non-institution it would permit UNCED's Agenda 21 to be exposed on an annual basis to people who really count — not just Ministers of the Environment and heads of diplomatic services. Then, within this kind of non-institution, if you achieved a consensus among the world leaders on climate change, deforestation, or whatever they decided was the major issue of the day, you would have the possibility of carrying that decision on down through different levels of government bureaucracy. Furthermore, it doesn't require long negotiations to set up, nor does it require a vast Secretariat. You just do it.

If this group included 15 countries and two of them objected to the conclusions of the majority, could they veto the outcome?

Usually decisions in similar groups are by consensus, but opposition on a given issue would have to come from one or two pretty powerful countries to veto an outcome. That is the way most international negotiations work. If any one of the five permanent members of the Security Council does not like something they can veto it. If the U.S. does not like the way in which the World Bank is behaving toward country X, it can veto that, because of the way the voting mechanism is set up. The U.S. has 30 to 40 percent of the votes on the World Bank Board of Directors. So, in a sense the problem with any international negotiations is that if one of a number of powerful countries — of which there are about 10 or 12 — is absolutely dead set against something, it can usually prevent it from happening.

How would the developing country representatives be chosen for this non-organization?

It would require some sort of consensus. It would obviously need to begin with India, Brazil, perhaps Mexico and Indonesia. And then whoever set this up would have to sit down and confer with the G-77, the Commonwealth, the Francophonie, and some of the regional groupings like the Organization of African Unity (OAU). They might ask: "What would be a reasonable number of African states to have represented in this non-institution, assuming that we cannot have any more than 25 countries in all. How do we arrive at a sense of which ones ought to be included? I would think, with Africa, that you would have to start by including Egypt and Nigeria, and then negotiate about what the other one or two would be. In the case of Latin America you would clearly have Brazil, and I would think Mexico, and then you would have to negotiate about which the other one or two would be. In Asia you would have China because it is a permanent member of the Security Council. And you obviously have to have India, and I would think Indonesia. Then you would have to decide whether to include others. Of course, all the permanent members in of the Security Council would have to be involved. This would not be simple. It is a very tricky, prolonged, and difficult negotiation.

Do you see this as an interim step? This non-organization could certainly happen more quickly than some of the other steps you have identified such as the reform of the Security Council, or the creation of an Environmental Security Council.

In the best of all possible worlds what I am suggesting is simply a transitional institution. I think the ideal arrangement is to reform the U.N. system so that it is capable of discussing these and other issues in a way that reflects the current distribution of power, population, and military balance. My preferred solution is to modify dramatically the current U.N. institutions. But there is no conceivable way that will be done between now and Rio, no matter how rosy a scenario you paint.

What will be feasible by Rio? At the Preparatory Committee final session, in New York, in March, there is going to be a discussion of institutional reform. Will issues such as using the "empty vessel" of the Trusteeship Council be proposed as a focal point for the promotion of sustainable development after the Earth Summit?

I don't know what is going to happen. My bones tell me that what we will get is one of these "patch and fix" operations. Someone will put together a coordinating committee so that all of the various U.N. agencies will allegedly talk to each other about what they are doing in the field of environment and development. We will get some pious wishes expressed that when reform of the U.N. is considered over the next four or five years, consideration ought to be given to the following issues: reform of the Security Council, transforming the Trusteeship Council into Trustees of the Earth, and so on.

What do you think should happen?

One of the things that should happen right now is that, as Secretary General of UNCED, Maurice Strong, and a number of others have pointed out, there is a good deal that the Secretary General of the U.N. himself can do to sort out some of these problems, particularly in making the U.N. system more efficient, and more coordinated. •

What are some of the things that the Secretary General could do?

The Secretary General has the power to deal with the U.N. bureaucracy. He has the power to coordinate the heads of all the specialized agencies — at least on paper. And he has his own convening power as the Secretary General of a world organization. Up until now, as a group of people including Brian Urquhart have pointed out, we give less thought and consideration to picking the head of the U.N. than most medium-sized American universities do to picking their presidents. If the major powers are serious about the "new world order" and the newly emerging importance of the U.N. system in the new world order, then they had better be a lot more careful about selecting a Secretary General who is chosen for competence.

Step number two involves the post of Director General for International Economic and Social Cooperation (DGIESC). The person who fills this post would be the second in command at the U.N. and reports directly to the Secretary General. The DGIESC would be responsible for coordinating all of the economic and social activities in the U.N. system.

What would this person have to do with the U.N. Economic and Social Council (ECOSOC.) Would this person be the head of ECOSOC?

No. In the same way that the Security Council has an elected president, ECOSOC also has one. But the DGIESC commands that part of the U.N. Secretariat to which ECOSOC reports. This DGIESC is potentially a very powerful position, but it won't be unless (a) the Secretary General wants to put his own power and prestige behind it; and (b) governments make a real attempt to pick somebody to fill that number two post who believes in sustainable development and is prepared to knock heads together within the U.N. system to bring it about. Those two things can be done without any deliberation at UNCED, without any change of the U.N. Charter, and they could make a big difference — not the only difference, but a very big difference.

Are you suggesting that this DGIESC could coordinate the promotion of sustainable development issues within the U.N.?

And knock heads together. One of the problems of the U.N. is that the heads of U.N. specialized agencies tend to be the equivalent of European medieval barons. They are a law unto themselves. They report to their own governing bodies. They have very little to do with the Secretary General. They have very little to do with ECOSOC. They put up with ECOSOC because they have to report to it. But they don't pay any attention to it.

Why is that permitted?

There are two reasons. One is the failure of the Secretary General and his deputy to have any real clout to deal with these people. The second is the failure of our own governments to take anything that remotely resembles a consistent position. So, for instance, the Government of Canada sends someone from Agriculture Canada to the governing body meetings of the Food and Agriculture Organization (FAO), which deal with forestry. But we also send somebody else to the governing council of UNEP, which also deals with forestry. And we are perfectly capable, as are other governments, of sending off the FAO representative with one set of instructions and the representative to UNEP with another. As long as this goes on, the heads of specialized agencies are able to play governments off against each other. There is very little within the system to cajole, persuade, force, or bully the head of the World Health Organization (WHO) or FAO into doing what the Security Council has decided, or what ECOSOC has decided, or what the Secretary General has decided, because each agency has its own governing body and its own source of funds.

There are plenty of mechanisms that have been suggested to deal with this problem. One that I like, which again does not require anything of a legislative nature, would be for a number of governments — and there is no reason why Canada could not do this — to say: we are going to centralize within our own bureaucracy the responsibility to define a concrete coherent Canadian international position on sustainable development. We are then going to force each of our representatives to the governing bodies of each of these specialized agencies to push that position. We might even go so far as to sit down and combine with a number of other like-minded countries to introduce exactly the same resolution in the governing body of each of the U.N. specialized agencies. This coalition would require the Director General or Secretary General of that agency to play a proper part in a newly reformed coordinating mechanism. This reformed coordinating mechanism would be headed by the DGIESC, whom I think should be called the Director General for Sustainable Development. The DGIESC could then get a program carried through in each of the governing bodies. The head of each agency would be told by his or her governing body that he or she must go to these meetings, pay attention to them, and become part of a system that coordinates across various specialized agencies. The reason this is necessary is that sustainable development is a lateral concept.

This would be hard to carry out politically, but it does not require reforming the U.N. Charter, or anything outside of seven or eight governments standing up and saying: "We met in the corridor yesterday and we decided that we are going to do the following."

What you are saying is that it would be hard for the Secretary General to do that on his own, but if he received help from a coalition of governments, he could require these specialized agencies to all pull together on sustainable development initiatives?

That's right. The Secretary General can do a good deal on his own in reforming the U.N. bureaucracy, changing people's terms of responsibilities, and persuading a number of heads of specialized agencies to cooperate. But at some stage he needs a stick. And given the relative independence of the governing bodies of each of the specialized agencies, the stick will clearly have to be provided by governments who for once must rise above sectionalism and say: "We want a proper policy."

As I understand it, you are saying that as we move towards the Earth Summit in Rio, one thing we can be working on is this non-organization with a G-7-like format that is focused on sustainable development. We could also be laying the groundwork for a Security Council that would define itself more in terms of environmental security, and would include Japan.

Or a Trusteeship Council. I don't think it matters that much mechanically where the sustainable development portfolio goes. What is important is that we provide a forum that will allow these issues to be discussed at the highest international levels. I have no personal view as to whether the Security Council or the Trusteeship Council is necessarily the best body for that. But we do need to have something of this kind in the central part of the U.N. system, in an organ that is at the same level as the Security Council.

Reforming the Security Council or the Trusteeship Council so that they promote sustainable development has the advantage that neither would require creating a new institution. The creation of an Environmental Security Council, suggested as another possible option, would constitute a new institution, would it not?

I would assume so. It has been discussed in a number of ways. I think it was originally invented by the British and the Soviets, who have been playing a major role as well. I think you can view it as one of two things. An Environmental Security Council can either be a separate council, or it could be a permanent high level committee, or subcommittee, of the Security Council. I suspect you could have the latter simply by decreeing it. I presume the Security Council could set up as many committees as it wanted.

Making the Trusteeship Council into the "Trustees of the Earth" would require a charter revision. I would guess that making a new Environmental Security Council would also require a revision of the Charter.

The Security Council could probably turn around tomorrow and decide to be the Environmental Security Council. But the developing countries are very suspicious of the Security Council acquiring more power than it has now. They do not feel they have much of a voice in it, and they feel that it does not reflect the realities of the latter part of the 20th century. They are right. I think they will resist any attempt by the permanent members to give the Security Council any more power until some effort is made to reform the membership to include more permanent members from developing countries, or more temporary members from developing countries, so that it reflects a more contemporary view than just the postwar realities of Europe in 1945.

Developing nations might be comfortable with a completely reformed Security Council, but it would be difficult to negotiate. Which of these other options for institutional reform might satisfy developing nations?

I don't think anyone has really looked at this very much. When it comes to the reform of the U.N., particularly the reform of the Trusteeship Council and the Security Council, we are in somewhat the same position that we are with UNCED. The developing countries have responded to most of the issues by saying that these bodies are not representative. Until we begin to get serious discussions about providing for more representation for the rest of the world on these bodies, little progress will be made.

The developing world will look kindly on any effort to reform the Security Council, or any proposal that begins to make the senior organs of the U.N. more responsive to them. The real resistance to reform of the Security Council will come from the permanent members, particularly those whose membership is more questionable than others. Nobody would question the fact that China, the U.S., and even Russia should be permanent members of the Security Council. That is not only appropriate to 1945, it is also appropriate to 1995. But if you were picking a European representative tomorrow you would not pick either the British or the French. You would pick the Germans. And you would certainly have to include Japan. And then you would have to talk about some of the larger developing countries. Now the British and the French, currently both permanent members of the Security Council, are not going to be wildly enthusiastic about losing their seats.

Reform of the Security Council is apt to be a long and a difficult negotiation. But there are other options that you have identified. Tell me more about the Sustainable Development Council that you said came out of the World Bank. This is a meeting of the Finance Ministers, is it not?

Let us assume, in the best of all possible worlds that we get this "G-7 Plus" non-organization together, which allows the very senior political leaders in the world to meet once every two years to talk about environment and development issues, and UNCED's Agenda 21. That solves one of our problems, which is: how do you get people who are important to focus on this issue? The second problem — how to get the international system to pursue sensible solutions in this area — is partly resolved by picking a proper Secretary General and a proper Director General. But I suspect that these problems won't be entirely resolved until you get the Finance Ministers to take a watching brief over how the system reacts to sustainable development initiatives. The World Bank and IMF already have the Development Committee, which in several ways has some of the powers of those two institutions during the time between the annual meetings.

Isn't it called the Development and Interim Committee?

That's right. By tradition it is chaired by a Finance Minister, always from the developing world. Its other members are, on the whole, finance ministers. Some of them may be governors of central banks, but they are the heavy-hitters in the economic sphere. I was trying, perhaps, to be too clever, but I think you can kill two birds with one stone here. First you can get the Finance Ministers together to talk about these issues because they are already together in this committee. And second, you may begin to get closer coordination of activities between the World Bank and those of the U.N. system. Lack of this kind of coordination has been a longstanding problem, particularly in the environmental field.

The Bank does not like to be regarded as part of the U.N. system; in fact it isn't in the U.N. system. Therefore most exercises that have been designed to ensure some sort of coordination, or cooperation, or even regular exchange of pleasantries between the World Bank and U.N. haven't worked. One way to get them to work might be to get the finance ministers to encourage the Bank and the U.N. to work together.

But there are not a few critics of both the World Bank and the Finance Ministers of the world, critics who claim an unholy alliance already exists between the Bank and these Finance Ministers. The Bank funnels enormous amounts of money to the Finance Ministries of various countries, and out of these loans come projects that are frequently not very sensitive to the environment.

Yes. It's like letting the fox into the pigeon coop. But I am assuming that sustainable development is never going to work unless the environmental community, and public opinion, and the press are able to convince those who make economic decisions to make better ones. If you put this Development Committee group of Finance Ministers together tomorrow they probably would not, on the whole, make very good decisions in terms of the environment. But it is this very group that has to begin to make better decisions in terms of the environment if we are to get out of this mess.

Are you suggesting that it might help to name them the Sustainable Development Council in order to be able to criticize them for not living up to their name?

You've got it. That's exactly what you do. You also begin to get some of them to realize that there are links between decisions that are now taken for strictly economic reasons, or strictly political reasons, and for the environment, which have not traditionally been recognized. Agriculture ministers have not traditionally sat around and asked: "What is going to be the influence of this fertilizer subsidy on the environment?" That is not why they place subsidies on fertilizer. That is not why the U.S. subsidizes the production of beet sugar. Or why Western Europe subsidizes the production of beet sugar.

Over the next 10 or 15 years we have to get Finance Ministers and CEOs of large corporations to ask these sorts of questions. We need to have the Secretary of Agriculture in the U.S. sit down and say: "Does it make environmental sense for us to subsidize farmers to grow beet sugar, which is environmentally very damaging in terms of its refining?" Or: "Does it make more sense to purchase sugar from Jamaica, or Cuba, or wherever else they can grow it cheaper than we can, or where it is more environmentally sensible?" If we cannot get people to start asking and answering these questions, I think we are dead.

We dodge the bullet every time we refrain from facing up to CEOs and Ministers and getting them to make these choices. So, I am suggesting that we recognize that these Finance Ministers are the critical ingredient in making development more sustainable. We have to start putting them in situations where we can hold them responsible for making their decisions properly. They have to be told: "Look, you are not just creating GNP anymore. You are creating sustainable development, which we have to measure differently in terms of national accounting and in new ways of measuring growth in gross national product." In other words, we have to reform the world's economic system. And if we cannot fundamentally reform the world's economic system, we cannot get out of the environmental mess we are in now.

How will institutional reform put pressure on the richer nations to change, in terms of their profligate use of resources and energy? It is fairly clear how this "non-institution" might focus on sustainable development issues, but it is not clear to me that it would have the power to force the U.S., for example, to change its energy policy.

It wouldn't. The only people who are going to force the U.S. to change its energy policy are the American people. And if we are in the business of trying to change the way the U.S. does particular things, 90 percent of that is going to have to come from Americans through the ballot box and censure in the press. Some pressure can also be brought to bear on the U.S. from outside, from other countries, and from demonstrating that it is possible to use a whole lot less energy and not starve to death or live in caves.

International institutions are going to be, at least in the foreseeable future, a reflection of the policies of the governments that belong to them. I don't think we are going to create international institutions that are going to force the U.S., Western Europe, or Japan to do anything they don't want to do. They can bring to bear moral suasion, which can sometimes be very effective. They can bring to bear the court of public opinion, which can sometimes be very effective. But I don't think we will be able to move toward the sort of institution that the French were promoting at the time of the Hague Summit, which would not only set standards for carbon dioxide emissions and deal with climate, but also have some kind of punitive powers that could be enforced by the World Court. I cannot see the U.S. Government ever agreeing to that; I can't see the Japanese Government agreeing to that. That just won't happen.

I spent a good deal of time at the second and third Preparatory Committee sessions in Geneva talking with non-government organization (NGO) activists from the developing world. Many of them are critical of both international institutions and international treaties because of their "from the top down" system of governance. What we really need, they argue, is for people at the community level to have more say in how their resources are used. Vague declarations at the international level rarely get implemented at the community level in a sensible or enforceable manner, they observe.

I have argued with that position, contending that a good international treaty could help communities control the sensible use of their resources. Is there necessarily a conflict between international agreements aimed at promoting sustainable development, and community control of resources?

I think you need both. One of the interesting things about sustainable development is that it is paradoxical. It is a top-down concept, but it is also very much a bottom-up concept. The people who tend to be most abused by it are the people in the middle — the bureaucrats. Community control over natural resources is one of the key ingredients — if not the most important ingredient — of sustainable development. But, I don't see that community control of resources is incompatible with reforming the international institutions and international processes.

In the voluntary movement, the 1980s were really years devoted to empowering local communities. The emphasis of NGOs in the field, and of NGOs that sprung up in the Third World, was to find ways to give rural communities — groups of farmers, disadvantaged groups such as women, and indigenous people — a much greater say in their own lives. That is quite a critical ingredient. But I have had a lot of people from a number of these grassroots groups come to me and say: "Look, we are now beginning to understand that you can create the world's best agricultural project in region x, and yet if the decisions being made in the capital city about agricultural pricing policies, marketing boards, and marketing arrangements are no good, then this project is dead. If the price structure is wrong, how will people sell their output and have enough money to make a living? What you need, it seems to me, is a combination of more community control in natural resource management, with some sense of how you write that into the policy process on a much higher scale.

The best prepared project, in the absence of a decent national economic policy, is simply not going to work. I hear this same analysis from all over Latin America, from groups that detest central authority, distrust the traditional political establishment, and dislike the World Bank and IMF. You should ask these NGO activists how many of them are in favor of the World Bank structural adjustment process, because certainly the World Bank structural adjustment processes in most of their countries has had a profound effect on the people with whom they are working.

Many of them hate structural adjustment programs.

They may hate them, but they cannot ignore them. And that is the lesson. If you hate structural adjustment programs you had better figure out a way to change them. But you can't just stick your head in the sand and say that the only answer is community control.

Many Third World activists argue that structural adjustment programs are the source of many of their problems.

That may well be true, but the only way to deal with that is to fix the process. You can't just ignore it and go back to the village and continue with your program.

At what point do you see these international institutions and international treaties beginning to have in them a component that strengthens community control of resources, and use of them in a sustainable fashion?

I am not sure that you will get that in international agreements. You may get exhortatory phrases, but I think that will have to be fought out at the national level. There are certain things that outsiders can do to either facilitate the process or at least not hinder it. Some of the aid agencies, particularly the Scandinavians, have been relatively successful in targeting a lot of their foreign assistance to regions and countries that have agreed to that sort of thing, and made it a criterion of assistance that local control over the designated resource must exist.

The other thing one is seeing, at least in Latin America, is that with the advent of far more democratic regimes, in order to preserve the democracy a number of the governments are starting to take serious action about local and state government, which for years has been a farce in Latin America. Newly elected governments are beginning to see that one of the long-term safeguards of democracy, in Brazil and Argentina, lies in devolving considerably more power to states and municipalities. If it is done properly, that means more control by local people over their own resources. Local control may be corrupt, it may be badly run, but so what? North American communities can also be extremely badly run. If it operates correctly, it does give people in the smaller units more control over what is actually happening in their day-to-day lives. In some countries in Latin America that trend may be becoming irreversible. It would be difficult for a military coup to totally dismantle that type of structure. But you can't write that into an international agreement.

When you write about strengthening the UNDP as the lynchpin of sustainable development, what do you mean? There is considerable criticism today about the kind of development promoted by UNDP. Can you spell out what strengthening UNDP would mean, other than a larger budget?

I think it might mean that UNDP needs a new mandate. It may well mean that it should become the United Nations Sustainable Development Program (UNSDP); it may be that its mandate has to be rewritten. UNDP has a number of strengths; it also has many, many weaknesses. None of these international institutions is a paragon of virtue. They all have something wrong with them, and many of them have serious managerial problems.

But UNDP has a number of strengths. The first is that developing counties trust it. UNDP is an organization in which developing nations have had a reasonable say for a number of years; they are more likely to trust it than most other institutions that have money. The second strength is that it has an extensive international network. It has a representative in most countries, and anybody who works in this business will tell you that the best kind of UNDP resident representative is the most valuable contact an outsider can ever find in that country. They are a sort of chief-of-mission for the U.N., a person who is probably acceptable to the government, who talks to all of the aid agencies, including the World Bank and others. The job of UNDP is to help countries develop their own capacity to plan and implement development projects. Capacity-building is critical to sustainable development in a number of areas — technology transfer being among the most obvious.

Were UNDP given additional resources and its mandate rewritten, what would it be doing in these countries that it is not currently doing?

If it had further resources there are a number of things it could do. A paper was presented to the third Preparatory Committee session about capacity-building and creation of networks for sustainable development. This paper, I suspect, was written personally by the Secretary-General of UNCED, Maurice Strong. It talks about networks for sustainable development among other things. That is the kind of thing UNDP could do quite well. It would involve everything from helping to construct networks of NGOs concerned with sustainable development issues, to strengthening universities, and strengthening policy research institutes that are relatively independent in the various developing countries. This way you could strengthen sources of opinion and policy on these issues that are independent of the government.

I think it can also help to do a number of other things. How do we take people who are in government bureaucracies, who make economic decisions, and persuade and train them to analyze the environmental consequences of decisions before they make them? Let me give you an example. Suppose I were to come into country X and the president embraced me and said: "Runnalls, you are the prophet of sustainable development. You say that all our finance bureaucrats should know about the environmental consequences of their actions. I have seen the light and I agree. Where do I send them to school?" I haven't the faintest idea. We don't know how to do that. We certainly don't know how to do it in Canada. But if we are going to behave more sustainably we are going to have to figure out how to do it. How do you reform the economics profession? How do you reform the managerial ranks? How do you start environmentally friendly industries? How do you begin to make available to developing nations a reasonable flow of relatively clean, non-polluting technologies that they are ready to absorb and cope with? One of the biggest problems of technology transfer is not things like intellectual property rights and who owns the license. The biggest single problem is having the necessary intellectual and physical infrastructure to absorb new technologies in developing nations. That requires training, and capacity-building and manpower development, and research — the "soft stuff" with which the development banks have traditionally not been much involved. This does not involve building a dam, power plant, or port, or a new railway line. It involves enriching existing educational institutions, creating new ones, devising new training programs, and trying to change mindsets.

Now, at the moment, there is no unit within UNDP waiting to do all these good things. They are no more qualified to do this than anybody else. But they do have the right sort of access and the right sort of respect on the part of developing countries, and they do have it in their mandate to deliver technical assistance. So, they are the logical candidate.

You are suggesting that a good deal of the funding could go through UNDP to help various countries create a human infrastructure for sustainable development.

Yes. I have a very dogmatic view about the relationship between sustainable development and environmental management. There are a number of people who suggest that with sustainable development you don't have to do the old tasks of environmental management any longer.

I am worried that if sustainable development becomes an acceptable way of doing things, and some sort of a plum within government that people bid for, suddenly a lot of environmental agencies will become sustainable development ministries. That is fine. But then, at that stage, who is going to look after the environment? I believe that UNEP should do that. That is what UNEP has done up until now. I don't think UNEP should be in the business of implementing sustainable development. I think the World Bank should be doing that; I think UNDP should do that; I think the other specialized U.N. agencies should do that. I think UNEP should continue to be the "environmental conscience" of the system; I think it should get a whole lot more money to monitor, and evaluate, and assess the state of the global environment.

Are you suggesting that UNEP should be a kind of Environmental Protection Agency (EPA) for the world?

Yes, it ought to be the EPA of the world. I think it ought to be the U.N. Environment Program not the U.N. Sustainable Development Program. And I think it is a critical player in all this, and that its budget should be significantly increased so that it can play that role properly. But I do not think it should be in the technical assistance business; I do not think it should be in the implementation of sustainable development business. I think it should watch the others to make sure they are doing it properly.

Sustainable development work isn't obvious. You don't get it in a kit and put it together. It is not clear to me what the appropriate balance is between traditional environmental protection and sustainable development. All I know is that if everybody goes crashing off after sustainable development, then nobody will be there to make sure that water pollution and air pollution are dealt with. Sustainable development has to be done in addition to a very beefed up form of the traditional environmental monitoring and regulation; that is what UNEP ought to do.

When you talk about UNEP as the EPA of the world, it suggests not only greater cooperation, but really a new level of international regulation, not only monitoring but some kind of enforcement mechanism. Are we headed in incremental steps towards a much greater level of global governance?

I think the answer to that will be in the outcome of the climate change negotiations. They are going to require something that won't be called regulation but will masquerade under some other name. We are not going to deal with climate change without dealing with all greenhouse gases, particularly carbon dioxide emissions. Some time, probably not by the time of the summit in Rio, during the next five or six years, I would predict that we will be in a position to require countries to have some sort of quotas, caps, targets, or whatever you want to call them, on carbon dioxide emissions. At some stage we will have to decide that the U.S., for example, will emit no more than x tons of carbon equivalent per year.

And if the U.S. does emit more than its quota, what will be the consequence?

There will have to be action of some sort. I don't think it will mean that the U.S. will be dragged through the World Court, but I think it will have to cost the U.S. some money. This may be 10 years off, but we may be nearing the stage where we begin to talk about such things as tradable permits for carbon dioxide emissions. There has been a lot of discussion about that. Those permits will have value. They will be like the tradable permits under the U.S. Clean Air Act. If the U.S. exceeds its allocation it will have to pay, and pay quite a lot.

The system of tradable emission permits only works when there is an agreed upon cap on total emissions. They only have value if there is an established upper limit on how much of a pollutant can be emitted. There also has to be an enforceable penalty assessed against those who exceed it.

The cap itself will have to be established. It will be a messy process. It will have to be established in international negotiations, that will take at least 10 years to pull together, I am sure. We are talking about gross measurements here; it should not be difficult to measure. You are not going to have U.N. inspectors sitting on top of everybody's smokestack. Monitoring will have to be done by very rough measurements such as: there are x number of cars in the U.S. driven an average of y miles a year that emit z amount of greenhouse gases. The U.S. Bureau of Statistics can tell you those figures with a high enough degree of accuracy. In China they know the number of industrial boilers in the country and the number of coal fired generating stations. This is not going to be an exercise in enormous precision. It is not going to be nearly as precise, for example, as the sulfur dioxide figures in the U.S./Canada Clean Air agreement, or the figures in the U.S. Clean Air Act, because I don't think we can measure to that degree of accuracy at this stage.

What will happen if year after year the U.S. exceeds its allocation of carbon dioxide emissions?

It is going to have to buy up other people's permits.

And if it doesn't?

I don't know. If that doesn't happen there may well be sanctions applied. In the U.S. there are all kinds of other remedies one could take if the U.S. signs a treaty that is enforceable in U.S. courts.

What I'm trying to get at is whether or not we are really moving toward a new system of global governance under cover of sustainable development and sensible international environmental policy.

I don't know whether it is "under cover" of sustainable development. I can repeat the endless cliches about globalization, and increased telecommunications, and the fact that there are no borders, etc. The fact is that in terms of capital flows, and even in terms of migrations of skilled people, there really are no national borders any more. If you have money you can move it back and forth anywhere you want. And people do it all the time. If you have a highly marketable skill, nobody's immigration policy is going to keep you out. Companies are becoming much more sophisticated in deciding where they are going to locate facilities, based on labor costs, and telecommunications, and many other factors. Those processes themselves are leading to a stage where we are going to have to have a much more substantial form of global governance, simply because, if not, the whole thing will come unstuck. The fact that we have gotten over the immediate hump of the Cold War is leading people to think more about international cooperation to solve some of the other problems we have.

I wonder what would have happened if someone had sat down ten years ago and written about a world in which all of Eastern Europe suddenly became a set of market-based liberal democracies; a world in which the U.S. and former Soviet Union began to disarm themselves at a fairly substantial pace; a world in which an agreement was reached on the Soviet withdrawal from Afghanistan; a world in which there was a Middle East conference with some prospects of settlement; a world in which the South African apartheid regime had finally self destructed. The changes we have seen in the last couple of years are totally unprecedented in the last several hundred years.

We are now faced with more of a tabula rasa than anybody would have thought possible We are faced with the prospect of how we actually construct a whole series of mechanisms to get us through the next millennium without a lot of the baggage of the last 50 years. The shackles on government and on people we had over the last 50 years have kind of fallen away. And one can optimistically think that progress will happen in a halting way. Things will go wrong. Progress will not happen nearly as fast as anybody wants it to. Things will appear to fall apart. Nevertheless, we are groping toward a system in which the international institutions will become more important in the running of the world. And the financing of those institutions and the governance of those institutions will be something that will occupy the minds of statesmen for the next 25 to 50 years.

I am not saying that the millennium for world federalists is just around the corner. But we are clearly moving to a stage in which these international institutions become more important. And making those international institutions more accountable than they are now, as they get more and more money, will be a critical question for politicians.

Are you suggesting that sustainable development will be central to that new international formulation?

The thing that drives sustainable development more than anything is the threat of major changes in climate. And the answer to the climate change problem is sustainable development. Because that is the only way you can cope with it and still offer the peoples of the developing world the prospect of a better life.

Hillary F. French:

Assessing International Environmental Treaties

 illary F. French is Senior Researcher at the Worldwatch Institute in Washington, D.C. She is author of *After the Earth Summit: The Future of Environmental Governance* published in March, 1992 as Worldwatch Paper # 107. In addition she has written *Clearing the Air: A Global Agenda* and *Green Revolutions: Environmental Reconstruction in Eastern Europe and the Soviet Union.*

Steve Lerner: What is the area you focus on at the Worldwatch Institute?

Hillary F. French: In general terms I focus on international environmental politics. This last year that has meant looking in depth at international institutions, treaties, and how well they are working or failing to work in the environmental area. I have also done quite a bit of work on the environmental problems of Eastern Europe and the Soviet Union.

You have suggested the possibility of grafting a sustainable development component onto existing institutions that have an important impact on the global environment. How do you see that working?

Some of the institutions that would fall into that category are the World Bank, the International Monetary Fund (IMF) and the General Agreement on Tariffs and Trade (GATT). The issue is how to take these institutions, which are unquestionably major players in the international economy, and integrate some concerns about environmental sustainability into their programs. There has been quite a bit of attention paid to how you might do this with the World Bank — with mixed success, but certainly, one would have to say, some success, although there is a lot more room for progress.

The IMF is uncharted territory in this domain. The Fund has a huge impact around the world through its structural adjustment lending programs in Third World countries where, in exchange for access to balance of payments stabilization funds, developing countries agree to put in place a whole host of policy reform measures that will, in theory, make them more creditworthy so they will pay back their loans. One thing the IMF could do would be to integrate environmental sustainability into the very essence of its structural adjustment program. Policies such as environmental taxation might be suggested. That might sound like a radical proposal, but if you buy the logic of sustainable development, that a country's future economic health depends on its ecological resources, then it really makes a lot of economic as well as environmental sense to do this.

That might work when we are trying to promote sustainable development in the Third World, because there is leverage with these countries when they are requesting financial aid. But when it comes to promoting sustainable development in the industrialized countries it seems more difficult to find the necessary leverage. Might the GATT be able to exert some pressure on developed countries to pursue sustainable development policies?

That is a possibility. I think the first priority with the GATT is seeing that it does not serve as an obstacle to legitimate, environmentally motivated policies around the world. There have been a number of worrisome incidents in the last few years. The most prominent was the ruling in September by a GATT dispute resolution panel that a U.S. law, the Marine Mammal Protection Act, was in violation of the GATT because it imposed an embargo against tuna from Mexico caught in ways that killed more dolphins in the process than U.S. fisherfolk are allowed to kill. This sent a signal to the world that the GATT could be a real obstacle toward putting in place some of the policies that we need. Even provisions of some international agreements, like the Montreal Protocol on Ozone Depletion and the Convention on International Trade in Endangered Species (CITES), might be deemed at odds with the GATT. There is considerable concern that some provisions of these international agreements will be challenged under the GATT.

So, the first priority is to amend the GATT so that legitimate environmental goals are recognized to be as important as free trade goals. As it is now set up free trade is viewed, at least by people who participate in the GATT talks, as sacred. It is difficult to challenge the worthiness of the free trade goal, but I think nations do have to accept that there may be cases where constraints on free trade are justified due to environmental or other considerations

But beyond stating that nations have the right to set their own environmental policy, even though it might occasionally be a constraint on free trade, nations are likely to move toward common standards negotiated through trade bodies. Governments are already voicing support for this idea. They call this harmonization. If common standards exist, then there is no trade barrier created because everybody is playing by the same rules and you can sell your product anywhere. If these common standards were set at a high level, then you would have a movement toward stricter environmental protection that would be driven initially by trade considerations.

The difficulty is figuring out at what level these standards should be set, and ensuring that they do not serve as a brake on countries that want to have more progressive legislation. There are means by which this can be done. In the European Community it is clearly stipulated that countries can go beyond a common standard, even if having a stricter environmental standard does sometimes act as a trade barrier. There was a ruling a few years ago by the European Court of Justice concerning Denmark's desire to mandate the use of refillable bottles. Some people saw that ruling as a real victory for the environment. But it was presented in other places as more of a victory for free trade.

I spent quite a bit of time investigating it and found that the ramifications of this ruling had been misreported in some of the ecological press. As a result there are a lot of misconceptions about the ruling. What I found was that even among some of the most vociferous environmentalists from Denmark, this particular ruling was viewed as a victory for their environmental policies. What the ruling said was that Denmark could go ahead with its returnable bottle program even though it did have the effect of discriminating against foreign bottlers. The court ruled that the environmental goal could, in this instance, take precedence over free trade.

That ruling sent a signal across the continent that countries would be able to set standards that were higher than the European Community's common standard. As a result, governments have been forging ahead with some very strict policies in Germany, the Netherlands, and Denmark in particular. Germany has now proposed a strict packaging law under which all kinds of wastes would have to be recycled and collected by industry. As with the Danish case, there were questions as to whether Germany's stricter packaging standard would constitute a trade barrier. But what seems to be happening is that the European Community feels that it cannot challenge the German program as a trade barrier because of the precedent created by this Danish returnable bottles case, as well as the language in the E.C. treaty itself. Instead they are writing common E.C. legislation that is modeled on German program. That means that the whole E.C. will have to approximate Germany's very progressive law. So a country can have standards stricter than the E.C. standard, but no nation can go below it. This works best when you have countries that are basically at the same stage of development to begin with, as in the E.C.

You have pointed out that international treaties to protect the global environment have some problems as tools for preventing environmental degradation. These treaties often take a long time to negotiate. Treaties subscribed to by large numbers of countries also often end up with the "lowest common denominator" effect where the standards adopted are those of the most reluctant member. As alternatives to treaties you mentioned the role of unilateral action by a country to goad other na-

*tions into taking action. Could you tell us a little more about what you
see as the alternatives to the treaty process?*

The alternatives have to, and do, go hand in hand with the treaty process. There is no escape from the need for international treaties on global environmental problems. Sometimes you don't have to have the
whole world participating in a treaty. If the issue is saving the Baltic
Sea, of course, all you need is the countries that border the Baltic Sea,
and that makes it a lot easier to get agreement. In fact there are not that
many issues that do require the agreement of the entire world, at this
point. That simplifies it greatly by narrowing the range of players to
those that are really affected by a given problem.

The question is: What can nations do to push the process forward if
they see it moving at a rate that is too slow for their taste? One thing
nations have done is either made a unilateral pledge, or gotten a number
of other countries to go along with them in taking a particular action,
before there is an international treaty mandating it. For example, the
E.C., in the global warming talks, has agreed to a stabilization of carbon
dioxide at 1990 levels by the year 2000. They did that completely apart
from any international treaty. This kind of initiative was taken in the
European acid rain negotiations as well; several countries got together
and agreed to go well beyond what some of the more laggard countries
were willing to agree to. Then, in subsequent years, there was a tight-
ening of the entire agreement. So, setting a positive example has been a
useful tool.

Incentives or penalties can also be used to get reluctant countries on
board. One type of incentive would be the creation of a fund that would
allow poorer countries to participate. Here the line gets a little blurred
between the negotiating phase and the implementing phase because the
incentive can involve both: it can be a way of getting countries to join an
agreement and a way to help them implement it.

The penalty approach has also been used in a number of cases. The
U.S. imposed trade sanctions on Japan, for example, to try to get them to
join in the ban on commercial whaling. This is a controversial course of
action mainly because the powerful countries have a much greater ability to use this "big stick" approach than do the less powerful countries.

Did it work?

Yes, it did work. That is the key thing. Trade sanctions tend to work.
Developing countries are not at all in favor of the use of this tool, but by
the same token, if you have an environmental goal that is important to
you, trade sanctions are, in many cases, the only way you can get other
countries to go along with it. I also think they are fair game in the sense
that what trade sanctions often do is simply say that a country trying to
sell its products in your market has to meet the same restrictions that
your own producers meet.

I think that countries should have the right to control the means by which something is produced that is sold within their borders. But trade agreements don't generally recognize that right. The GATT, at least in the recent tuna ruling, distinguishes between a product itself and the means that are used to produce it. So it would be all right with the GATT if a government wanted to require a certain fuel-efficiency standard on cars and make that standard legally applicable to domestic built and imported cars. But it would not be acceptable to the GATT if that government wanted to require that cars sold in its territory not be produced in a way that creates a terrible toxic contamination problem. That is where the GATT draws the line. And I think that is an artificial distinction.

What do you think about the proposals for the reform of the governance of the Global Environment Facility (GEF)?

I think we have to expect that the governments that give money will want to retain some control over how their funds are spent. However, I do think governments should include recipients of that money in the decision-making processes determining how the funds will be spent. There is clear justification for this. Brazil, for example, is likely to be on the receiving end of a large share of the funds for the GEF, at least those devoted to biological diversity and forest preservation. Brazil is going to be asked to put in place a lot of projects that are intended to help the global cause of protecting biological diversity. So it should logically have a role in designing these projects. Indeed, in practical terms, Brazil's cooperation is needed to carry the projects out.

Even some of the donor countries, including the U.S., are willing to consider alternative means of distributing the voting weight within the GEF or another kind of Green Fund. In the Montreal Protocol ozone fund, developed and developing countries have equal voting power. This is an interesting model. One other idea would be to consider a country's ecological assets, as well as its traditional economic ones, in apportioning voting rights. Under this system a country like Brazil, which harbors a large share of the world's biological diversity, might get credit for that when the voting powers are divided up.

Do you feel we are at the beginning of an intense era of negotiation on international environment and development issues? Do you feel these environmental negotiations are going to make big headlines in the years ahead?

I think there is no question that these issues are going to be big news in the years ahead. The problems we face are very urgent. Global warming stands to inundate coastal areas and decimate agricultural productivity in certain parts of the world. The loss of biological diversity is staggering if you look at the rate at which species are being lost that could harbor important agricultural strains or medicinal values. Deforestation is proceeding at rapid rates. So, if nations want to solve these problems that are so closely tied to the welfare of their people, they really have no choice but to cooperate through international treaties and institutions. The winding down of the Cold War provides room for these issues to emerge onto the international agenda.

Do you get the sense that we are moving toward some kind of global governance on these issues?

We already have global governance on many of these issues. The fact that nations have already agreed to over 170 international environmental treaties, and that more than two-thirds of these have been reached in the last 20 years, is a sign that governments are recognizing that they have no choice but to come together in new forms of international agreement on the issues before them. Probably the most far reaching of these agreements is the Montreal Protocol on Ozone Depletion. This has affected important industries in countries around the world. They are being forced to completely shift away from chemicals widely used in a number of industrial processes, toward totally different forms of production. World production of CFCs is already down more than 40 percent from its peak in 1987. So, I think the process is really already underway. Governments are gradually delegating to international institutions authority to help them combat shared threats of great concern to their citizens. I think this process will continue.

Is the United Nations Conference on Environment and Development (UNCED) dramatically different than past environmental negotiations?

I think UNCED is a relatively unique event. The scale of it is unprecedented in the history of international environmental negotiations. In the past we have worked on one treaty at a time, whereas with UNCED we are faced with an enormous list of issues that we are trying to resolve by June, 1992. There is some precedent for UNCED in the Stockholm Conference held 20 years ago, but that was a very different kind of event. For one thing, there were just two heads of state in attendance compared with the over 100 expected to participate at the Earth Summit in Rio. The breadth of the issues on the table at UNCED is also very different, with the climate change and biodiversity treaties up for discussion, and the incorporation of development into the agenda.

Has grouping this number of issues together in the UNCED negotiations proved a fruitful approach? Have the linkages been made between the environment and development issues?

That is a key question and I waiver in my opinion. On one level, the range of issues being discussed at UNCED seems too broad. I tend to view the real priority as coming up with institutional frameworks that will enable the process to continue over the long run. There is certainly no way we are going to solve all the problems on the UNCED agenda before June, 1992.

From that standpoint, I would like to see a narrow focus on the institutional issues and on the financial resource and technology transfer questions. On the other hand, it is possible to argue that form should follow function and that we should know what we want institutions for and what programs we need them to implement. Certainly there is a value to trying to get governments to grapple with this complex of issues as a whole, to force them to grasp how all of the issues connect.

What would be the best institution to focus attention on sustainable development after UNCED?

The question is not what a new institution is called, but rather what it is supposed to do. Whether the United Nations Environment Program (UNEP) is given a lot more money and significantly new powers, or a Commission on Sustainable Development created, or a Committee on Environment and Development, as the U.S. has proposed, the key issue is that it must have resources and clout. The powers it needs would be in the area of facilitating treaty negotiations — perhaps using various forms of majority voting if necessary, monitoring compliance with treaties, and marshalling financial and technological assistance. These are all powers that are currently diffuse in the United Nations system.

How can we judge if a proposed institution is likely to be effective at promoting sustainable development? Does it matter where this institution is located in the U.N.? Or should we be looking at its budget?

One of the hallmarks of an institution that could deal with these issues seriously would be that the governments were willing to give it a significant amount of money to.

What would be a significant amount?

UNEP's budget was $59 million in 1989 and is now supposed to be about $150 million. The budget needs to continue to increase. Then there is the related question of the Global Environment Facility (GEF) and funding for on-the-ground programs such as the trust funds that might be created under any new treaties, or to carry out Agenda 21. Those would require a much higher level of funding.

Would it really be enough to simply increase UNEP's budget and mandate? For one thing UNEP is located in Kenya. Would it not be awkward for an organization headquartered in Nairobi to coordinate the work of other U.N. agencies?

Yes it would be. The U.S. has proposed giving UNEP a greater presence in New York, and I think that would make some sense.

So UNEP would not move out of Nairobi but it would have an expanded office at the U.N. in New York.

Yes, UNEP already has a small office here, but the U.S. proposes creating an office in New York, where UNEP's Executive Director would spend a significant amount of his time. It would also be helpful to strengthen the UNEP office in Geneva. The developing countries are not thrilled with this idea because they see it as symbolically important that UNEP is headquartered in Kenya. Anything that is done to diminish that is not looked upon with favor. However, it would help for UNEP to have more of a presence at U.N. headquarters in New York, just in terms of small but important things like making documents more rapidly available.

Are you suggesting that one of the real contenders for sustainable development coordination after UNCED is a strengthened UNEP?

Yes, it is a strong contender. It will not be the only institution charged with this role, but it will be one of the important ones.

What other institution might become a focal point for coordinating sustainable development work?

I think it is likely that there will be some board or commission that is created to monitor the follow-up to UNCED and Agenda 21. That would be a body separate from UNEP. It might be through the Economic and Social Commission. It might be a Committee on Environment and Development, as proposed by the U.S., that would combine three pre-existing committees under the General Assembly. The three pre-existing committees, according to the U.S., are not currently fulfilling a very important function.

Would this Committee on Environment and Development be at a lower level within the U.N. than the proposed Commission on Sustainable Development?

As far as I know there is no clear ranking difference between a committee and a commission. However, there is a danger with either proposal that any body created will lack real clout. For instance, if the new committee meets just once a year, which I think is what the U.S. is talking about, there is a high probability that it will not accomplish a great deal. The committee would get governments together annually to review what has happened, but it would not have the power to do anything proactive. In fact, that is what happened with the follow-up to the 1982 U.N. Energy Conference. It is ironic that one of the committees the U.S. wants to reconstitute into this new Committee on Environment and Development is the Committee on New and Renewable Sources of Energy, which was created after the 1982 U.N. Energy Conference to oversee follow-up.

Did it ever do anything?

No. The whole reason that the U.S. is proposing meshing it into this broader effort is that the U.S. describes it as moribund. One of the members of the U.S. delegation even went so far as to call it comatose. There is the potential that a similar thing could happen to the proposed Committee on Environment and Development, particularly if its whole mandate is to "review and advise," as the U.S. suggests. In recent discussions there were clear distinctions made between countries that wanted to keep words in Agenda 21, such as "verify" compliance with treaties, as contrasted with the U.S. position which pushed for "reviewing" compliance. There are significant differences in what is implied by those terms. It's unlikely that this committee or commission would actually have the power to go to governments and ask them to supply evidence that they are complying with Agenda 21 commitments, as is really needed. Instead, governments might all just get together once a year and listen to what governments themselves say about what they are doing.

In your paper, After the Earth Summit: the Future of Environmental Governance, *you suggest that while compliance is a problem with many treaties, they are not complied with any less than are many national laws. If we are going to improve the enforcement of treaties there are several things we can do: (1) monitor compliance, (2) issue annual reports about compliance, and (3) resolve disputes through the World Court. What do you think is the best strategy for improving compliance with international environmental treaties?*

There is some precedent for what needs to be done in some of the systems that already exist both within the environmental domain and in other fields of international relations such as human rights and labor laws. For example, the Convention on International Trade in Endangered Species (CITES) has a secretariat — an office — charged with implementing it. This secretariat has powers that, as far as I know, no other environmental treaty secretariat has. These powers include not only serving as a repository for reports that governments are asked to submit, but the authority to go to countries, if they have reason to believe a government is not implementing the treaty, and ask them why. The secretariat can also bring this non-compliance to the attention of other governments, which can in turn use the force of international persuasion and diplomacy to bring about a change in the behavior of the offending nation.

I think this is an interesting model for the kinds of provisions most treaties should include. However, governments have traditionally been resistant to entrusting these kinds of powers to an international agency. They would rather keep it within the control of what they call the "conference of the parties," which is composed of the governments that have signed onto the treaty. Governments would prefer to let these annual meetings of governments deal quietly with any compliance problems. But it is unrealistic to expect that governments gathering once a year are really going to be able to be on top of these kinds of issues.

Would it help to delegate more power to the governing bodies of international environmental treaties so that they can set new environmental standards as conditions in the real world change?

The main advantage of delegating to governing bodies the power to up-date treaties is that it speeds up the whole process. Negotiating a treaty can take years from the time it is proposed to the time it is ratified. In fact, some of the major environmental treaties that have been negotiated are still not in effect. An example of this is the Law of the Sea, which has been languishing for over 10 years awaiting enough ratifications. The Basel Accord on Hazardous Waste Export is another one that has not yet entered into force. The main advantage of delegating this power to governing bodies of treaties is that you can do away with the ratification process and set in motion a more flexible instrument that can be easily adapted.

Is one of the problems with many of the existing environmental treaties, that their secretariats are not equipped to monitor compliance?

Yes, that has been a real problem with most of the treaties we have on the books. The problem is twofold. First, the secretariat of the treaty has often lacked resources, budget, and staff. The other problem is that the secretariat often doesn't have the authority to do the job. In the environmental realm, the CITES secretariat, as far as I know, is the only secretariat allowed to go to governments and request information about whether or not they are complying.

Do you think there is a need for a single institution to coordinate the negotiation and enforcement of international environmental treaties?

I think, ultimately, that may be what is required; in fact, it is likely to happen at some point in the years to come. However, it is a long way from where we are right now, and I think we have to move forward one step at a time. Governments have to gradually become accustomed to the idea of delegating some of these powers to international institutions. As they do they will realize that there are tremendous economies of scale to centralizing the whole process.

There are a couple of parts of the process that could be centralized now. The process doesn't have to be centralized all at once. For example, the negotiating end of the process could be centralized. Some countries are in favor of doing this, although not enough of them to make it happen immediately. It would make sense to have a central negotiating body that would be in charge of facilitating the negotiation of the various treaties that are now before us.

As the system exists now, a brand new international committee is frequently put together for the express purpose of negotiating a given treaty. An example of this is the Intergovernmental Negotiating Committee (INC) set up to marshal the climate change talks. This is a very cumbersome way of going about it, and makes it difficult for many developing countries to adequately cover all the different negotiations that are underway. If the process was centralized in one place it would be easier. We are beginning to do this, though, as far as I know, not by design. The fact that the climate change negotiations and UNCED negotiations are happening in New York one right after the other may cause some people to realize that this is a more efficient way of doing things.

The other function that could be centralized is enforcement. Enforcement could be centralized if the secretariats for all the treaties were in one building somewhere rather than scattered in little offices all over the world, as they now are.

There seems to be a double bind in designing enforceable treaties. If they are too strict they scare countries off and few countries sign them. If they are too lax the treaties are hardly worth the paper they are printed on. Is it true that at the moment we really don't have an enforcement mechanism for these treaties?

In large measure that is where we are. There is a trade-off. Some countries argue that strong enforcement mechanisms, and strong targets, and timetables in treaties will discourage nations from participating. There is some legitimacy to that argument. But I also think that one should not be in too big a hurry to have a treaty just for the sake of having a treaty. If you have a global warming treaty that doesn't have any commitments to reduce emissions of the main greenhouse gas, carbon dioxide, then what is the point of having the treaty in the first place? There is nothing wrong with holding out for a treaty that has some real substance to it, rather than trying to reach the common denominator that everyone will be ready to agree to.

The other element that should be brought into this discussion is the importance of financial and technological transfers as a way to prevent countries from being afraid of taking responsibility for compliance. If a treaty contains strict monitoring, compliance, and enforcement mechanisms, developing countries might have good reason to shy away from signing it, because they lack the technical and financial means to implement it. However, if these countries were provided the resources to implement the treaty, then I don't think they would be so worried about signing it.

You wrote that "Paradoxically, one way to make environmental agreements more effective is, in some cases, to make them less enforceable." What did you mean by that?

I was thinking of the use of so-called "soft law" which is largely composed of action plans and declarations, as opposed to legally binding treaties. I was pointing out that such instruments can be useful by laying the groundwork for future agreements of a more binding nature, and creating an international consensus on an issue without scaring countries away. So, there is a fine line between deciding when you do want international agreements to have teeth and when you want to leave them, for the time being, at the action plan level.

Do you see the General Principles on Forestry being negotiated at UNCED as the kind of soft law that may lead to a forestry convention?

My impression is that the U.S. is still very keen on eventually having a legally binding treaty on forestry. The question is whether or not the United States is willing to have the convention's rules applied to its own forests, and take real action at home as part of that effort. I think there is reason to believe that the U.S. is not ready to take these kinds of action at home.

An effort to negotiate a treaty will backfire if it is perceived as an attempt to impose conditions on the Third World without any willingness to do the same thing here in the United States. I am skeptical that the U.S. would agree to a treaty that could be used to pressure it at home. Perhaps that skepticism is unwarranted, but that has been the pattern with many of the negotiations that are underway. There is an effort to get developing countries to do things we in the North would like to see them do, yet an unwillingness to accept any constraints on our own actions, such as our voracious energy appetite.

How can inter-treaty bargains be made without an institution that bridges the various environmental treaties?

International agencies will need sufficient powers and resources if they are to serve as mediators between the various nations. However, UNEP has already played this role in several important instances. Mostafa Tolba, the head of UNEP, is credited by many people with playing an important role in the negotiations over an ozone treaty in Montreal in 1987, and also in the talks at the Basel Convention on Hazardous Waste Export. He struck the deals behind the scenes.

This is the kind of service an international agency can provide. It can act as a credible third party that can broker agreements among governments. This could be done more efficiently and effectively if there were strong institutional backing, and someone with real stature. I am thinking of the role being played by the European Community's Environment Commissioner, Carlo Ripa DiMeana. He has been a bit of a surprise. Environmentalists didn't know what to think of him when he came on as the Environment Commissioner of the E.C., but he has risen to the challenge and is a very visible figure in trying to get governments to put forth innovative proposals. For example, he has been a key player in the effort to get a carbon tax implemented in the European Community. If we had someone like him at the international level, it could help mobilize governments.

Scott A. Hajost:

Lobbying at International Environmental Negotiations

cott A. Hajost is International Counsel at the Environmental Defense Fund, and a representative to UNCED from the Consortium for Action to Protect the Earth (CAPE '92) and the Climate Action Network (CAN).

Steve Lerner: You have been active in a variety of international environmental negotiations in different capacities: You were with the State Department and the Environmental Protection Agency (EPA), and now you're at the Environmental Defense Fund (EDF). How does the United Nations Conference on Environment and Development (UNCED) rank in terms of importance?

Scott A. Hajost: I think you have to say it is important because it is the first effort in 20 years to link development and environmental issues. The challenge for both non-government organizations (NGOs) and governments is to try to find what can be accomplished. General Assembly Resolution 44/228, which created UNCED, laid out a daunting task. One can argue that everything in the world is probably linked in one way or another, but the particular challenge for UNCED continues to be to define a realistic set of goals that can be set in motion by 1992.

Do you think that UNCED's scope was too broadly defined? Would it be more successful if some priorities had been made early on, forcing delegates to focus on making progress in a few discrete areas?

It is my personal opinion that UNCED is a bit too much of the "kitchen sink". Where do you draw these lines? There is no easy answer. At the UNCED negotiations there is very little time to talk about an incredible array of subjects. Take energy policy, for example. The U.S. delegation didn't say much about energy. They had to be reminded that energy goes well beyond climate change and that energy is a development issue and a standard air pollution issue.

Why wasn't the discussion of each nation's energy policy, and its impact on environment and development, made a top priority at UNCED? It seems as if this is the issue that cuts across all others.

I think it has been a priority for the secretariat. UNCED Secretary General Maurice Strong has seen this issue as crucial. While the secretariat would not say this, I think there is a perception that the climate treaty negotiations probably will not get beyond a framework convention, at least in the first stage. The reason for this is that there is a significant divergence of opinion on what kind of carbon dioxide commitments various nations are willing to make. Therefore, it was thought that UNCED could be a useful fall back position for the climate treaty negotiations, filling in the gaps through an Agenda 21 programmatic agenda.

I think the UNCED secretariat originally imposed too narrow an interpretation on the climate convention. A climate convention should create not only a legal mechanism but also a framework to address programmatic areas of energy relating to climate change and carbon dioxide. The climate treaty was being viewed as a fairly narrow legal instrument when we still have to engage in a large variety of other programmatic initiatives. That happened as a result of not knowing how far the International Negotiating Committee (INC) would get. Since that time there has been a lot more collaboration between the INC and UNCED. At least now there is agreement that energy is a crosscutting issue that is fundamental to development and environmental protection. Under this definition of the issue, UNCED does not have to interfere with the climate treaty negotiations at all.

One of the great challenges that confronts us is to transform the global energy supply system. We need to move from fossil and nuclear fuels to renewable energy sources. Why was the challenge of transforming the world's energy system not given a higher priority at UNCED?

I think it is because a lot of countries, including the U.S., were fearful of having to fight climate change issues on two fronts: at the climate change negotiations and at UNCED. For better or worse, the positions various countries take on energy related issues at UNCED are being defined by their climate negotiators. They are not looking very far past climate change treaty negotiations, nor do they seem to want to stake out positions that go beyond it.

However, at the third Preparatory Committee session, it seemed as if the U.S. agreed to talk about energy in some fashion. They have actually put some decent positions on the negotiating table. I think energy should be right there at the top of the agenda because it cuts across so many sectors. In the oceans area, for example, the more you reduce reliance on fossil fuels, the less you have to worry about oil spills in the ocean — and the less you have to worry about Antarctica being opened up to potential oil drilling 50 years from now. In the Arctic as well, there has just been an environmental protection strategy adopted by the Arctic rim countries. So I think energy will be addressed, but it is taking a while.

Some activists from developing nations think that there was a conspiracy from the outset of the UNCED deliberations not to put energy at the top of the agenda because many of the most powerful nations do not want to make sacrifices in their use of energy.

There is probably some truth to that. That is a point that U.S. environmental groups have made as well, particularly in relation to forest protection issues. A perception has been created that the U.S. position is to some extent "sink driven," in other words, driven by a policy of enhancement of forests. Clearly, stopping deforestation is critical in its own right. But the U.S. isn't prepared to face up to the negative consequences of its energy consumption patterns.

There has been a suggestion about creating a new U.N. presence on energy issues. The International Atomic Energy Agency (IAEA), of course, deals just with the nuclear aspect of energy. Yet IAEA is the only international body that deals at a global level with energy issues. Otherwise you have the Organization of Economic Cooperation and Development/International Energy Agency (OECD/IEA) which has been in large part focused on security of energy supplies. But we don't really have anything in the U.N. system that is effective in the energy arena.

The most important U.N. related body in terms of energy policy today is the World Bank and its lending programs. If you don't get the multilateral development banks moving on the right path in energy lending, then you are not going to be really successful. The discussion continues about the World Bank's Global Environment Facility (GEF) and how it might be reformed. There are also discussions about how projects will be funded under the climate treaty. Both the INC and the UNCED Preparatory Committee are grappling with how to address a revised GEF funding mechanism. Basically we have to change the way energy is in used the South, but, more importantly, in the North, including in the U.S.

One of the difficulties that UNCED faces is that it can almost always be said that an issue is being covered by some other negotiation or U.N. agency, and therefore that UNCED should not discuss it.

Yes, an example of that is the whaling issue. Some countries are frustrated by the International Whaling Commission (IWC) and foresee a possible end of the commercial whaling moratorium. Representatives of these nations would like a review of the IWC to come out of UNCED. Other countries resist this. Similarly, countries that would like to ban radioactive waste disposal at sea and want to amend the London Dumping Convention, would like to see UNCED initiate something in this area. The London Dumping Convention parties have had a dispute for nine years on radioactive waste disposal at sea. Are they likely to find a way out of their impasse? Should UNCED say anything about it?

But states that don't want new negotiations in this area resist this approach. They point out that radioactive dumping is being taken care of outside UNCED. Another example involves whether or not there should be a discussion of reforming the World Bank at UNCED. Some argue that reform of the World Bank should happen within the World Bank and that UNCED shouldn't discuss it. Another question is whether

UNCED should talk about trade issues and reform of GATT.

You have just come from the negotiations in Nairobi on climate change. Is there going to be a climate change convention signed in Brazil in June, 1992? If so, will it be a convention without target reductions of carbon dioxide? If it does not include specific targets for carbon dioxide emission reductions, will it really help control global warming?

I think there will be some form of climate treaty signed in Rio. There is enough political momentum to get agreement. There are, however, a lot of pitfalls along the way. If you look at the developing country role in the climate treaty negotiations, it is anything but monolithic. Argentina is already splitting ranks with the Third World and is trying to move towards the developed world. The Association of Small Island States, worried about going under because of sea level rise, wants everyone to stop squabbling and agree to an effective climate change treaty.

The major stumbling block has been the squabble between the U.S. and the rest of its OECD partners. The South, which is not monolithic itself, looks at the North and says: "You guys cannot reach agreement about what you ought to do. You talk about the high costs of doing anything about global warming, yet you use 10 times more energy than we do. Then you question the science of climate change. What are we supposed to think? Climate change may not be our top priority. We have to worry about poverty." The fact that the North does not have a united front on this issue makes it more difficult to reach a negotiated solution.

One of the biggest problems we face in negotiations is the fact that the United States does not have a good energy policy and does not subscribe to any form of targets or timetables for limiting the emissions of carbon dioxide.

So, there will be a climate change treaty. How far it goes, however, remains a question. I would hedge my bets and say there will be some shift in the U.S. position. There may be something that allows the White House to slide away from total opposition to any form of targets and timetables. States are not going to agree, however, in the first phase to a 20 percent cut in carbon dioxide emissions, which is what we at EDF, CAPE '92, and CAN think is necessary. There are some states, including Germany, calling for actual cuts in carbon dioxide emissions. From the perspective of the environmental community, the first phase of the climate convention is not going to go as far as we think it should to make economic, technical, and scientific, as well as environmental sense.

But I am an optimist, no matter what I am told by my sources in the Administration. The White House perception on the climate change negotiation is that it is going to have a negative impact on the economy and, therefore, is bad. I think the Administration is going to hear a lot more from the American people and from Congress on this issue. The President is going to face pressure to attend the Rio summit during the UNCED and climate change sessions in New York.

237

I think something will be put on the negotiating table that will create a process for making progress on the climate change issue. The treaty may make some minimum progress towards limiting greenhouse gas emissions, including carbon dioxide. I hope it will set out an agenda for action so that things won't just stop once the treaty enters into force. There needs to be a process by which, within a couple of years, we can return and negotiate a much more detailed subsidiary agreement to the climate change convention that will actually involve some real cuts in emissions of greenhouse gases.

What do you think of the U.S. position that we don't have to set targets for the reduction of carbon dioxide emissions because we are controlling other greenhouse gases through the Montreal Protocol and through the Clean Air Act? Is that a reasonable position to take, or is it a refusal to face the crisis that confronts us?

In the long term we have to control gases other than carbon dioxide, although carbon dioxide is the most important of the gases to control. The Intergovernmental Panel on Climate Change (IPCC) tells us that we have to cut a variety of greenhouse gases and address a variety of sinks and sources. To do that we have to enhance forests and halt deforestation. But the bottom line is that carbon dioxide forms the bulk, particularly from the energy sector, of the greenhouse gases and must be given priority along with methane.

We in the environmental community think we ought to stay within certain rates of temperature change. We see a certain concentration in the atmosphere of carbon dioxide, as well as other greenhouse gases, that require that we make some significant cuts in carbon dioxide. Does that mean a 60 percent or 50 percent cut? There is room to maneuver if you include methane, for example, in your calculations. But, the bottom line is that if we are going to halt global warming, we have to act on carbon dioxide from the energy sector.

To environmentalists it is not an all or nothing question. There can be a phased approach. As you learn more about these sources and sinks you can build a more comprehensive approach over time. We know enough about methane from industrial sources, for example, and the technologies and the economics of it, that we can make reductions. In fact, EDF and the Natural Resources Defense Council (NRDC) have sent joint comments to the EPA on proposed landfill regulations on non-volatile organic compounds. We argue that there is both an economic justification and a climate change justification for obtaining methane reductions from landfills.

The calculation about the various ways of reducing emissions of other greenhouse gases is complicated. How much does the Clean Air Act reduce U.S. emissions of greenhouse gases? There are lots of numbers games, but the bottom line is that there should be no double counting of emissions reductions — a practice that has been described as "double dipping." Montreal Protocol gases are regulated by the Montreal Protocol and reductions under this treaty should not be counted as greenhouse gas reductions. I think that the U.S. has not been able to face up to doing something in the energy sector and as a result has resorted to a "comprehensive approach" that involves double-dipping. That is changing, however, now that assessments under the Montreal Protocol and the IPCC have concluded that the warming impact of CFCs is offset by cooling from ozone depletion. Thus CFCs are not as important as a greenhouse gas and that should force the U.S. to rethink its position.

Is a substantial reduction of carbon dioxide emissions the most significant action the United States could take to convince developing nations that we are serious about entering into a partnership with them to halt accelerating environmental degradation?

From many perspectives that would probably be the best thing the U.S. could put on the table. If the U.S. were to say that it will do its part to reduce consumption of goods and resources, the first reform (for a gluttonous, fossil fuel addicted society such as ours) would be to minimize our use of fossil fuels. Oil producing countries do not necessarily like to hear that. But it really comes down to our saying: "All right. We hear you. We are ready to stop pumping these greenhouse gases and carbon dioxide into the atmosphere, and that means we are going to find ways to price fossil fuels better, become more efficient and reduce our emissions of carbon dioxide." The U.S. committed itself at the G 7 Summit in London to realistic, full-cost pricing of fuel. But where is the beef? We haven't seen it yet.

One can become involved in deep philosophical discussions on this subject. The attitude of the South has been, if everyone is emitting the average per capita amount of carbon dioxide of someone in India, we would not have a global warming problem. It is the excessive emissions in the North that are causing the problem. One can also take an historical perspective on greenhouse gas emissions. But some claim that can be rebutted through an examination of the benefits of the industrial revolution. The argument tends to spiral. The fact remains, however, that we currently have a very unequal use of energy and a very unequal production of carbon dioxide among the world's citizens — with the U.S. being the gluttonous hog.

If the Chinese began to emit carbon dioxide at the rate that Americans do, we'd all be in serious trouble.

That's true. That is also the reason that the U.S. likes to point to the fact that emissions from developing countries are rising. This is true, in one sense, but developing nations have legitimate development interests. A more practical and positive approach would be to say: "Let's find ways to cooperate so that the Chinese develop in ways that give them access to energy-efficient technologies." The Chinese are going to have to burn coal as efficiently as possible. They will burn coal unless someone comes up with some absolutely whiz-bang solar technology.

What should be addressed at the climate negotiations and UNCED is the need to meet the legitimate energy needs in the developing world in a way that minimizes climate change and other environmental effects. Here, developing countries have some responsibility to look at energy programs and projects that make long-term economic sense such as investments in energy efficiency.

Some have said that the negotiations on the preservation of biological diversity are stalled. Others have described them as making very little progress. Do you think a convention will come out of these negotiations that might be signed at UNCED? Will it be signed at the Earth Summit? And if so will it be a valuable contribution to the canon of international law?

That is a big question mark. My sense is that the U.S. has been very hard on the financial issues in the biological diversity negotiation. There has been resistance to granting the developing countries greater intellectual property rights and control and value over some of the biological resources that have been taken from them. The biodiversity negotiation has always been on a slower track than climate change, partly because it is trying to define what the convention is suppose to do in the midst of climate and forest principles negotiations. Furthermore, I don't think there has ever been as much political commitment to that treaty as to the others. If you look at the London Summit Declaration itself, you will see that biological diversity is put, in essence, in the third tier of priorities. There is a big question mark about whether we are going to see a biodiversity convention, and if it will be a skimpy thing by Rio.

While most people know that there are supposed to be two treaties signed at the Earth Summit, few understand what Agenda 21 is. A lot of Agenda 21 is still bracketed text, up for negotiation. Do you, nevertheless, get the feeling that Agenda 21 is the sleeper at UNCED, and that many people may be surprised by the scope and potential impact of it? Or is Agenda 21 just a long shopping list of initiatives that the international community thinks should be done at some point in the future?

The challenge is, how can we build political support and institutional mechanisms to actually implement Agenda 21? Without support, Agenda 21 becomes sort of a grab bag or wish list. Look at the report of the Stockholm Conference. That contains all kinds of recommendations and some means of implementation. The trick is taking that kind of action plan and commitment and getting governments to actually move on it. If we haven't done that, then it does become a wish list. The challenge remains to make Agenda 21 real. UNCED delegates still have a lot of negotiating left to do on it. The forest principles, for example, could be something potentially useful or they could be pabulum.

A question remains in my own mind about exactly who is going to implement Agenda 21, what is going to be done with it. Is it just going to remain a piece of paper? Looking at the oceans section, for example, if the delegates really want something serious on the land-based source of marine pollution, it will require that someone really take it on and say: "Two years from now we will need a diplomatic conference to adopt some legal instrument on land-based sources of marine pollution."

A lot of people still don't understand Agenda 21, no matter how many times Maurice Strong explains what it is about. Agenda 21 is a nice catchy phrase, but show me what it means, show me the substance of it, show me how it is going to make a difference in my daily life, in the world's daily life, and in the protection of the planet. The treaties are available and people can judge them. But with Agenda 21, particularly when you get to some of the cross-cutting issues, it becomes a little bit more invisible.

There are some good environmental housekeeping provisions within Agenda 21 and mechanisms suggested for their implementation.

Yes, there are a lot of what they call "options."

What progress do you think will be made on these forestry principles that are under discussion?

There are big differences among the delegates about how to proceed on future negotiations of a forest convention. Should the forestry issue be included as a set of principles in Agenda 21? Thus far there hasn't been anything put on the table about a follow-up process to negotiate a forest convention. There has been no agreement about when, where, and how to do that. Do we go back to the General Assembly and create an Intergovernmental Negotiating Committee on Forests, as we did with climate change, with definite target dates about when to start and finish negotiations?

There is pressure for such an approach. The World Wildlife Fund has taken a very strong position, charging the UNCED delegates with having failed miserably by not agreeing on negotiating a forestry convention by 1992. At least the delegates could set up a clear basis on which to move forward on the forestry issue after Rio. Hopefully, they will recognize the rights of indigenous people to address underlying problems of deforestation, debt and trade inequities, as well as make a start in halting further primary forest loss in the North as well as in the South.

Do you think all these international environmental treaties are really going to work?

This is an issue within EDF. Before coming here I did most of my work on treaties and international agreements. When I arrived at EDF, Bruce Rich, who closely follows the activities of the World Bank and other multilateral banks, asked me what all these international environmental treaties really accomplished. The question required that I examine nine years of my professional life. When it is all finished, what have you really got after these international negotiations except the piece of paper, he asked? You have all these agreements, you've been to all these nice meetings, but what has it actually produced?

I had to think about that. I gave him what I thought was a pretty good answer. I said that the Montreal Protocol on Substances that Deplete the Ozone Layer (1987) was one good example of an agreement that has had a real impact. In our discussions Bruce made clear that his strategy is to go where the money is. He tries to make an impact on the World Bank, the multilateral development banks, and the International Monetary Fund (IMF). With this strategy one sees immediate paybacks and results in terms of dams that are shut down and people who are saved from being displaced.

The institutional reform issue will be taken up last because many northern delegates feel it necessary to decide on the substantive issues before deciding which institutions should handle them. CAPE 92 calls for strengthening the United Nations Environment Program (UNEP) with vastly increased powers to oversee environment and development policy within the U.N. or a new institutional body. Among the options for institutional reform being discussed are: reforming the U.N. Economic and Social Council (ECOSOC), creating a Commission on Sustainable Development similar to the Commission on Human Rights, and establishing new Secretariats and trust funds within the secretariats for each of the different conventions. These are critical issues if you consider that Agenda 21 will be no more than a piece of paper unless there is institutional support for this agenda for change. What do you see coming out of UNCED in the way of institutional reform?

I don't see any major institutions coming out of UNCED. Maurice Strong has been clear about this. Governments don't want to take any drastic or innovative steps and say they want no new institutions.

There are several pieces of this we should understand. First, there is a fairly clear agreement that UNEP will receive more resources and will be better funded. Kenya will probably help provide better communications capacity. No one is going to suggest that UNEP move out of Kenya, but there will be efforts to make it more effective. Right now its budget is less than Greenpeace International. The deal is going to involve a significant increase in the amount of money and political support for UNEP's efforts. I could very well be wrong, but I don't think we will see any immediate changes in UNEP's legal status as a program of the General Assembly reporting through ECOSOC.

There will be greater collaboration between UNEP and the United Nations Development Program (UNDP). That is absolutely critical. UNDP is a body that NGOs have not given as much attention as they should. The critical issue on the table is going to be: What type of body, if any, should be created for follow-up? Should it be an interim secretariat for UNCED that will oversee and coordinate Agenda 21 until we go through more of a U.N. reform process? This might be a body that would keep more of a spotlight on Agenda 21. I don't see a lot more happening on institutional issues at this point.

I have heard some enthusiasm for a Commission on Sustainable Development. Clearly there has to be an institutional focal point for experts and diplomats who are going to continue to promote the implementation of Agenda 21. Otherwise we will wait another 20 years before there is a high-level focus on solving global environment and development problems.

We can't afford to wait another 20 years. We must find some type of body that will bring together cross-disciplinary political impetus to keep Agenda 21 moving. That will require greater attention to these issues within the U.N. itself, including greater attention by the new Secretary General. The General Assembly itself will likely accord more priority to environment and development issues and there is always a reformed ECOSOC.

We must foster the notion that we are in this together and that we have to find ways to make the world's trading system responsive to environment and development concerns in a way that it has not been before. There must be a greater recognition that the whole macro-economic setting is entwined with these environment and development issues. We must have an institution that is trying to shape and move that process forward.

What institution would that be?

It could be a high-level Commission on Sustainable Development. I think that would be a step forward. But my own view is that the U.N. system is not the be-all-and-end-all answer to everything. It doesn't cover all the agreements; a lot needs to happen on the ground, regionally and nationally. The U.N. system will only permeate so far. We need to have people, communities, governments, and regional groupings actively involved in promoting some of the objectives that were stated for UNCED.

So, where do you think the institutional reform issue is headed?

There are three themes here on the institutional front. First, UNEP should be strengthened, including its financial resources, and should be given greater political weight for its catalytic and coordinating role. Second, more emphasis and meaning should be given to the coordination mechanisms within the U.N. system and within regional groups. Third, some serious deliberations should take place about the need for some body or mechanism that will oversee the implementation of UNCED's Agenda 21 and its connection with the U.N. institutional reform deliberations.

Those who are talking about change in the Security Council say that UNCED should not deal with that now because we have U.N. institutional reform coming up in 1995. Tampering with the U.N. Charter is as sensitive an issue as amending the U.S. Constitution. There has been some talk about expanding the responsibilities of the Trusteeship Council. The general view is that to do something with the Trusteeship Council would require a modification of the Charter, even if the Trusteeship Council has practically nothing on its agenda. Hopefully, the Security Council will also give greater attention to environment and development issues in the post Cold War period.

We already have a long list of U.N. agencies and international environmental agreements. Has any one looked to see if these agencies are doing their job effectively and if the provisions of these treaties are being carried out?

One of the things CAPE '92 put on the table is to have some outside, independent auditing mechanisms that can help evaluate whether organizations and agreements are meeting their stated objectives. At the Oceans Working Party at UNCED, the Secretariat was asked to put together an evaluation of just how some of the international agreements had been working in the oceans sector. Outside consultants were asked to try to evaluate how effective some of these institutions and agreements have been, because the organizations themselves could not do the job.

If an outside group of experts did an evaluation and found that the Food and Agriculture Organization (FAO), for example, is not doing an effective job at promoting sustainable agriculture, what would be the mechanism for doing something about that? Don't we need an independent institution on sustainable development that will have the muscle to do more than simply write a report?

We have had some lengthy discussions within CAPE '92 on that issue. It boils down to how ambitious you want to be in revising treaty structures. There is a provision in the U.N. Charter dealing with specialized agencies that allows them their own fiefdoms. To change this, governments would have to make some serious reforms, such as the proposals on common budgetary provisions for the U.N. system, which would include the specialized agencies. I would imagine there would be a lot of political resistance to such a proposal from the individual agencies; they can muster a lot of influence. Often the secretariats of these agencies are in control of this process, while governments are not necessarily well informed about what is going on. So, real change will require that governments agree to change some of the legal arrangements

I would presume that governments are not just going to give this portfolio to some entity that will direct them. They are going to want to sit in on the process in some fashion. Will there be someone to say to the International Maritime Organization (IMO), and all the parties to it, "you have not yet done your job right?" That is the difficult part.

Do you think it will require an ecological disaster before we see substantial cooperation among nations on the promotion of sustainable development? If sea levels rose and Hawaii, the Netherlands, some Japanese islands, and other areas went under water; or if the hole in the

ozone got so bad that the public noticed a widespread increase in the incidence of skin cancer and cataracts, would we see more rapid progress? There is a certain impatience with the U.N. process. I understand that the U.N. moves very slowly because it relies on consensus building. But the evidence suggests that we are facing survival issues as both a species and as a planetary web of ecosystems. Do you get the sense that the scale of the problem and the urgent necessity to arrive at remedies has been recognized by government delegates?

No, I really do not think so. I think that the governments as a whole have really not stepped up to the table and met the challenge of creating institutional mechanisms that will allow us to move rapidly to address these problems. There was an interesting editorial in *The Washington Post* the other day observing that the ink was not even dry on the signatures of the Montreal Protocol, in 1987, when the clear link was made to the Antarctic ozone layer hole. The Montreal Protocol was barely amended when we had new science requiring us to adjust the amendment again. Similarly, on climate change, the science tells us that climate can change very rapidly and that at some point in time it will be too late to do anything about it, regardless of how fast the world then moves.

We have to be able to create mechanisms, procedures, and institutions that anticipate the problems we have, and take aggressive and decisive action. My own viewpoint, as an international lawyer, is that sovereignty, rather than being a benefit to the protection of the environment, can create a hindrance in dealing with some of these global problems.

I have heard sovereignty used more frequently as an excuse not to do anything in the UNCED process, and in climate treaty negotiations, than I have heard it used in my previous nine years in government. Sovereignty is used to protect national interests, sometimes legitimately. Developing countries have big forests. They look at the North and see that we have chopped ours down, and they say: "Don't shift your problems onto us." But, on the other hand, sovereignty is also used to prohibit public participation or to deny the rights of indigenous people.

The U.S. Government position always has been that you cannot separate the sovereign right to exploit resources from the concomitant obligation not to harm the environment outside your jurisdiction. Now the U.S. and China are beginning to say: "It is our sovereign right to use our coal." I hear sovereignty used as an excuse for inaction all over the place.

Do you think we are moving toward a new form of global governance? Is that where all these treaties you are interested in are heading?

Over time I hope that will be the case. There has been improved international cooperation in some areas. But building international agreement on these issues is a one step at a time process. I am more of an incrementalist as an international lawyer, not someone who thinks we can go out and get it all at one time. What we can't afford is paralyzed decision-making. I believe in international law, but we cannot wait for a climate convention to enter into force before we start doing anything to implement it. We have traditional notions like "interim implementation", but I think we must negotiate legal instruments that provide a framework from which to operate. Maybe we can do more with institutions. My own sense is that a lot of the governments in the climate treaty negotiations don't want to give authority to central institutions, or even the conference of parties, to make decisions. They want to reserve it very much for themselves; they are all protecting individual economic interests. We need to move along a path that allows us to make decisions and take action, while not confining us to normal sovereignty and treaty relationships, and that also involves the public at all levels.

To my mind, the way people judge the progress at UNCED is almost like an ink-blot psychological test. Those who have high expectations of UNCED are disappointed by the glacial pace of U.N. decision-making. On the other hand, those who come to the UNCED negotiations with the expectation that this is the beginning of a process are less disappointed. Where do you see yourself fitting into that continuum?

I fit more toward the latter scenario you described that sees UNCED as the start of a process. My expectations are that UNCED itself is not going to solve all the problems of the world. But the UNCED process should not end after the signing of a couple of treaties and a nice little Earth Charter that do not say a lot. There has to be something more than that.

UNCED must set in motion a process which, in the short term, fosters public participation and helps identify ways that more money can be effectively put into developing countries. It is not just a question of money, because some of us are fighting against the World Bank investing more money into bad projects. It has more to do with how money is spent. At the same time there have to be other minimal commitments, including a commitment on carbon dioxide and energy and a commitment to integrating environment and development.

Do you think that President Bush will attend the Earth Summit in Rio?

Between CAPE '92 and CAN we have a convergence of groups that work together on climate issues and UNCED. One of the dominant themes you will hear from these two groups is the question of whether President Bush will go to the Earth Summit in Rio. When is he going to commit? The sooner he commits the better in terms of the success of the conference. A commitment that he will go would also provide the U.S. with impetus to try to find something creative and useful to do at UNCED for which the President can take some credit.

The clear message to the President is: "George, the planet is at risk. Where are you? We need you. Make a commitment to go to the Earth Summit, step up to the table and set targets for the reduction of carbon dioxide emissions." We feel that the President has to become engaged, has to go to the Earth Summit, and has to try to make this conference a success rather than an exercise in damage control.

What would make Bush go to Rio?

I think it's a political call. He has to be convinced that it is more in his interest, in terms of the reelection campaign, to be at Rio than it is not to be there. Some advisors to the President may tell him that the way they see the UNCED conference shaping up, they don't recommend that he go. Or, they could argue that if the President made a commitment to go to Rio, the U.S. delegation could shape some agreements that would be in the U.S. interest and would change the tide. His advisors could argue that the U.S. could offer more financial resources in exchange for progress on forests. But that would require that we look at U.S. old-growth forestry policy. Basically, it will probably turn on whether he can sign a climate treaty that he can get a little credit for.

Outside of Alaska we have, by some calculations, 2 to 3 percent of our old-growth forest left.

That's right. And we are ready to chop down some more. That is where you have a clear nexus between domestic policy and foreign policy. The U.S. wants to push the forestry issue internationally, but does not want to talk about its policy on old-growth forests at home. The U.S. also does not want to talk about climate much in the context of forests. And the U.S. does not have an energy policy. At UNCED the U.S. wants to make progress on an international forestry agreement, but we don't have much money to put behind it — and we definitely haven't done our own job in the U.S.

Is there some interest at UNCED in pollution permit trading? EDF has been in the forefront of pushing for pollution permit trading as part of the Clean Air Act. Are you lobbying for similar market mechanisms to clean up the global environment?

We at EDF think that, in the long term, we are going to see a lot more financial resources and technology transferred to the South if we create tradeable permit schemes. This may not work in every sector, but our senior economist in New York believes that we are going to end up with a lot more money going to developing countries more quickly through tradeable permits than by setting up government controlled funds.

How would that work? Are these tradeable permits in carbon releases?

In its simplest form we propose a global cap of some kind on carbon dioxide emissions and/or a couple of other greenhouse gas emissions. Then you create entitlements that could be allocated in ways that would be negotiated. These entitlements would be traded. Countries could purchase or sell entitlements. It is very similar to what is in the acid rain portion of the new Clean Air Act, in which we had a 10 million ton reduction of emissions, a cap, and entitlements.

Tradeable pollution permits only work if first there is an international regulation creating a cap on total emissions.

Yes. You have to have the regulatory mechanism in place. The U.S. Government has talked a lot about emission trading. The problem is that until we get to the point of saying that we have caps and some real commitments, there isn't anything of value to trade. Groups in the South are suspicious of this concept, but we are starting to engage in a dialogue on it and governments are starting to think about it.

When we talk about finding the financial resources for sustainable development, should there not be some focus on the Official Development Assistance (ODA) levels and the fact that the ODA of the U.S. is 0.33 percent of GNP while the U.N. has asked for 0.7 percent?

There are only a couple of countries that are meeting the U.N. ODA target. More importantly, we should examine what our ODA is being spent on. Is it being spent for defined political objectives? The bulk of the U.S. ODA assistance goes to Israel, Egypt and Turkey. And how much of it is being spent on the military? Peter Thatcher at the World Resources Institute sounds this theme at almost every meeting I have been in. What is bilateral assistance used for? Does it have implicit ties to technology purchases on the other end?

At some point there must be a critical look at the exact nature of bilateral assistance, and the fact that we are spending it on things that we really should not. Bilateral assistance is targeted more at political ends than at sustainable development. That is why the Development Assistance Committee guidelines that came out of the OECD are important. Clearly it would be better if the OECD countries had a better sense of how they spent money and coordinated their bilateral assistance.

We also have to look at the type of environmental conditions we put on bilateral aid. That is one of the important themes NGOs put forward at the London and Houston Summits. As we look at additional aid to the former Soviet Union and Central Europe, let's make sure that there is a clear, coordinated environmental component.

You have been involved in these international negotiations on the environment for the last nine years in various capacities. Let me ask what may sound like a silly question. When you go to bed at night and think about the fate of the earth, what do you think is likely to happen? Were you to have children, what kind of future would you imagine for them?

That is not a silly question, particularly when you work in this area every day. I think about it. I'm something of an optimist. We are late in finding solutions to these global environmental problems; as a result, it is going to cost us a lot more to solve them. Nevertheless, I think we will be able to tackle these problems. I think there will be some type of habitable world to live in. I think we are not entirely stupid.

I probably worry more, even with the change in the relationship between the U.S. and the USSR, about some type of nuclear catastrophe triggered by a non-superpower than I do about environmental degradation. My real concern is about Africa. That is where there is a real worry. The biggest concern is how do we move out of the downward spiral that Africa is in without writing Africa off as a basket case? The challenge is how to bring people out of this cycle of poverty.

Do you think that in the future the majority of the world may remain habitable, but that we might have continent-size areas of intense poverty and environmental degradation?

At EDF we are discussing the population issue a lot. We have seen how complicated an issue it is. It is not just a question of literacy and distributing condoms. There are broader demographic and social issues. In the near term it is going to be the impact of population growth that we have to deal with.

My last trip to Kenya, including my last days going through the Nairobi Game Park, showed me that there is tremendous development pressure on the land outside Nairobi. There are developments right up to the corridors that the species have to pass through. Even though "ecotourism" is the number one foreign exchange earner in Kenya, the population pressure on the land is tremendous now — and Kenya is supposed to be the gem of African countries. I am worried about whether there is going to be wildlife in Africa 20 to 30 years from now. How do you come to grips with the inequality of wealth that this situation implies? How can we help bring the people of Africa out of the cycle of poverty? I don't have any great sanguinity that we can achieve that.

I think we can stop the pollution of the oceans. At some point in time we will find a way to stop pumping greenhouse gas into the atmosphere and eliminate emissions of CFCs, even if we are late and there continue to be harmful impacts from the thinning of the ozone layer. I think we will find ways of avoiding the creation of landfills. We may pay a heavy price in the process, as we have in the U.S. under the Superfund.

I have the same problem when it comes to the food supply question. Some people argue that there is not a real problem with food, even with climate change, because we are going to be able to produce enough. But the problem of distribution remains. We may have an overall stable global food supply and we may even increase it, but how do we distribute it to the people who need it? We already face that problem.

Now that I am out of the government I can start asking some of these questions. For instance, when I went to one of the game parks in Kenya with members of the delegation at the climate treaty negotiations, I asked what progress had been made in the last 10 years. We pumped a lot of money into Africa, but I see no indication that the problem is turning around. One thing I have learned since coming to EDF is to look at the people side of the equation.

Others would say that we should avoid taking a completely human chauvinist perspective and lose sight of the many non-human species that are going to become extinct in the coming decades.

I think we are going to keep track of biodiversity one way or another, although maybe not as well as we can. But I agree. We have an obligation to other inhabitants of the planet and, in fact, if the world is truly going to link environment and development, the human dimension has to incorporate the environmental dimension.

Do you mean that the spotted owl is going to do better than the poorest people in Africa?

I'm sad to say that it may. Look at fund raising. Look at the political pressures on where our aid and resources are going. The new focus is on Central Europe and the former Soviet Union. Why wasn't Africa a real concern? How do you mobilize concern about that? I *do* think that the spotted owl is going to get a lot more attention in some ways than whether or not someone in the developing world has enough food to eat or enough health care. Look at the cholera spreading through South America because there is not enough primary sewage treatment. What are people going to put money toward? If I put out a proposal to deal with land-based sources of marine pollution and coastal sewage systems, as compared with a plan to save the spotted owl, which one do you think would get funded?

Wildlife scientists at EDF point out that while we may do all kinds of things to save the spotted owl, if we have serious increases in temperatures we may not be able to save the forests that the spotted owl lives in. As a result there has been a lot more thinking about migration corridors.

Migration corridors? Is this the so-called "adjustment approach" to global warming, where instead of trying to stop it from happening we come up with strategies to minimize the damage from it? To mitigate the loss of biodiversity from global warming, it has been suggested that we create North/South corridors so that as the temperatures rise, animals will have an escape route on which they can flee to the North. But is it not hard for a coral reef to flee to the North?

Yes, coral reefs can't flee North and are one of the most sensitive indicators of change. That is one reason EDF marine scientists are spending so much time on coral reefs. Yet some land use planners consider that if we are not going to do enough to stop global warming, it will be important to allow routes for species to move North. That means North/South corridors. We may have lots of forest cover in the U.S., but a lot of that forest area is fragmented. So the question remains as to whether species will be able to leapfrog the areas of development as they attempt to move North.

That's a depressing thought.

William R. Pace:

The Hague Declaration on the Environment

illiam R. Pace is Director of the Center for the Development of International Law, co-chair of the International Task Group on Legal and Institutional Matters, and chair of the U.S. Citizens' Network's Working Group on Legal and Institutional Issues.

Steve Lerner: Do you think the United Nations Conference on Environment and Development (UNCED) negotiations have opened up opportunities for strengthening international law, particularly as it relates to environment and development issues?

William R. Pace: The UNCED negotiations and the Earth Summit are bound to contribute to the development of international law, but so far it appears that both the nation-state delegates to UNCED and non-government organization (NGO) representatives and activists are failing to take advantage of the truly historic opportunity for achieving fundamental progress. Instead they are taking business as usual, tiny-steps-for-tiny-feet approaches that fail to adequately confront the issues being negotiated at UNCED.

During the UNCED negotiations there have been some of the most remarkable proposals for legal and institutional reforms of international law and institutions since the founding of the United Nations half a century ago. These proposals come at a moment of extraordinary historic opportunity, which is due, in large part, to the unprecedented geo-political developments of the last five years.

In stark contrast to these options for reform has been the dictum by the U.S. and the U.K. against any additional financial resources or new institutions. To complete the gridlock at UNCED has been the Group of 77 (G-77) developing nations' refusal to seriously discuss new international environmental laws and institutional authority until the equity issues — poverty, trade, resources and technology transfers, debt, and the issue of fair participation in decision-making — have been addressed. Thus, the minimalists on both sides are the victors.

Unfortunately, most of the progressive government and non-government proponents of fundamental reforms are caving in to "reality" and are beginning to argue about what tiny steps should be taken.

What are some of these progressive proposals for the reform of international law and institutions?

Many of these proposals are found in *Our Common Future,* the report of the World Commission on Environment and Development. These include the establishment of an Environment and Development Commission or Sustainable Development Commission based on the Human Rights Commission and International Labor Organization (ILO) models. Forty-three nations have signed onto the Declaration of the Hague on the Environment, which calls for establishing a new global institutional authority for protection of the atmosphere. There are proposals for reform of the U.N. Trusteeship Council, and The Economic and Social Council (ECOSOC). And there are a variety of proposals for new institutions: an Environmental Security Council, an international environmental court, transboundary environmental rights and obligations, a global Environmental Protection Agency, "Green Helmets," a Planet Protection Fund proposed by Rajiv Gandhi before he was murdered, and a Green Fund proposed by some 40-50 nations at a meeting in Beijing. There are also proposals for creating emission credit banks, global electrical grids, and global conventions on climate change, biodiversity, and forests. Important proposals were also made during and after the third UNCED Preparatory Committee session. Among these are France's proposal for a Commission of the Earth, "Commission de la Terre"; Norway's call for a Sustainable Development Commission; and Costa Rica's request that UNCED support the creation of an independent Planet Earth Council, "Consejo del Planeta Tierra." Several of these proposals, if enacted, could cause fundamental reform in the international legal order. Last spring another remarkable proposal, the Stockholm Initiative on Global Security and Governance, was issued by 36 current and former world leaders from all regions of the earth.

Does UNCED's focus on global environment and development issues give nations a special incentive to cooperate on an unprecedented scale?

The root cause of this extraordinary summit is the recognition that there are certain global environmental catastrophes threatening our planet that can only be avoided through an intensification of international cooperation on an unprecedented scale.

I had thought that the need to deal with global environmental challenges was one area in which nation states would be willing to give up or rather expand their definition of sovereignty. I believed that some of the transboundary atmospheric and ocean pollution problems were so great that nations would recognize the need for transboundary legal and institutional mechanisms in order to take restorative measures. That was why I felt that international environmental law provided the greatest opportunity for major improvements in strengthening the international legal order. I am now less convinced that that will be the case. In fact, it appears that peace, disarmament, and collective security may well be the area in which we will succeed in strengthening international law.

Some argue that Maurice Strong, Secretary General of UNCED, has taken on so many issues that very little of a practical nature will come out of these negotiations. Others think that UNCED has done a good job of making nations recognize the linkages between environment and development problems. What do you think?

There are tremendous pressures to compartmentalize all issues. One of the more amazing aspects of the UNCED negotiations is that they have taken on a wide array of complex interrelated issues. If UNCED retains its huge agenda and the linkages between these issues all the way through the Earth Summit and beyond, it may be one of the most important summits in history.

The Brundtland Report and other world commission reports have irrefutably demonstrated the linkages between such issues as protecting the oceans, protecting air and water, energy and food production, preserving the rain forests, indigenous peoples' rights, cultural and biological diversity, desertification, eradication of poverty, population planning, human settlements issues, and finding sustainable development paths. These issues *cannot* be dealt with separately or by individual nations. In order to deal with these challenges, we will have to address the fundamental way in which the world community makes decisions and operates economically and politically. Our failure to begin meeting these challenges will not be a failure of Maurice Strong or UNCED, but of all of us.

Unfortunately, too much of the official response at UNCED meetings has been rhetoric. A legitimate complaint about the United Nations is that it is a place where rhetoric is reality. If UNCED never gets beyond the rhetoric, it will be a failure. If that happens it will not be just another unsuccessful conference, but a colossal failure, because the global threats UNCED addresses are real and in some ways more insoluble than war. We are losing somewhere between 20 and 100 species a day; and certain processes of degradation to the oceans or atmosphere could become so advanced they may be impossible to reverse.

You have written that the pace of progress towards international agreements is proceeding by "slow, slight and hesitant modifications to existing programs and bureaucracies that is unworthy of the tasks before UNCED." But this is the first time that the international community has grappled with many of these issues. To me it seems unsurprising that progress has been slow on forging an international consensus.

The delegates are dealing with UNCED in the same way they have dealt with U.N. business in the past. There is no recognition at UNCED either that there have been dramatic geopolitical changes or that these challenges deserve more than a business-as-usual approach. As Albert Einstein said about the dangers of atomic weapons in 1948, "Everything has changed except the way we think." The format used at the U.N. and UNCED of bringing 160 nations and 20 or so international organizations together in general debate for 4 or 5 week preparatory sessions leading up to a general conference or summit is failing.

How could progress be made more rapidly?

This may seem unrealistic, but an important first step is to acknowledge that there is a fundamental crisis in the U.N. decision-making process. In addressing this issue within the existing U.N. system, it is vital that the involvement of non-governmental organizations (NGOs) and peoples' organizations be formalized. There also needs to be a commitment made to provide the necessary resources to keep to keep an amended UNCED process going for 2-5 years. The June, 1992, timeframe has allowed only enough time for us to begin to seriously address the issues before UNCED.

Do you expect the UNCED process to be extended after the Earth Summit in Rio?

It has to be extended in some fashion. Algeria has proposed followup summits every 5 years; Argentina proposed that Agenda 21 be adopted every five years by an intergovernmental conference. On a very practical level there is no more important measure of success for UNCED than the interim and long-term follow-up mechanism.

Some have warned that excessively vague agreements will give the appearance of progress without solving real problems. Is there some danger that the UNCED negotiations will actually delay progress on environment and development problems?

If we allow the Summit in Rio to end up as an empty set of declarations, without trying to postpone, prevent, or condemn it, we may have done damage by participating in UNCED. If that happens it might have been better had UNCED never occurred. It would be tragic if Rio became a giant photo opportunity for heads of state who fraudulently claimed that great progress had been made in overcoming global environment and development emergencies.

But is there not the danger of setting our sights too high? The end product of the UNCED negotiations will likely be a mixed bag. There may be a global climate change convention, although it may not have the targets for reduction of greenhouse gases that we would all like to see. There may be a biodiversity convention of some kind, although it will certainly not be as evolved as we might wish. There may be a vague Earth Charter. There may be a long Agenda 21, which may or may not be implemented. But if we take the position that the whole UNCED process was a mistake and become overly critical of it, would that not undercut the positive aspects of it?

I agree that we should not condemn the whole UNCED process. I believe the "genius" of UNCED is that it may well be the largest conference and summit ever attempted by the U.N. on the widest array of issues. But it now appears that there will not be enough time, and that the process is too flawed to expect UNCED to achieve substantive agreement on its major goals. As a result, UNCED will fail unless heads of state agree to reform the process for a follow-up to UNCED and make the kind of commitments in institutional authority and financial resource that are necessary.

For example, in my area of interest — legal and institutional issues — no one is holding out much hope for any substantive progress. Some people argue that an agreement on a framework convention is a step forward. But it won't be if we give the impression that we have a method by which we can solve some problems when we really don't. One problem with the framework convention approach is that scientific evidence is changing, and environmental degradation is sometimes happening so fast, that you cannot, under our current treaty-making process, accommodate these changes.

On the other hand, if the climate change negotiations lead to an effective institutional framework to protect the atmosphere, and if we begin to put into place some of these broad decision-making mechanisms so that this institution will have adequate scientific expertise, access to information, and the necessary administrative authority and resources, then that alone would be a major success. Unfortunately, it is exactly those elements of the agreement that are getting pushed off the negotiating table. Instead, delegates are fighting over how many and what kinds of treaties will be enacted and what kind of emission levels and target dates established. But how we are going to implement these agreements is left undecided.

Part of the reason for this is that the U.S. says that we must proceed with "substance before form": We need to discuss what we are going to agree to, then we will discuss how we are going to do it. The U.S. negotiators say that the U.S. does not enter into treaties with the kind of insincerity that characterizes Europe, Japan, and other countries. If the U.S. enters a treaty, it means to enforce it and obey it, U.S. delegates argue.

Yet, this argument is hypocritical because the U.S. is unwilling to discuss any of the substantive issues. For example, The U.S. opposes both hard and soft law status for the Earth Charter and Agenda 21. The U.S. has been stonewalling most of the central issues in the climate and biodiversity conventions, standing almost alone in the international community.

The problem with this approach is that delegates from many developing nations cannot afford to participate effectively in the negotiations. For many of the poorer countries the financial, institutional, and resource issues *are* the substantive issues. They want to know how they are expected to comply with these new international environmental laws and commitments that will be imposed on them. They don't have the resources to attend these negotiations, much less enforce the new laws at home and make changes in their national legislation and institutions. So, if delegates from developing nations cannot talk about some of the resource issues, then they cannot go along with these treaties.

Why are you so enthusiastic about the Hague Declaration on the Environment among the options that exist for strengthening international law and reforming international institutions?

The Hague Declaration on the Environment, signed in March of 1989, is an astonishing document. Here is an extraordinary declaration calling for the establishment of a major new global environmental authority to protect the earth's atmosphere. This is not an initiative put forward by a bunch of environmental extremists or cranks, but rather an initiative of heads of state and foreign ministers.

In calling for an institutional authority to deal with the atmosphere, does the Hague Declaration go beyond the global warming convention?

Yes. The parties to the Hague Declaration endorsed a fundamentally new kind of global environment authority that goes beyond existing treaty secretariats. While it was to be established within the U.N. system, it was not necessarily to be within an existing U.N. institution, such as the United Nations Environment Program (UNEP). The reason for this, I suspect, is that most of the leaders who participated in the drafting of the Declaration did not think that an existing institution would be capable of such a quantum leap.

Were they suggesting the creation of an Environmental Protection Agency (EPA) for the global atmosphere?

Yes. The Declaration called for a strengthening of the enforcement mechanisms of the World Court, the International Court of Justice. It called for decisions to be made, in some cases, without unanimous consent. It was an astonishing document for heads of state to propose. But it was opposed by then Prime Minister Margaret Thatcher, who blasted it the very afternoon it was released. And it was opposed by the U.S. Administration, so it just sank.

How does the Hague Declaration propose to provide the financial resources necessary for helping Third World nations meet new international atmospheric regulations?

It calls for countries that have the greatest resources to provide the majority of the funding to help Third World nations meet these new commitments. It also states that the most industrialized and developed countries are largely responsible for the degradation of the atmosphere. The Hague Declaration reached a level of agreement that has not been attained since. This is the kind of extraordinary institutional proposal, the kind of initiative and leadership, that is necessary to respond to global environmental threats.

Is it your contention that UNCED delegates should have espoused an agreement similar to that reached in the Hague Declaration?

The Hague Declaration has now been signed by 43 countries and the process that it began should be carried forward either in UNCED or in the climate convention negotiations. When I was permitted to address the UNCED delegates of the institutional working group in Geneva last August I tried to contrast the difference between the Hague Declaration and the tinkering with bureaucracy proposals that the UNCED delegates were offering.

Why is the Hague Declaration on the Environment not being debated on the floor of UNCED?

There are a number of reasons. One primary reason is the UNCED dictum imposed by the U.S. and U.K. that there will be no additional funds and no new institutions. This dictum has set up a negotiating impasse which, combined with the normal depressing effects of achieving consensus on issues among 160 nations, is producing a lowest common denominator effect. Many documents being submitted by the U.S. and other countries, relative to the Earth Charter and Agenda 21, are actually reversing agreements and commitments made 20 years ago in Stockholm.

The Hague Declaration called for the World Court to play a central enforcement role. Did that not scare off many nations that might have otherwise signed onto it?

Yes. I think the greatest obstacle to strengthening the international legal order is the unwillingness of nation-states to consider obeying the same principles of law that they legislate and enforce among their own people. We have a large body of international law, but we don't have the institutions with adequate authority to back up international law: institutions of administration, enforcement, and adjudication.

But what good would it do if the World Court were to convict the U.S. of not having met its CO_2 reduction target? Who will impose sanctions on the U.S.?

You are getting at one of the most fundamental obstacles in current international treaties and agreements. There is no effective enforcement of international agreements. We had a remarkable precedent-setting example this past year in what the Security Council did in imposing sanctions on Iraq in the Persian Gulf. The world's most powerful countries have been willing to apply automatic sanctions to South Africa and other small countries, but the question remains whether they will be willing to apply these same principles to themselves.

This is exactly the issue that the southern NGO activists have raised with northern NGOs and the northern governments. In effect they say to us: "You can't tell us that you are going to solve our problems, when the source of many of these problems is in your societies." Whether it is in the Security Council or the Group of Seven (G-7), powerful nations are going to have to agree to obey the same laws and principles that they impose on others.

What kind of sanctions might work? Obviously, we will not have a police force that will come out and arrest the President of the United States because the U.S. is emitting more than its share of greenhouse gases. The human rights struggle demonstrated that exposing and embarrassing governments can be very effective. So, even if we arrive at a point short of police power, we can develop sanctions against non-cooperation.

What about economic sanctions?

Economic sanctions could be automatic. If one country is destroying the air people breathe, we ought to be willing to do what is necessary to stop it. But we need a process that is able to adapt to different individual, regional, and cultural situations, just as we have in local and national law.

While the five nations that constitute the U.N. Security Council may have reflected the political and military powers at the end of World War II, many agree that they no longer do. Will a serious reform of the U.N., aimed at promoting sustainable development, require a reform of the Security Council?

The current reorganization of the U.N. Secretariat by the new Secretary General and the discussions about the 1995 review of the U.N. Charter are having an important impact on the UNCED negotiations. This is especially true for the U.S., the U.K., and other permanent members of the Security Council. The U.S. and the U.K. foreign affairs officials insist that we cannot open up the U.N. Charter for debate because it is a Pandora's Box. I disagree. Not opening up the U.N. Charter for debate is the Pandora's Box.

It is not acceptable that five victors of a war that took place 50 years ago continue to veto the will of the rest of the world at the United Nations. It is untenable that two countries — the U.K. and France — retain a veto while unified Europe itself does not have a veto. Nor can we expect Germany and Japan to provide $20-25 billion for future collective security operations if they are not allowed to participate in the Security Council deliberations. We may not have seen the end of the question of who gets the Soviet veto. And neither Africa nor South America have permanent members on the Security Council.

What was important about the Stockholm Initiative on Global Governance and Security?.

There were four major world commissions in the 1980s: The North/South Commission headed by Willi Brandt; a Commission on Disarmament directed by Olaf Palme; the South Commission of Julius Nyerere, the former President of Tanzania; and the World Commission on Environment and Development, the Brundtland Commission. In the aftermath of the proclaimed end of the Cold War, a number of those involved in these commissions wanted to revisit some of the fundamental issues about security, protecting the environment, and the disparity of wealth between nations that affect both environment and security. They made a number of recommendations, including the creation of a Commission on Global Governance in 1995 that would prepare for a Breton Woods level summit meeting, such as the one that set up the U.N. following World War II.

The kind of process that would make everyone in the world feel included might be similar to the process followed by the Brundtland Commission. The Brundtland Commission included representatives from various backgrounds and sectors of 21 nations from all regions of the world who came together to make recommendations.

World leaders might adopt a new plan in a manner similar to the way in which the United Nations was created. Among other things, the U.N. was originally designed to control nuclear energy and create an International Court of Justice with binding authority and jurisdiction. While the 46 nations in 1945 failed to establish a United Nations that could effectively make, keep, and enforce peace and security, perhaps it can happen in this decade.

But even if we establish a Commission with good geographic distribution, its recommendations will ultimately be put through the filter of power politics.

Lawmaking at any level is often painful and ugly and at any time brute power may come into play. But our best hope is that something will occur similar to what happened in Philadelphia 200 years ago. I contend that something similar happened in a modest way at the Hague in 1989 when a diverse collection of heads-of-state transcended the forces of nationalism, mediocrity, and selfishness by calling for an enlightened mechanism for global decision-making. There you had a lot of interesting men from many different backgrounds make the right decisions in many ways.

What do you think of reforming the Trusteeship Council and turning it into a Trustees of the Earth Council? Do you see any advantage in taking the Trusteeship Council as a vehicle and transforming it into a forum for these kinds of issues?

We need a cluster of reforms both within and without existing organizations and institutions. The proposal to transform the Trusteeship Council, which has almost finished its work on decolonization, is another good idea, but it would have to be done in combination with a number of other important reforms. It has been suggested that a Sustainable Development Commission or an Environment/Development Commission might report to the Economic and Social Council, the General Assembly, or the Trusteeship Council. How this Sustainable Development Commission would be constituted would have a dramatic impact on whether the reform of the Trusteeship Council would work or not. If that Sustainable Development Commission were based on a model similar to the International Labor Organization or the Human Rights

Commission then it could be very effective. Non-government representatives should also have a formal role in the deliberations and perhaps even in decision-making. This might be accomplished through an arrangement similar to the tripartite mechanism in the International Labor Organization (ILO) that is composed of one-third governments, one-third labor, and one-third business representatives.

There are also proposals for strengthening the role of certain under secretaries of the U.N. There have been proposals for an ombudsman for the environment. The list of numerous and exciting proposals addressing many of the aspects of environment and development that need to be discussed makes it apparent that we can't do all of them; but we will have to do several of them. Those initiatives we do pursue will have to have a synergy amongst them so that the whole is greater than the sum of the individual parts.

There is even a "green helmets" proposal for a humanitarian peace corps, or environmental peace corps, that could exert international moral pressure on belligerents and say to them: "You are not going to destroy this historic city or this national park that has value to the global community." The Green Helmets could be modeled after refugee relief organizations and deal with environmental disasters. Each of these proposals has merit and we should not give up on them just because of opposition from the U.S.

Anil Agarwal, an NGO activist from India, is not enthusiastic about international legal edicts handed down from a distant bureaucracy. He prefers that local people have control over local resources so they can make sensible decisions over the resources that support life in their area. Do you actually think that the development of international law will help local communities gain control of their resource base?

Those of us who argue for the development of international law and international institutions agree with activists such as Agarwal that there is an economic model unleashed in the world that is consuming the resources of the least powerful countries. The First World is currently consuming up to three-fourths of the resources of the entire planet. So 20 percent of the people are consuming 75 percent of the resources.

Where do you get those figures?

Those are figures from the World Bank's 1990 report. The same annual report indicates that the poorest nations of the world transferred $47.2 billion net in debt payments to the wealthiest nations. And this does not count several times that net amount in transfer of natural resources, food, lumber, and minerals. Perversely, the poorest nations are currently subsidizing the wealthiest nations. That is the status quo and this year we are celebrating the 500th anniversary of this transfer of wealth.

Many people are not aware that this transfer of wealth from South to North is taking place. Where I come from, in Colorado and Wyoming, the vast majority of people are convinced that the U.S., far from making hundreds of millions of dollars a year from the poorest countries, gives away that much in charitable aid. But the reality is that we are forcing Third World leaders to starve children in their countries in order to make debt payments. I argue that we need some mechanism of international law that can force the most powerful nations and multinational corporations to stop practicing this kind of exploitation.

Do you think that NGO activists from developing nations recognize that, if properly designed, international agreements can be useful to people at the community level?

At the UNCED negotiations this last summer, activists from indigenous groups and southern NGOs often objected to new institutions and new international laws. The one exception was in the area of human rights protection. They all agreed in the value of international human rights protection. Maybe those of us who have been arguing for greater environmental agreements at the international level should be advancing them instead in the context of human rights. Perhaps breathable air should be a human right instead of an environmental right. Perhaps drinkable water should be a human right. If these human rights are enforced, perhaps there will be some spin-offs that are important to environmental protection.

Human rights protection works partly because of the efforts of strong NGOs, such as Amnesty International, that monitor, report on, and embarrass governments about human rights violations. A parallel "Amnesty for the Environment" movement might be useful.

Some southern NGO activists are skeptical about UNCED and are looking for ways to use these negotiations to strengthen their community struggles to protect their resources. What I'm understanding from you is that there has to be progress at both the local and the international level, and that organizing at the local level will not suffice to solve the large scale problems that we face as a global community.

These grassroots groups do not have a chance against the forces that are aligned against them. For the planet to effectively arrest the forces of environmental degradation we are going to have to strengthen communities and institutions at two levels: the global level and the local level.

By the end of the U.S. Presidential campaigns of 1968 and 1972, I came to believe that we could not solve problems at the nation-state level. Because of the accumulation of power at the nation-state and multinational-corporate levels, I believe that establishing strong global laws and institutions is the only way we can restore the flow of power, resources, and self-determination mechanisms to the local communities. This leads me to believe that the two levels at which society needs the most investment of creativity, energy, resources, and commitment are the neighborhood or village level and the global level.

In the U.S. the deterioration of the neighborhood as an important social unit has led to a disaster of incalculable dimensions. Almost every problem that we need to solve manifests itself at the neighborhood level: drugs, crime, homelessness, care for seniors, childcare, and improving education. Until we begin to deal with these problems in our neighborhoods or villages, assume community responsibility for these things, and accept the moral bond that we need to have with the people we live with, we are not going to make much progress.

A bright economist, I suspect, could demonstrate that the same economic model used by the World Bank that has so devastated Third World economies is the model that devastated Denver and much of the U.S. In the 1970s scores of mega-development projects were built in Denver. The city allowed all kinds of high-rise office and residential buildings to be constructed. Many of us living in Denver questioned why the city was subsidizing, much less permitting, the destruction of many of its old residential and downtown neighborhoods, single family homes, and historic storefronts. We asked who these new buildings were for and where the people were who could afford to live in them.

Tragically, like the unsustainable development projects built in the Third World, the projects in Denver were wildly wrong. The new buildings soon went bankrupt and brought down property values of entire areas of the city. Adjoining older buildings, neighborhoods, schools, and local banks all collapsed or suffered badly.

How did you become involved in the promotion of international law? From what you have told me it sounds as if you worked first at the community level in Denver. What made you shift your focus from community work to pushing for greater justice at the international level?

The two levels of society that most desperately need to be strengthened are the local level and the global level. I believe that the neighborhood, village, or rural community is the most important social unit in human society. It is at this local level that we develop our sense of moral bond or community. Yet, for most of my life, the sense of community at both of these levels has been systematically weakened.

I grew up and spent most of my life in Wyoming and Colorado where I was involved in education and local community politics. After college I worked with an inner-city high school during a time when Denver was experiencing serious desegregation problems. I was also involved in resisting the destruction of the old neighborhoods in Denver. In addition, I was active in a number of initiatives in Colorado against nuclear energy development and the Rocky Flats nuclear weapons plant. At one point during the energy crisis of the 1970s, there were actually plans to detonate nuclear weapons underground in Colorado to open pockets of natural gas. Even then, I was interested in the linkage between environment, unsustainable development, and disarmament.

My interest in international law really became a passion while resisting service in the military and opposing the war in Vietnam. In the late

1960s I came to believe that religion and nationalism caused more wars than they prevented; and that mutually assured destruction, as a global nuclear defense policy, was unadulterated insanity. Civil laws and the institutions of law based on universal moral principles are the most powerful civilizing agents in society. They are necessary to maintain order against brute power, anarchy, and violence. In my readings at that time, I found Albert Einstein and Bertrand Russell utterly convincing in their contention that mankind would either outlaw war, or perish. It seems to me that the way to pull back from the policy of mutually assured destruction is strengthening international legal mechanisms to bring about disarmament, prohibit the production and trade of weapons, and essentially outlaw war.

But, strengthening the United Nations peacekeeping capacity depends on the development of world law. We can't just do it by treaty. World law will have to be administered, adjudicated, and enforced. So, about 20 years ago, I began to believe in and work for a strengthened international legal order, and the strengthening of global institutions to achieve very limited goals, such as peace and disarmament. At that time I had not foreseen international environmental challenges as a principal activity of global institutions.

A few years ago I was asked to work for Amnesty International in London and New York on a campaign celebrating the 40th anniversary of the Universal Declaration of Human Rights, the highlight of which was a rock-and-roll concert tour across 16 countries. After that I helped organize a parallel NGO meeting in Europe in support of an initiative of foreign ministers of the Movement of the Non-aligned Countries to strengthen the World Court. Subsequently a London-based environmental organization asked me to open an office for them in Washington, D.C. For the last couple of years I have been director of the Center for the Development of International Law.

Stephen Collett:

Quakers Facilitate Informal Discussions Among UNCED Diplomats

Stephen Collett is the Friends World Committee for Consultation (Quakers) Representative at the United Nations, and Director of the Quaker U. N. Office.

Steve Lerner: What do the Quakers do at the U.N. and what has been your involvement with the UNCED negotiations?

Stephen Collett: The Quaker Office has six people working full time in New York and a sister body in Geneva with about the same number of people. I am often asked what it is that we do at the U.N. and whether or not it is lobbying. I don't really think that it is lobbying. That is not the term that best describes the non-government organization (NGO) role, and certainly not our role at the U.N. The U.N. is quite different from a parliamentary body. In a parliament or congress you have various proposals that can be passed by a majority or a two-thirds vote, and it is useful to argue the case to individuals who will be making those votes. In a congress or a parliament you can sway someone, or use other means of bringing pressure from his or her constituents to say we want you to vote this way or that way. That is not at all the way the U.N. operates.

At the U.N. you have resolutions passed or decisions taken. Some of these are action oriented. They implement or initiate some kind of action, such as the holding of a conference on environment and development. But that would not be of any value if the decision had not been made by a near consensus. To win a vote by a simple majority is not good enough, unless it is a seating question. Questions of credentials have to be passed by a two-thirds vote, for example. But anyone sponsoring a serious issue would back off if they did not have near unity or a very large majority on the subject.

The purpose of the U.N. is to identify issues of common concern, and ways in which those problems can be treated in the world community, by making recommendations for government policies. Some decisions will affect how U.N. funds are spent, for example, or what kind of U.N. support will be set up to accomplish a certain goal. Governments must be in agreement, by and large, about what the problem is and the way it must be solved. That is how a decision or resolution in the U.N. takes place. It works by consensus politics.

The issues taken up by the General Assembly of the U.N., as critics often point out, are often the same issues year after year. In fact, the agenda does not change very much. A few new agenda items are added each year. But, that is the point. What a vote really represents is a kind of straw poll of the degree of international unity on a subject. That helps to lead international opinion. I think it is quite influential in the shaping of government policies and how an individual government relates to the consensus on a particular subject.

What has your work been in relation to consensus politics?

The Quakers have supported a comparatively large office here at the United Nations because we support the process through which it works. We think this is the right way for countries to go about things. Quakers have a strong historic peace testimony, as we call it, a tradition of pacifism. We believe that peace requires a building of international institutions. Peace doesn't just happen. It is not just the absence of war, as Martin Luther King, Jr. said. It is a situation of security, in the broadest sense of the term, where people are secure in social and economic terms, and their rights are protected, and they are at peace with their neighbors. That is a situation that will lead to an abiding peace and that is the purpose of the United Nations: to work toward peace on a global scale.

I view the charter of the United Nations as one of those strokes of genius in the history of humankind when a new vision arose, much like that of the U.S. Constitution and the Bill of Rights. The U.N. Charter is a very concise document about what kind of world order we want. It takes time to build the institutions and laws required to support the vision embodied in the Charter of the United Nations and the Statute of the International Court of Justice, as it did to build the institutional support for the U.S. Constitution. The history of the United States is a building up of a national government, in all its parts, to make possible the vision described in the Constitution. The same is true of the United Nations, although we are not yet very far along in that process. The U.N. has been in existence only about 45 years. In those 45 years I think we have come a long way. The United Nations has been supremely influential and important in the history of the last 45 years, much more than it has been given credit for. I believe the United Nations is as responsible for the absence of a war since World War II as is nuclear deterrence. In fact, I think it has been more important.

To understand the importance of UNCED, I think some history is useful. When the U.N. began, some of the framers looked ahead and identified the two most difficult problems that the world faced: decolonization and disarmament. They thought that disarmament would be the easier of the two problems to solve. The reason was that the 51 states that founded the United Nations were the winners of the Second World War. All that was necessary was to establish a common security system based on the U.N. Charter; to gradually disarm themselves, and move over to a new system. In that fashion the earth would come to be governed in a new way. Decolonization, on the other hand, was seen to be the tougher challenge. While the founders thought disarmament might take 15 years, they saw decolonization as requiring from 75 years to a century. Considering how many centuries had gone into acquiring those colonies, seizing them, and protecting them, how could the U.N. ever convince the colonial powers to give them up?

Because of unforeseen problems in the aftermath of the war, it turned out, of course, to be the other way around. The United Nations collected information on all aspects of our world and on all its members, including information on the colonies. The colonial powers had to submit information on the status of health, education, resources, and trade in their colonies. This body of information created a snowball effect. From this pooled information it became clear who was doing what to whom, and the nature of this colonial system in relation to the U.N. Charter that the members had signed was clarified. Eventually, the colonial powers realized they could not continue in this fashion. The colonies also realized that they had no reason to continue to accept the situation. So the vision of the United Nations had an impact, as did its function as a body that collected, disseminated, and analyzed information. This may be parallel to the kind of impact UNCED has.

Some non-governmental organization (NGO) activists from developing nations would argue that while decolonization took place politically, the economic relations between the colonial powers and their colonies have not changed.

I certainly agree with an analysis that perceives the world today as strongly influenced by neocolonial structures. I think that underdevelopment is a structural problem; it will take centuries to reform that system. This is partly what UNCED is about.

What is the importance of UNCED in this context?

The importance of UNCED can hardly be overestimated. We cannot see it yet, but it is an undertaking to identify and initiate the next stage of world order beyond the U.N. Charter. The chapters of the U.N. Charter are taken up mostly with a global security system. We have a long way to go to fulfill the vision that is in that charter, but we have come a long way in two years. We could move rapidly to a new and better understanding of that system and use of those ideas. I hope that happens. There is a lot of potential that is still unused in the Charter as it is.

If you look at economics, the U.N. Charter says that the U.N. will support economic cooperation for development. It also ties together (in ways that proved to be prophetic) the human rights, development, and security issues that were not recognized or used until the Helsinki final act of 1975. The whole Helsinki process recognized the integral relationship between human rights, democracy, security, and economic cooperation among states. It recognized that these aspects are linked, and need to be built on together, and will hold each other in place in a network of true security. Between neighbors and in regions this has to occur, and that is what the U.N. Charter says in calling for regional support for neighbors and then the global system that supports that kind of regional development.

UNCED represents the recognition, forced upon us, that our economy is out of balance and out of control in terms of resource use. UNCED suggests that we are driving ourselves to ruin because we do not have a system of clear rights, principles, and commitments to an international economic system. We have not generally realized that economic activities of nations can affect the living standard and the ecology on the other side of the world. That is why I believe that the UNCED negotiations are the most important negotiations the U.N. has undertaken since it was founded.

You say that the U.N. Charter was a stroke of genius. Do you see the same kind vision emerging out of UNCED?

UNCED will really begin a process of redefining the vision. The document that we have as the mandating resolution — U.N. Resolution 44/228 of December 22, 1989 — is a very significant piece of work. There are parts of it that are fuzzy, but it lays out most of the elements that needed to be included.

At the UNCED negotiations, members of the Preparatory Committee have experienced a sense of growing vision as they have proceeded with their work. I think U.N. Resolution 44/228 was frightening to many countries that participated in it. That was the case with the Stockholm document that came out 20 years ago from the U.N. Conference on the Human Environment. After that conference, by the time it got to the General Assembly, there was a retraction of some support from its final endorsement. Some countries asked: "What have we done; are we going to commit ourselves to this?" That has been true during the UNCED Preparatory Committee meetings as well.

The significance of the third Preparatory Committee negotiating session held in Geneva in August, 1991 was that countries finally bought the idea of Agenda 21 and engaged in the process of writing an Agenda 21. Going into the August negotiating session many were not sold on the idea that their task for 1992 was to write a comprehensive agenda for the next century. That was a little scary. Could they accomplish it, is one question. Would they want to commit to it, is another. Would they even want such a process to get under way? Because, as the decolonization issue has shown, these things take on a life of their own. And when you start looking at these issues, the information you assemble begins to build up its own rationale.

That is what is happening to the delegates at the Preparatory Committee meetings. It is hard for us as public interest groups (if you can refer to the non-governmental community as public interest groups) to see this process. It is hard for us to see that there has been much progress. Yet I believe that a lot has been accomplished. I believe the collection and analysis of information by the UNCED Secretariat is a major achievement. That work, of course, is of varying quality. We know a lot about some of these subjects and less about others. However, the way it has been presented has generally brought governments along to the place where they can understand now what would go into an Agenda 21.

The question of institutions is always the caboose. You can't know what you want in the way of institutions until you are sure of the things you want to do and the relationships between them. You have to take up institutional questions last.

The financial issue is at the top of the agenda. An agreement on finances seems to be what is holding up a breakthrough. Developing countries have been saying that they will not make commitments to conventions when the resources to meet the new standards have not been identified. The industrialized countries say they will not put up a large sum of money when they don't know what it will be spent on. How will they solve this conundrum?

The money on the table is most directly represented by the Global Environment Facility (GEF). The Beijing Declaration calls for a Green Fund, that will finance development, whereas the GEF has been targeted at global environmental issues. I think that the negotiation will bring those two ideas together into one solution. That would mean a GEF Green Fund that would have numerous windows and would be able to address many of these problems. It would have a very different governing structure than the GEF. Currently the GEF is chaired by the Vice President of the World Bank, and is mostly a World Bank operation, even though the United Nations Environment Program (UNEP) and the United Nations Development Program (UNDP) are participants. A compromise might be something more like the Montreal Protocol Fund where decisions are made by a board of seven industrialized countries and seven developing countries. This would avoid the problems posed by having a commission on sustainable development and then a separate decision-making group on funding. The idea would be to put them together. This format would also provide a much more democratic governance structure than has been common in funding mechanisms of the World Bank. Problems remain as to how to combine different treaties under one fund.

This suggestion would meet one of the U.S. positions requiring that there be no new institutions created to carry out the work of UNCED. If instead of building a new institution you took the GEF but agreed to reform the way in which it was governed, that would not count as a new institution. I think there have been hints that the U.S. might be open to something along those lines.

Industrialized countries, which are the largest donors, have suggested that they are not willing to discuss the governance of the GEF at UNCED. I don't think that is a position they can maintain. The governance mechanism will have to be discussed. The GEF is a pilot project with a three-year life running about $1.3 billion. It would end a year and a half or two years after the Earth Summit in June, 1992. It is clear that they are going to have to discuss governance; that is why I think the Green Fund idea is a good negotiating position for the G-77, though not all that sound in itself.

Is there a need for a new institution?

Perhaps an institution that would evolve out of present institutions; I think that is the key to the problem of "no new institutions." I hear a desire for "no new institutions" from all sides. The G-77 is very protective of UNEP. They don't want any new institution supplanting UNEP. For other reasons the donor countries don't want new institutions. What would be best is a revitalized U.N. system with a new rationale of sustainable development.

How much money will be needed to finance the first stage of Agenda 21? What kind of financial resources should we be looking for to carry out a credible sustainable development program? Where should this money come from?

The $1.3 billion that the GEF represents is peanuts. It is not where the major money is. The amount of aid given by governments, the Official Development Assistance (ODA), is now around $50-55 billion. It has been that for about a decade, which means that its real value has been sliding.

As I understand it, the U.S. ODA is about 0.2 percent of our GNP. And the U.N. has asked countries to raise their ODA to 0.7 percent of GNP.

Although the U.S. has never agreed to 0.7 percent of GNP, it is the generally agreed target for ODA. Several Scandinavian countries and Holland have achieved 1 percent of GNP. Going to an ODA of 0.7 percent of GNP would double the $50 billion currently available. So compared to a GEF, that is significant money. It is money that could be well spent in the interest of a more equitable, better working, and peaceful world.

And one can argue for it out of self interest?

I think so. There would be a lot of multiplier effects from that money.

Do you see that happening?

I'm looking at what cards are available. Trade is another card. The value of trade is larger than ODA. The multiplier effects would be stronger. In many ways, trade is better than aid.

Do you mean a reform of the trade arrangements? When you suggest that we "play the trade card" what does that mean? Does it mean commodity pricing that is more favorable to developing nations?

Yes, better markets for commodities. That would mean in this country that we would have to do away with subsidies that support non-cane sugar and a number of other things you could identify. GATT is talking about a freer, more open trading system which justifies prices on trade advantages that are rational. In many areas that the developing countries trade in we, in the North, have not allowed that to happen — in agriculture, for example, commodities are the large one. It means that the Common Agriculture Policy (CAP) of the European Community needs ongoing reform. The U.S. also has enormous agricultural subsidies that skew commodities trade. We have created a club of tariff reductions within GATT; it is not a level playing field by any means, if you look at the larger world situation. These are very complex issues. I do not believe that the advantages that we enjoy will be given away in UNCED, and I have no illusions either about immediate action on ODA or trade concessions.

But, you ask what could be done. What could be done is that governments like the U.S. could make gestures indicating that the ODA and trade issues are negotiable, and that we are willing to work on trade issues and increasing ODA, and are willing to work on the debt problem, which is the third macro money-maker. They could say that ODA, trade, and debt are negotiable in many different fora, not just in UNCED. If we gave that signal it would have a tremendous impact on the UNCED process.

The industrialized nations are asking a lot of developing nations to keep large areas in their countries forested and spend money to adopt cleaner technologies. You have mentioned several things that the North could do, such as debt relief, leveling the trade playing field, and increasing ODA. Progress in these areas would demonstrate to developing nations that we are serious about moving toward sustainable development. In following the negotiations in a number of different areas at the United Nations, what sacrifices do you sense the North is willing to make?

I think that is a very important issue. It is tied to how successful the whole UNCED process will be in this first round. It will also be part of the enormous task that will remain after UNCED. After UNCED we will still have to educate governments and the general public about what a new world order based on sustainability really means. I think it is a revolution we will enjoy. It is a revolution of values. People will not have such a difficult time identifying with those values. Business will find that espousing positive values is good. I think the cutting edge of industry is going to be the massive social/economic conversion that is required of us. If you have to retool and reform the system there are going to be some start-up expenses. There certainly are going to be expenses in cutting way back the enormously wasteful military complex we have shackled ourselves with. There is pain in conversion as well, but there is a lot of business opportunity and jobs. There will be a tremendous economic resurgence when we start getting sustainable development on track.

Some NGO representatives from the developing world have stressed that they need more accountability from their leaders as to how aid funds are spent, and agreement from them on a more democratic process, in which people have more influence on the economic policies that affect their lives. These questions of democracy and accountability have always been seen as matters to be worked out in a national context, yet it is clear that a democratic process is necessary for sustainable development. Do you see UNCED having a democratizing impact?

Definitely. Democracy is necessary for ecological management, because for it to work, people have to be responsive at the local and individual level. If they are not, how will we manage things? Progress toward sustainability will require the democratization of societies around the world, as well as democratization of the global process. That could be an important benefit of the UNCED undertaking.

What role are the Quakers playing in the UNCED process?

We follow a range of subjects and try to understand enough about them to run alongside the diplomats. We engage these diplomats, we talk with them about specific questions, we distribute materials both of a scientific nature and illustrating the views that are circulating.

The Quakers provide space for off-the-record discussions. That has been one of our chief contributions. We arrange meetings both on the small scale of lunches and teas, and on the larger scale of weekend conferences. At these gatherings diplomats are able to get together, often with members of the U.N. Secretariat, and sometimes with a few outside experts. We invite diplomats to explore each others' thinking and to look ahead on these issues. We guarantee that these are confidential discussions.

We don't have our own axe to grind. Thank heavens for Amnesty International, which goes around and points the finger. We don't often do that. We do sometimes have to "witness" when we think something is dead wrong, and we feel obliged to tell a government that we don't agree with its policy. But that is not our usual practice. Most of the time we listen and discuss these issues to understand what various parties need in order to move further on a particular agenda item. Then we can structure a meeting that will set up a conversation at the right time, with the right people, on the right topic, and pitched in the right way. We have held meetings of this kind for diplomats in the UNCED process, and will continue to.

What topics are these meetings organized around?

We have been organizing smaller meetings on such topics as the role of women, human rights, and environment. We also have had a program of four week-end conferences over two years for senior negotiators just prior to sessions of the UNCED Preparatory Committee.

Our practice is to write an agenda for these meetings, together with participants, by circulating and discussing drafts with them. The programs for week-end colloquia have closely tracked the agenda of work for each upcoming PrepCom: where we are in the process; what are our options and problems; how shall we go about negotiating them? We have brought in outside experts on science, local communities, and development. We have also used U.N. agency expertise, and we have relied heavily on UNCED Secretariat participation to lead off discussions. We gather 35 to 40 delegates, with another 5 to 10 from the Secretariat, and simply open matters for discussion after a lead-off speaker introduces a topic.

Over two years I feel we have seen quite a degree of convergence on the issues from the environmental side of UNCED. The economics are more difficult and we probably know even less about them. But, in the process, all sorts of economic issues are coming to life within the policy debate of the U.N.—as well as human rights and security issues. Rio can only begin to deal with these problems, but it is remarkable to see countries begin to work on these issues seriously.

Peter J. Davies:

The Greening of U.S. Development Organizations

 eter J. Davies is President and CEO of the American Council for Voluntary International Action (InterAction).

Steve Lerner: If you were a lobbyist at the United Nations Conference on Environment and Development (UNCED), what would you lobby for?

Peter J. Davies: I would lobby very hard for population concerns to be considered. I do not think we should accept the excuse that the population issue will be handled somewhere else. Second, it is not enough that the developed countries commit themselves to putting some technical assistance and some money toward encouraging developing countries to do something about their environment. Industrialized nations must commit to reducing their own overconsumption. We must focus on the fact that oil energy is overconsumed in the North. We must control our own overconsumption of world resources. We lecture others about preserving their forests, but we are not doing nearly enough to conserve our own resources. We are not prepared to change our own habits.

There are many northern international development organizations going to the South to do development work. Why are they not doing work also in the North with the industrial nations, many of which have farther to go to achieve sustainable development?

There are a number of U.S. private voluntary organizations (PVOs) that have programs in developing communities within the U.S. For instance, they try to bring grassroots development to Mississippi or wherever. The work of the Highlander Center is an example of this.

But is that enough? As you point out, one of the greatest threats to the earth's ecosystems results from overconsumption by affluent people in the North. It follows that development work has to be done not just with the poor, but also with those who consume too much? It may sound strange, but should we not have a new kind of development worker going out into the field in the North (maybe setting up shop in some of our shopping malls) to work with those who consume too much. Is it not necessary to teach those who overconsume that they are, in a way, un-

272

derdeveloped, and that they have to evolve beyond consumerism? It would be good for Americans to hear that while we may be accomplished consumers, in terms of sustainable development we are underachievers.

Yes. We have to change our way of relating to the environment.

Is there a growing interest in that sort of work in the development community?

Yes. There is. InterAction is composed of six groups, at least. There are the pure development or relief groups, those that do virtually nothing except respond to disasters. CARE does a lot of disaster emergency response, but it is also engaged in longer-term development including environmental afforestation projects, for example. There are many development groups engaged in long-term development programs and projects that, for example, work on child survival and women's projects. There are the refugee resettlement groups, some of which become involved in environmental issues, because many of these refugees are essentially economic migrants and are forced to move because of population pressure.

There are also what we call the development education non-government organizations (NGOs), which are focused on educating the American public about global interdependence. The End Hunger Network, Bread for the World, and Results are very much involved in development education activities. Quite a few of our development members are becoming more involved in development education. We at InterAction argue that they should educate Americans about global interdependence, and the necessity for reducing our own consumption instead of pushing for economic growth. Then we have the environmental groups, such as the Sierra Club and World Wildlife Fund, that are now members of InterAction. Because of the diversity of the membership, and the interaction and networking that takes place, we are beginning to raise some of these issues and get a healthy dialogue going between environment and development organizations.

Many activists from the developing world complain that the development model that has been foisted on them for the last 40 years is an inappropriate and destructive one. InterAction represents some 135 PVOs. Does this complaint apply to some of your members?

Yes, absolutely.

What success have you had in trying to introduce the concept of sustainable development to your members? I understand you have a Sustainable Development Task Force.

Our Sustainable Development Task Force is small and it is starting slowly. We have a Task Force that brings together those member agencies that are interested in sustainable development. That does not include all our members. The Task Force went out and formulated a three-year project to get people undertaking sustainable development projects, in which environment and population issues are part of the program design, to share their field experiences on what works and what does not work. The idea is to hold workshops in Latin America, Asia, and Africa where people who do field work discuss their experiences gained from projects that integrate environment and development, population and development, or population and environment. That project is just starting. The first workshop will take place in Costa Rica in early 1992.

We at InterAction are undertaking this project in partnership with our Latin American counterparts. The idea is to do case studies of successfully integrated projects and disseminate them as learning aids among other members. For example, many of our development members recognize the importance of integrating family planning and population concerns into their programs. Yet, they don't know how to do it and have never done it. Because they have never done it they are scared of the political fallout of doing it. We will also try to identify the necessary ingredients in a successful sustainable project. How can you make certain that a project builds into its design a concern about its own environmental impact? We are hoping that some common principles will emerge out of these case studies.

People in the field are already doing a lot of this integrated development. But they are not people who take that information and put it down on a piece of paper and put it into a case study format, or share it with other practitioners. Therefore, we will have a facilitator and case study writer in each of these workshops.

I notice that you shy away from the term sustainable development, preferring the term "integrated development programs." Is there some subtle difference between the two?

No, I just think the term sustainable development may mean different things to different people. I come out of a rural development background focused on organizing and encouraging people to recognize that they have the power to do something about their own environment. Sustainable development is just a phrase, so I talk about integrated development —integrating the various components that make a successful program work. In this formulation the three legs of the stool are: environment, population, and development, but people are the central focus.

How has this message of integrated development or sustainable development been received by the members of InterAction?

It is vital that our members recognize the importance of promoting a sustainable variety of development. However, not everyone has bought into that yet. At our board meeting two years ago, we presented a statement on sustainable development principles to the full membership of InterAction. We put it before the group to be adopted as official InterAction policy. Our by-laws require that such a decision be unanimous.

The main point of contention was the issue of population control. Our population groups wanted firm language about population control, but our Catholic groups and some of our Evangelical groups did not want the word control used. We finally settled on the use of the word population without the word control. Passing that statement was an enormous leap forward for us. The most radical of the population groups abstained because they did not feel it was strong enough. The most radical Evangelical groups abstained to allow us to reach a consensus. For a membership organization that is a very important thing to have achieved. That statement is now official InterAction policy.

How is the critique of the development model that is being made by activists from developing nations being processed by your membership?

The word processed is a very good one. It is a slow process. We have held a forum every year at which we invite the South to speak out so that all of us northerners are not just talking to one another. As a result, some of our more conservative organizations hear the voice of the South insisting that we in the U.S. reduce our overconsumption. They also hear people from the South say that the economic growth model may not be the most appropriate model for developing countries. I think this has caused a reexamination on the part of a few of our members of the partnership programs that they are involved in. They are also taking a more careful look at the environmental impact of what they are doing and have focused more on organic agriculture, for instance, instead of using pesticides and chemical fertilizers.

Take, for example, Winrock International on the Rockefeller estate in Little Rock, Arkansas, which is a major player in agricultural development. It has a farm and AID contracts to undertake agriculture development programs. I believe it is hearing this critique and beginning to examine its own programs and projects in this light.

What options do you see for not only changing the amount of money that is devoted to sustainable development, but also changing the way the Global Environment Facility (GEF) is administered?

I have just come from a meeting devoted to the issue of popular participation in World Bank projects. We want to keep the focus of the Bank and our NGO/World Bank Committee in two equally critical areas: first, on the adverse impact of structural adjustment on the poor; second, on the process of getting more popular participation in World Bank projects. It is very hard to get the Bank's operational people to spend time on this when they have to spend their time pouring out a lot of money in loans. They are concerned about slowing the process down. They sent us a series of 21 questions that focused more on the internal workings of the Bank process than they did on some of the development philosophy issues such as bringing local people in on the design of projects at an early stage.

But I think we have to recognize that the Bank is a major player. The Bank influences governments by lending them money. NGOs have expertise on community development issues such as grassroots organizing, training, and human resource development. They should bring this expertise to bear on operational people at the Bank. It will be an uphill battle to influence the key operational people at the Bank, but it remains a useful effort.

The donor countries want the money for sustainable development to be channeled through the World Bank's GEF. Since without the cooperation of the donor countries there will be no money, is it not a good bet that this is how it will work?

I will go even further than that. The World Bank is a major player today in international development. Its influence goes beyond AID or any of the multilateral regional banks. It influences the regional banks. Therefore, if you really want to have an impact on putting funds into use effectively in the environmental area, you might as well play with the big boys and do it with the Bank. If you were to set up a separate structure, or try to find another house for it, you would probably not make as much headway as you would with the Bank. To be sure, an educational job has to be done within the Bank and I don't envy whomever is going to be faced with that. The Bank is not homogeneous and one must work with and support those who want to see resources spent wisely by NGOs on people-oriented programs.

The U.S. UNCED delegation seems to be hinting that while they are not willing to discuss new and additional resources for sustainable development, and while they do not want any new institutions created to promote sustainable development, they might entertain suggestions for the reform of the GEF to make it more transparent and democratic. Are the development groups trying to get a unified position together on how the GEF should be reformed?

You never get a unified position from the development groups. We have not come together yet and taken a position on GEF. The environmental groups are probably much closer to doing that than are development organizations. But PVOs interested in sustainable development are very concerned that the GEF become an effective vehicle for environmental funding and not another bureaucratic entity.

The Group of 77 (G-77) developing nations argues that the Green Fund should not be administered by the Bank. The Group of Seven (G-7) industrialized nations wants the money to be administered by the World Bank. Is there a possibility that the new GEF fund could be administered differently so that it is not exclusively the donors who decide how the money is spent?

We call that popular participation.

But banks are not well known for permitting a great deal of participatory democracy in the shaping of their loan agreements.

PETER DAVIES

I don't know enough about the mechanics of how things will be set up to have an opinion. I think it is important that the developing countries should have more of a say. Maybe the board of the Bank should not be as unequal as it is in allowing the developed countries to call the tune on most lending decisions. It would probably be possible to build in some controls that ensure a more democratic structure for the GEF. But I'm skeptical that this will occur, given that the new World Bank president has a financial background, as opposed to someone with a development background.

What I understand you to be saying is that the development community has not come up with a suggestion for what institution should handle large amounts of money for sustainable development. And I have yet to hear from you any ideas that the development community has come up with about the reform of U.N. institutions to help promote sustainable development.

Agencies that make up InterAction — such as CARE and WorldVision Church World Service, Save the Children, Oxfam, etc. — do not spend time and energy focusing on how the Bank funds its operations or how the multilateral institutions evolve. Most of the private voluntary organizations are so involved with raising money and running their operations that they spend very little time on broader policy issues. That may sound like a very cynical response, but I don't see much statesmanship among the private voluntary organizations. There were some statesmen in our community a few years ago, such as David Guyer of Save the Children; Jim MacCracken of Christian Children's Fund; and to some extent Charles McCormack of the Experiment in International Living.

If you were to give me a few names of people from the development community who are most knowledgeable about the GEF and institutional reform at the U.N. — who would they be?

I'd be hard pressed to come up with names.

That seems strange when the impact of these institutional arrangements is significant on the development projects run by members of InterAction.

That is exactly my concern. For eight years I was a CEO of a middle-sized PVO, Meals for Millions/Freedom from Hunger Foundation, and we were focused on integrated rural development programs. I have now been at InterAction eight years working with a large number of these organizations. I say to you carefully and advisedly that these organizations are very parochial and very slow to change. They spend a lot of time on strategic planning to narrow their focus and identify their targets for fund raising. They are not fully involved in the broader spectrum of development policies or influencing government policies that have an impact in the Third World.

Having said that, there are a few individuals who have focused on the broader picture: Dr. Paul McCleary, Executive Director of Christian Children's Fund, convinced his agency to focus more on Eastern Europe and the former Soviet Union. WorldVision recognized that one of the issues is scaling up so that they can have a more important impact on agricultural productivity or health, instead of having a lot of little projects. Paul Thompson at WorldVision is probably as broad in his thinking and as concerned about environment as anyone in the development field. But there are relatively few.

How is InterAction involved in the UNCED process?

It is my own strong sense, based on a lot of overseas work, that you cannot separate environment and population issues from development issues. Many of us recognize that for NGOs and PVOs working in development to ignore the fact that the UNCED process was taking place would mean that we would miss an opportunity to promote effective development that incorporates environment and population concerns. As a result, we decided to spend some of our very limited resources on paying the salary of a person to monitor the UNCED process part-time, participate actively in the U.S. Citizens Network on UNCED, and motivate a number of our members to participate.

I have to tell you frankly that there are relatively few members of InterAction who give a damn about being involved in the UNCED process. They see the U.N. process as hopelessly slow, painful, and unproductive. But it is important that our members not bury their heads in the sand. UNCED is here and NGOs have a role to play to influence their own governments and the UNCED process itself.

What is it that you think might come out of UNCED that would be of use to the organizations that you represent?

I am less concerned with service to our members (although that is important, also) than I am about what is happening out there in the world that is going to affect people at the grassroots level — those for whom my members work.

I hope there is some convergence of interests there.

Yes, but my mission, as I see it, is to convince my InterAction members that unless they change the way they do business, unless they integrate environmental concerns into their development programs, unless they focus more on strengthening the capacity of local indigenous institutions to carry out development, unless they focus on the population dynamic, unless they focus on the civil and social conflicts, and humanitarian rights issues — then all their development projects will not be effective and will not solve the problems that we face.

The bottom line is that NGOs — whether from the U.S. or developing countries — must not just work at the micro field level; they must also attempt to affect the unenfranchised at the macro level.

Harris R. Gleckman:

A Code of Conduct for Transnational Corporations

arris R. Gleckman is Chief of the Environment Unit, Transnational Corporations and Management Division (formerly Centre on Transnational Corporations), Department of Economic and Social Development, United Nations.

Steve Lerner: What do you do here at the Centre on Transnational Corporations?

Harris R. Gleckman: The Centre on Transnational Corporations (CTC) has been looking at the ways in which foreign investors, international trade, and the environment affect one another. For eight years, we have been doing studies on different aspects of by multinational corporations.

We look at the Brazil conference as an important time to articulate the corporate responsibility for global environmental protection. Of course, businesses have environmental responsibilities and obligations within a country. But we are primarily focused on the international environmental responsibilities of transnational corporations (TNCs).

How do you begin to make TNCs accountable for the impact of their operations on the environment?

We have approached this question in a number of ways. The CTC recently completed the Benchmark Survey of the major firms in the world, asking them how they are doing on global environmental management; to what extent they have company-wide policies for keeping track of their impact on the environment; and the extent to which they are trying to monitor from headquarters what they are doing, or whether they are letting local managers run their own shows in each country.

What is crucial about this piece of work is that the Earth Summit in Brazil, in June, 1992, will be an occasion for governments and international organizations to say what they are going to do to create a global environmental management system. But there is another set of forces at work in the world, in the private sector — the transnationals. These transnationals are developing global environmental management systems within their companies. They are doing this on their own as well as in response to public pressure and government overtures.

At the Centre on Transnational Corporations, we are trying to bring these two processes together. The intergovernmental negotiators working on a global environmental management approach, and the TNCs, which are doing global environmental management at the corporate level, need to see each other's efforts in a complementary fashion.

This survey you did is of voluntary initiatives taken by international corporations. Are you moving toward a written pledge by multinational corporations in which they agree to a code of conduct on global environmental management?

CTC has two avenues we are traveling on in this regard. One is within the Code of Conduct negotiations. The international Code of Conduct negotiations have been going on for 15 years. They concern the rules of practice of transnational corporations operating in host countries, and host countries' responsibilities to their foreign investors. The sections of the Code on environmental and consumer protection have been agreed to by the negotiating parties. There are three paragraphs on environmental protection and consumer protection that have been agreed upon. That is non-controversial text in the Code. However, the Code of Conduct negotiations as a whole are stumbling over other issues of international law, and over the effect of the Uruguay Round.

The other more directly relevant track to the UNCED process is that the governments decided last July at the Economic and Social Council (ECOSOC) that it makes good sense to have a chapter on multinational responsibility in the United Nations Conference on Environment and Development (UNCED) agreement to be signed in Brazil. They asked the Executive Director of the Centre on Transnational Corporations to prepare action-oriented and practicable recommendations on ways to mobilize and encourage TNCs to contribute to global environmental protection.

Where would this separate chapter be placed? In Agenda 21? Or in the Earth Charter?

We envision it in both.

How is this different from the Code of Conduct negotiations?

If there is to be a new global partnership between the business community and governments, the governmental side needs to express its expectations of what the private sector and multinationals should be doing. Governments also need to make clear what they will be doing to create a framework to encourage clean investments, clean technologies, and economic growth with an environmental consciousness. The chapter that would appear in the Earth Charter or in Agenda 21 would be a much longer document than the reference to these issues in the Code of Conduct. The chapter on transnationals in the Earth Charter would attempt to express some principles stating that firms should operate with equivalent sets of standards or consequences of their activities in all countries of the world. It would also suggest that firms should use the best available technologies wherever they are operating. And, it would suggest potential new principles in the soft law area. In Agenda 21 there will be an effort to establish timetables and forecasts of what should be done over a number of years.

How much input will the TNCs have in shaping this document? You circulate the draft to them, they can comment on it; but if your executive director feels that their suggestions are inappropriate, do they get left out of the draft?

The drafting process is open to a number of different constituencies: TNCs, governments, environmental organizations, other professional experts, all of whose ideas will be listened to. The Executive Director of CTC needs to mold these together into a coherent package, not acting as a scribe for any one constituency, but trying to come up with a version that advances the discussions. What we are attempting to do is combine new ideas with previously accepted ones. There are those in the corporate sector, as well as in certain governments, who would like to say only what has been said before. They suggest that the International Chamber of Commerce's (ICC's) Business Charter for Sustainable Development should be adopted by governments.

Others object that this is not a legitimate process: one should question whether the text goes far enough. The text of the Business Charter for Sustainable Development uses the concept of sustainable development only in its title. The content returns to environmental protection. There are no development aspects in the body of the text. UNCED is a conference on environment *and* development. So there has to be something more substantial that brings those two concepts together. The Executive Director has to not only synthesize existing documents, but also try to move the discussion forward. The agreements to be made in Brazil are to be forward looking documents.

How would you describe the level of debate over this? Has it been very contentious? Have the TNCs come together into a unified bloc of some kind? Do they have an organization that speaks for them? Are they very concerned about this process?

There are a number of leading individual firms, environmental business organizations, and individuals in major corporations who are trying to think about these issues. They all have different primary concerns that they want expressed. There is not a homogeneous view.

So Shell is different from Exxon.

That's right. There are also firms that feel that the international community should do nothing, and that corporations should be allowed to do whatever they wish within the minimal laws of many countries; they think that is the nature of our laws. Suggestions that hold that there should be principles of international behavior in this area are seen by some as a bad idea. And they will tell the U.N. and the UNCED process that the corporations are interested in the environment and will do what they can to protect it, but governments and international bodies should say no more about it.

I don't understand the position that CTC occupies at the U.N. How do you deal with conflict and disagreement between corporations and environmentalists?

One way of describing our role is to describe ourselves as a consulting firm (which of course we are not) with two clients. We work with governments and we work with the corporate sector. With the corporate sector, we help explain the political process, the economic realities, the changes in the world's economy.

We articulate the political, economic, and social changes which are occurring, and help focus TNCs attention on what they ought to be doing. For instance, we talk to the corporations about the fact that in the future, standards for submitting test results for health and safety will be created in countries which frequently do not have them. As a result, instead of working with 30 different regulatory authorities, TNCs will be working with 160 in a short period of time. Given that reality, what are the ways a firm can make efforts to ensure that its labels are clear, clean, and accurate; can make sure that the contents of its products contain the least hazardous elements possible, so that one to five years from now they do not have to address the new regulatory authorities that will appear.

To the governments we give examples of the best corporate practice and a workable international business arrangement. And we need to learn from governments what initiatives they are taking, so that we can discuss and understand the consequences of their decisions. In the end, the stick is the national laws and regulations, and the threat of a proliferation of multiple sets of rules and regulations on a given issue. Water quality will be judged (and is presently judged in those countries that regulate water quality) in 20 different ways. Very shortly there will be 100 different ways.

And that is not in the best interests of TNCs.

No, it isn't in their interest. Therefore we advise the firms to look ahead and deal with their water protection plans around the world. We advise them to switch to a high standard now, because they are investing new capital, and it is cheaper to do it on a new investment than to retrofit an old plant. It is in their interest to realize that their water quality standards ought to move to a higher level so that they are adaptable to a changing set of rules.

Are you suggesting that there will be international regulations on water quality that the TNCs will eventually have to comply with?

Over time, in certain areas, there will be new international treaties depending on political interests and events in the world. Five years ago you wouldn't have predicted a Basel Convention on Hazardous Waste. We are working on agreements on chemicals that are banned or severely restricted in one country. In time, there will be whole new areas requiring international consensus, for example. Water quality is one example. The corporate sector needs to be aware of this happening. Companies should not be surprised by an international statement on it, and/or a series of new national laws and regulations on it, because water quality is an important issue.

Could there not be some international agreements on how TNCs themselves should be allowed to operate? Could the combined wisdom of the representatives of governments assembled at UNCED say that TNCs, wherever they operate, should apply the same environmental standards?

The core of our work is on generic standards. The structure of UNCED, however, is built on particular environmental crises. In some of the draft language of the Earth Charter we are trying to help evolve the minimal expected standard for multinationals to follow when local rules are nonexistent or are weak. We are trying to come up with a possible phrasing for that potential reference standard. These are some of the complexities and challenges that face us.

Three years ago, we looked at the question of international reference standards and published a document saying that there are difficulties with all the ones. If you adopt home-country reference standards, it causes problems. For instance, take the chemical industry in a developing country. There may be 15 plants from 12 home countries and they will be working with 12 sets of rules. In that case, the host country has multiple sets of standards being used. One solution is to set a standard of "best available technology in the sector," which does resolve some of the sectoral variations. But there is an ambiguous understanding of what is the best available technology.

Another alternative we have been working on is to say that there is a minimal set of standards that firms should follow analogous to the minimum accepted level of human rights. No matter what national law says, there is an international expectation that the minimum should be followed. For that approach to work we have to define the components of minimums. At the same time, we need to make sure that this minimum standard does not get misinterpreted as the maximum. This would suggest no need for improvement.

Which would you bet on: the minimal standard or the best available technology regulation; or could the standard be some combination of the two?

We are moving toward the minimal national environmental standards. One of those standards may relate to best available technology within reasonable financial terms. We will see what comes out of this process. There is a general acceptance that there ought to be certain sets of practices that firms follow everywhere, and that gross inconsistency on clearly hazardous activities is wrong.

So, what the international community is doing, and this in our view is central to the UNCED Summit in Brazil, is asking, what is that expectation? The Centre for Transnational Corporations sees it as part of its role to help articulate worldwide standards where a broad consensus exists about how firms treat human life. The challenge is to write that as a policy statement.

I noticed that in the CTC Benchmark Survey it appears that the firms surveyed were more interested in some areas than in others. For example, they professed to be interested in areas where there was strong national legislation; they were less interested in issues that they saw to be chiefly a problem for developing nations, such as preservation of biological diversity. Is the Code of Conduct or are the emerging minimal standards addressing the corporate responsibility to preserve biological diversity? For example, if you have a chemical plant in a developing country, should it have to be concerned with its impact on biological diversity?

On the subject of biological diversity, the Benchmark Survey found that three of the respondents were aware of surveys on properties that they own in developing countries. They should be aware of the elements of biodiversity that they have stumbled onto, and therefore what choices they need to make about the land that they own. Even if they make absolutely benign environmental products, there are other sets of issues that they need to look at.

For a given firm you have the question of priorities. One of the useful elements of the UNCED negotiations is that they point out to the corporate sector the topics of global concern at the moment, and advise corporations to take heed of this international consensus. You can interpret the product of UNCED as a moral statement, or you can also interpret it as a warning flag to the corporate sector that it should anticipate in the near future increasing domestic ordinances and laws on these subjects. This is going to affect the TNC production processes, their products, and their style of operating. Here you have an example of the dynamic between an international conference and its effort to define global management of the biosphere, and the corporate sector developing global environmental management on its own. UNCED will be a means for these two systems to talk to each other.

The TNCs have kept a fairly low profile at UNCED. How would you describe the manner in which TNCs make their views known at UNCED?

In 1972, at the Stockholm Conference, the role of the business sector was a single intervention by the International Chamber of Commerce that lasted around eight minutes. This time I think the situation is quite different. There are a lot of parallel events that are being developed, in which industry involvement is welcomed. The International Chamber of Commerce held a conference in Rotterdam called the World Industry Conference on Environmental Management, which made recommendations to the UNCED preparatory meeting. The Secretary General of UNCED has retained a senior industry advisor, Stephen Schmidheiny, who created an organization of 48 chief executive officers of firms from around the world (balanced North, South, East, and West) to come up with their recommendations through the Business Council for Sustainable Development.

Regarding specific concerns on the agenda, TNCs have made their views about that process known to their national delegations. In addition to their ability to intervene in the working groups, they, as other non-government organizations (NGOs), have the right to address the Working Groups.

We can add to that CTCs' effort to involve as many firms as possible in drafting the text for what might be an expression of multinational responsibility for environmental protection and economic growth. We sent a letter out to all the firms that have articulated a public environmental position and asked them to let us know what they think of our draft. So, we are drawing on the leading firms in the world.

I would expect that if the corporate world took UNCED seriously, and thought that something might come out of it that would affect operations in the future, there would be visible signs of lobbying by the corporate sector. I have not seen that. Is that because they work more effectively through channels to which I am not privy?

Different trade bodies and different firms have chosen different ways to influence the UNCED process. By and large, active participation in the Preparatory Committee meetings is not one of the avenues that they have chosen. There are trade associations that address the Working Groups on specific issues about land or water, protection issues that are in their sectoral interests. Each country's national delegation also provides a route for lobbying. Some of the delegations include corporate executives or retired corporate executives. There are sets of meetings between the Secretariat of UNCED and industry associations, in which the associations give their input into the UNCED documents. There are a number of different avenues.

The activist NGO community has the advantage of more familiarity with working with intergovernmental leaders, more openness about saying: "Here is what our views are." They are prepared to engage in a dialogue of confrontation with governments over their views. When looking over the list of the participants at the third UNCED Preparatory Committee negotiating session, there was a page of government delegates, a page of the international organizations, and six pages of the NGOs, some of which were industries. So, there are multiple avenues for influencing the process.

Some of the NGOs, particularly from developing nations, have a very jaundiced view of the operations of TNCs and the impact that they have had in the Third World. Many of them feel that the TNCs are not very worried about the UNCED negotiations because they don't see any agreements emerging out of them that will significantly transform the way TNCs do business. Some critics of the process even go so far as to introduce a conspiratorial air to their analysis. They ask, for example, why it is that UNCED did not, from the outset, focus on the impact of the energy sector on both environment and development? Some saw the invisible corporate hand keeping the energy issue from being highlighted on the UNCED agenda.

Everyone has a hard time striking a list of the primary areas to work on in a conference on environment and development. I have watched that over the last three and a half years. We are always caught on the new nexus between environment and development. What we have ended up with is a list of eight environmental areas and a list of 22 development areas for which we are invited to look at a matrix, which is 176 areas. That is a Christmas wish list. Why certain issues were not added on the environmental side or development side; or why some prioritization was not made is a fair and tough critique. And I think it should be made. Where would energy appear in the matrix: Would it be an environmental crisis or a development issue?

Both. I would have thought it would have been obvious, essential, and almost first on the list of issues to be addressed. I realize energy is now beginning to be addressed at UNCED in a piecemeal fashion, but focusing on the impact of the energy sector on environment and development has been largely ignored.

At the Centre on Transnational Corporations we have a long study out on climate change and the role of multinationals. In it we attempt to estimate what share of greenhouse gases have been generated by multinational activities, and we look at specific industry groups. This is a piece of work now available in draft form in the Climate Change negotiations, and at the second UNCED Preparatory Committee meeting. What was interesting in doing that study was that there was not very much literature on it from either the corporate side or the environmental critics' side.

This goes back to what occurs in the planning process for a conference. I would suggest that the environmental groups did not get organized early enough to define roles on the agenda that were felt to be important. It was a mixture of the financial weakness of environmental groups and their disdain for becoming involved in international discussions in many cases until it is too late. I think environmentalists also somewhat enjoy saying: "Look, it didn't happen."

There are also some hard questions to ask about how to argue and structure that debate. Not having done the economic homework is one part of that. You hear more on the energy issue if you listen to the debate on the atmospheric protection questions. There are concerns from the OPEC countries about proposals to radically switch sources of energy supply. In one part of the debate about atmosphere, one of the OPEC countries was saying in the open session that they thought the production of the document by the Secretariat — actually under the initiative of the Swedish chairman of the Working Group — had never been really asked for. Using that as an argument, they wanted to put a bracket around (delete) the entire document including the title of the document. Now, that is a reality of political national concerns about oil and energy policies. I think in part that the broader critique of that type of energy policy is not systematically being made, internationally. The number of the NGOs taking an active role in the climate change negotiations is not very large, given that it is central.

There is another side of the role of TNCs. Transnational corporations often have a better environmental record than do smaller local firms that have neither the resources nor the expertise to handle their wastes in a responsible fashion. So, there is an argument to be made that many TNCs already are doing a better job than many smaller firms in the developing world, and that TNCs are already in a leadership role.

There are two or three pieces of research being done on this. One piece was done by a part of the Centre on Transnational Corporations in the Economic and Social Commission for Asia and the Pacific (ESCAP), which tried to do a comparison between national and international firms in five or six ESCAP Asian region countries. They asked the firms what their perception was of the government regulatory system and what each of the firms was doing. What we found is that certain groups of firms that have to deal with environmental issues at home, in their major markets, are far more sensitive to the environment as a social/political concern than are many national firms that have not had the 20 years of pressure in the North on their major markets. They may have had only three to five years, and that clearly affects national consciousness within the business community about what the expectations are. One of the elements that needs to be included is that some of the areas where multinationals are involved — high-capital, high-risk, high-polluting industries — have a disproportionate impact on the environment. One needs to see if it is also the case that multinationals need to operate at a higher standard because they are larger facilities.

Often the discussion about TNCs focuses more on pollution than on sustainable development. Yet many TNCs use up renewable and non-renewable resources in a profligate way. While the focus is often on what they are doing with their waste, very little attention is paid to the fact that TNCs are feeding a consumptive pattern of behavior that is wasting the resources of the planet. Is the wise use of resources issue being brought up in the examination of TNC behavior?

CTC faced the challenging question of how to translate the concept of sustainable development into business terms. We worked for a year and a half to develop a set of ideas, which was called "Criteria for Sustainable Development Management", to help corporate managers who want to undertake growth for their firms, but aspire to do it in an ecologically sound way. We asked what kind of new ideas they need to think about in their new corporate culture.

In long-term planning one has to decide whether to take the current value of the natural resource, or whether to look at it over a number of years and take a different return from it. These are elements we thought were very important to introduce into a new business ethic and a new corporate culture that deals with environmental protection and economic growth. The core question was: How do we move the discussion beyond pollution prevention into the area of natural resource conservation. The hard part is that for the most part even the industrialized countries' governments still engage in environmental protection. They have not, as part of public policy, made the transition into natural resource protection and sustainable development. It is harder for the corporate community to react, because a clear public consensus on this issue reflected in laws, and administrative procedures do not exist in most of the major industrialized countries except for in a handful of countries like the Netherlands and Canada, that have seriously taken on what will be a sustainable growth track.

The managers of Shell Oil have realized that they are in the power business, not in the oil business. Are you working with other corporations to more broadly define their role in an ecologically sustainable fashion?

We see our Criteria for Sustainable Development Management helping executives think in those terms.

How do you see this area of soft law evolving? How will these principles you are developing for the behavior of TNCs play out after UNCED? Will these voluntary agreements have any practical results?

The results will come through a series of major events and consistent pressure maintained on these issues. There have been changes in corporate practices in the last five to eight years, internationally, that I would not have forecast, for example, the growth of the concept of global environmental management, progress on industrial safety and accident prevention, and a reduction in the toxicity of products. I think that is an indicator of what one can expect after the Earth Summit in Brazil. Brazil will be an occasion. The importance of the occasion is the build-up of ideas and setting on track a longer-term commitment to work on these issues. That includes public pressure on these issues and the realization that the problem is not solved. A momentum problem exists with international conferences.

What level of institutional follow-up will occur after Brazil? The Peruvian government released a paper at UNCED's third Preparatory Committee negotiation session that suggested an unusually structured review of the Brazil proceedings.

This is the International Labor Organization (ILO) model that they proposed.

Yes. One of the Peruvian suggestions was for a new council of CEOs, ministers, and leaders of NGOs to take part in a periodic review of the Earth Summit outcome. There were other suggestions from Peru about creating a corporate/governmental institution. We have to evaluate what kind of institutional mechanisms we are going to need to maintain momentum. That is going to be the test of what gets accomplished after Brazil. There will, of course, be an effort to indicate that we have taken care of the environment and that we should move on to other topics.

The power of TNCs is that they can decide where to locate their operations. If the rules get too restrictive in one country they can always threaten to move.

One of the advantages of international discussions on developing soft law is to say: This is a common basis for national environmental systems. Having a reference mark is particularly helpful in strengthening weaker developing countries. It enables them to object when companies try to lower environmental standards below a certain international consensus. This is the minimalist approach. It also reduces the pressure on individual countries that might be told by a multinational: "We are going to go to another country because their rules in this particular area are more lax." If the international community articulates where the common floor is, then it makes less effective the threat by multilateral corporations that they will move to find lower environmental standards.

However, it does not seem to us that environmental rules and regulations significantly influence where foreign investors put their operations. On a new plant for a high-risk activity, the incremental capital cost is 1 or 2 percent. Pollution prevention is not, all told, an expensive exercise — or enough to make a difference in where they locate. If you were to give corporate executives a list of 15 areas and ask them what factor weighs most heavily in the decision to locate a plant abroad, environment generally would fall below 10 other considerations. The labor costs, markets, access to materials and other considerations are more important to them.

In the public debate between the governments there is a lot of talk about this argument that does not match actual practice. It is also the case that environmental groups generally repeat this argument, which adds to its apparent veracity, although it still doesn't match practice. We came to this conclusion four or five years ago and the evidence suggests to us that it is still true.

There are industries where this is not the case: heavy metal production, dyes, asbestos, hazardous waste disposal industries in particular, where the cost differences are extreme. But that is not the dominant feature of the whole market. And it is a mistake to just look at those industries as examples.

To argue that firms might move discourages governments from making environmentally sound rules because it feeds the mystique that they are going to lose either the environment or the jobs. We argue that governments should regionalize environmental systems, because they need regional labs, but what long-term investors want is clarity and consistency in rules. If they are going to have to meet a lead standard they want to know what the lead standard is. If they are going to make a capital investment, and they are going to be there for 10 to 15 years, they want to know what rules they are going to have to comply with, and not have a lead standard change by one or two orders of magnitude.

So, our basic view is to advise countries to develop reasonable sets of standards that they articulate and develop and put in writing.

Afterword

he interviews in *Beyond the Earth Summit* provide the reader with a rich context in which to understand the historic significance of the United Nations Conference on Environment and Development (UNCED). In the aftermath of UNCED, three critical questions emerge:

- Was UNCED a success or a failure?
- What are the next steps for the UNCED process?
- Where do we go from here?

Was UNCED a Success or Failure?

It is difficult to decide whether a conference that has not, at the time these words are written, taken place, will be considered a success or a failure. A number of the interviews address the criteria for making this judgement. My own present view is that UNCED will probably be what I would call a "qualified diplomatic failure" if measured against the original objectives set for the conference. At a second level, however, I would count UNCED an inevitable diplomatic success simply because it represents an historic starting place for the global dialogue on sustainable development that must, as Senator Al Gore suggests, be the focus for the new order in international politics if a liveable world is to survive. At a third and perhaps most important level, there is widespread agreement that UNCED has stimulated the emergence of what one might call a global movement of non-government organizations (NGOs) for sustainable development. This global NGO movement is, arguably, one of the most important outcomes of UNCED. There is widespread agreement that NGOs have a critical role to play at every level of the global struggle for sustainable development, from grassroots to national to international spheres. To say that a global movement for sustainable development has emerged greatly strengthened from UNCED is not to say that this "movement" represents a single set of widely held views among the NGOs. Nonetheless, NGOs are able to move far more rapidly toward the shared understandings that must underpin the agreements of the coming decades than governments can.

What Are the Next Steps for UNCED?

There will be a great deal of discussion of this in the months following the Rio Conference, and many of the interviews discussed this subject. But there is widespread agreement that:

• UNCED is the beginning of the process of achieving global bargains on sustainable development;
• The success of this process will depend on strengthened international institutions to follow up on negotiations in process in Rio, monitor agreements made in Rio, and take the next steps on the long journey which the Rio negotiations have just begun;
• NGOs will be crucial to this process, and to the resolution of the tough debates reflected in these interviews over what the architecture of a sustainable future will look like.

Where Do We Go from Here?

The answers to the crucial question of where we go from here will be as varied as the prescriptions in these interviews. But we at Commonweal intend to explore the following:

First, we expect to stay focused on raising the level of public dialogue about the architecture of a sustainable future.

Second, we believe that some of the best organizing fora for doing this will emerge from UNCED and from the series of United Nations conferences scheduled or contemplated over the next three years: the U.N. Conference on Human Rights scheduled for 1993; the U.N. Conference on Population scheduled for 1994; and the U.N. Conference on Restructuring the United Nations contemplated for 1995, the 50th anniversary of the founding of the U.N.

Third, we believe that the evolution of the global NGO movement for sustainable development merits continuing attention and support. We plan to participate in it and report on it as long as it holds promise for playing a key role in global change.

Fourth, we believe that the "good news about sustainable development" that is emerging in grassroots, municipal and national actions in countries around the world is critically important. Because we are U.S. citizens and because the U.S. is currently the greatest obstacle to progress on sustainable development, we think it is particularly urgent to report on the good news about sustainable development that is emerging in communities and states across this country.

Fifth and finally, we believe that the struggle for a sustainable future is more than a social, economic and political struggle. It is also, as Senator Al Gore and many others have come to believe, a struggle of the human spirit. So we intend to continue to address not only the social, economic and political realities, but also the reality that humankind does not live by bread alone. Mahatma Gandhi once said that if God came to India he would have to come in the form of a loaf of bread. Gandhi was firmly rooted in the reality of the needs of India. That did not stop him from believing in, and calling upon, the human spirit to help meet those needs.

—*Michael Lerner*
President, Commonweal

About the Author:

Steve Lerner is Research Director at Commonweal, and an investigative journalist who specializes in environmental issues. He is former editor of *Common Knowledge,* a quarterly journal on environmental threats to health, and co-author of the Natural Resources Defense Council special report: "Healing the Hole in the Sky." He was principal investigator on the Genotoxin Survey Project, which published a map of sources of toxic chemicals in California.

Lerner traveled to Nicaragua in 1980 where he researched the dumping of mercury in Lake Managua. He subsequently studied heavy metal and toxic chemical pollution in the Philippines, Thailand, Malaysia and India for the Institute for Health Policy Studies, University of California, San Francisco.

A graduate of Harvard University, Lerner is a former staff reporter for the *Village Voice* and has written for *The New Republic, Audubon, The Amicus Journal, The New York Times Book Review, Ms., Omni* and other publications. He is author of a previous collection of interviews entitled, *Earth Summit: Conversations with Architects of an Ecologically Sustainable Future.*

Also Available from Common Knowledge Press:

EARTH SUMMIT

Conversations with Architects of an Ecologically Sustainable Future

"The Earth Summit to be held in Brazil in June, 1992 will be a significant test of this generation's resolve to address the seeming paradox of environment and development. Environmental protection and economic development can be mutually reinforcing. This collection of interviews will be enormously helpful to all of us who wish to realize this goal. These conversations illuminate both the problems we face and the solutions we need."
—*U.S. Senator Timothy E. Wirth*

"This book provides a guide to the key issues which will dominate the Earth Summit. By focusing on people in the Third World and the U.S. who are working now to protect the planet, it provides examples of how citizens can change society and thereby create an ecologically sustainable future. It belongs on every activist's bookshelf."
—*Michael Clark, President, Friends of the Earth, U.S.*

"Steve Lerner's thoughtful interviews on the Earth Summit provide a rich source of information and ideas about what is at stake at the 1992 U.N. Conference on Environment and Development, the high obstacles that stand in the way of its success, and what might be done to overcome those obstacles. He has tapped a rich vein of wisdom."
—*Philip Shabecoff, Executive Publisher, Greenwire*

"These interviews with 19 environmentalists are better than edifying. The topic of conversation—how to devise and enforce international covenants to save the earth—is radically sober, maybe intimidating. But the talk is rarely dull, for Lerner is a talented journalist who provokes imagination and candor. His subjects emerge as interesting, complicated people with various points of view, and engaging ways of setting them forth."
—*Conn Nugent, Environmental Program, The Nathan Cummings Foundation*

"Conversations is the operative term here. We are privileged to eavesdrop, as it were, on deeply thoughtful, deliberate and candid exchanges about the profoundly complex and interlocking issues that undergird efforts to move toward a sustainable future, as these are focused by those actively engaged in preparations for UNCED."
—*Donald N. Michael, Member, Club of Rome; Emeritus Professor of Planning and Public Policy, University of Michigan*

Cover Art by Karl W. Stuecklen

 Common Knowledge Press • ISBN 0-943004-06-3 • $9.95
Printed on Enviro-Text recycled paper

Order Form

Copies of *Beyond the Earth Summit: Conversations with Advocates of Sustainable Development* are available from Commonweal, Box 316, Bolinas, CA 94924. (415) 868-0970.

The price is $12.50. For shipment at book rate in the U.S. add $2.00, for Canada add $3.00. For shipment to all other countries by surface mail, add $4.00 postage and handling. All orders must be paid in U.S. funds.

Copies of *Earth Summit: Conversations with Architects of an Ecologically Sustainable Future* are also available from Commonweal. The price is $9.95 and the shipping costs are the same as those listed above.

Number of copies: *Beyond the Earth Summit:*_____

Number of copies: *Earth Summit:* _____

Total payment enclosed: $_____

Send to:

Name_____

Address_____

_____Zip_____

Comments: